D1066445

Merriman Smith's Book of Presidents

A White House Memoir

A. Merriman Smith's
Book of Presidents

A White House Memoir

Edited by Timothy G. Smith

with a Foreword by Robert J. Donovan

W · W · NORTON & COMPANY, INC ·
NEW YORK

E 176
.1
.S6 2

Copyright © 1972 by G. Timothy Smith

Library of Congress Cataloging in Publication Data

Smith, A   Merriman, 1913–1970.
Merriman Smith's book of Presidents

1. Presidents—U. S.—Biography. I. Title.
II. Title: A White House memoir.
E176.1.S62   973.099 [B]   73-39298
ISBN 0-393-07469-2

Published simultaneously in Canada
by George J. McLeod Limited, Toronto

Portions of this book originally appeared in:

Thank You, Mr. President, Harper & Brothers, 1946

The President Is Many Men, Harper & Brothers, 1948

Meet Mr. Eisenhower, Harper & Brothers, 1954

A President's Odyssey, Harper & Brothers, 1961

The Good New Days, The Bobbs-Merrill Co., Inc., 1962

PRINTED IN THE UNITED STATES OF AMERICA

2 3 4 5 6 7 8 9 0

Dedicated to
the White House Correspondents Association
for its administration and promotion of
the Merriman Smith Memorial Fund

Contents

Preface		9
Acknowledgments		13
Foreword by Robert J. Donovan		15
ONE	President-watching: The Trouble with Images	29
TWO	Some White House Styles	41
THREE	Backstairs at the White House	67
FOUR	People around the Presidents: Cronies, the Hired Help, and VIP's	85
FIVE	First Ladies	111
SIX	The Lighter Side	123
SEVEN	Presidential Campaigns: Getting to the White House	135
EIGHT	On the Road: White House Travel Yarns	153
NINE	Presidential Retreats: Custodial Coverage	179

CONTENTS

TEN   Two Deaths   195
ELEVEN   Post Mortems: The Traumas of
            Transition   215
TWELVE   Protecting Presidents   225

An Epilogue: Presidents and the Press   239

Illustrations Follow page 142.

Preface

IN THE SUMMER of 1964, *Esquire* attempted to classify and explain the workings of the Washington press establishment by using a complicated chart which covered a two-page centerfold. The diagram was full of lines and boxes with categories arranged by beat, type of medium, membership in the various news organizations, and so on. There was a section for the pundits—Lippmann, Reston, the Alsops. And for the foreign correspondents. Members of the elite Gridiron Club had their names underlined and the bureau chiefs—Wicker, Donovan, Lisagor, etc.—had their names starred.

The placement of Merriman Smith on this chart obviously presented a problem. He could be put down as a wire service reporter, the UPI man at the White House. But how to describe his place in Washington journalism? He was not a weighty analyst like some of the columnists, nor did he hold any particular titular position like the bureau chiefs or top editors. Yet, in his books and magazine articles and television appearances, he had become more than a straight news reporter. He had a special closeness and knowledge of the White House that were unique. So where to put him and how to describe his relationship to presidents since FDR?

The final solution was to construct a little box on one side of the chart. It was a special category entitled, "Friend of the Presidents," and a blue line ran from the box to a drawing of the White House.

Typically, Smith's reactions to the chart were decidedly mixed. He knew he was regarded as a White House fixture, and that was fine. When John Kennedy won the presidency and was having a victory party in Hyannis Port, he introduced Smith to Jackie: "I want you to meet Merriman Smith. We inherited him with the White House."

That was just about the way his considerable ego expected to be treated. As Pierre Salinger noticed in his book, *With Kennedy,* "he [had] a gentle disdain for a succession of Press Secretaries he believes have been put there to complicate his work."

On the other hand, he did not like the thought of being dismissed as just a crony. He felt his long tenure and constant, day-to-day exposure to presidents—under all sorts of conditions, in all sorts of moods—gave him insights into the men and into certain aspects of the office that others missed.

He was willing to leave analytical theory of the presidency to the theorists and definitive historical interpretation to the historians. What he knew best were the anecdotes and stories, which for him were important in understanding Franklin Delano Roosevelt, Harry S Truman, Dwight David Eisenhower, John Fitzgerald Kennedy, Lyndon Baines Johnson, and Richard Milhous Nixon as human beings, as people.

What were they really like? How did their White House styles differ? What is everyday life in the White House or on the road with a president like? What was it like to be there, in Warm Springs and then in Dallas, when a president suddenly died? What happens to the staffs, the people around the old and new presidents in a period of transition? What happens to a reporter? These were the types of questions Merriman Smith felt best equipped to answer.

Before his death, he had planned a final book of this sort. His notes made clear that it was not to be a definitive study of the presidency nor even of any of the men he knew who had occupied it—above all, "not pompous hindsight"—but rather, a book of "story-telling to make famous people and their times come alive in something like human terms."

This book is an attempt to fulfill those plans. Its material is drawn from many sources: not only from Merriman Smith's previously published books and magazine articles and columns, but also in large measure from unpublished memoranda, notes, correspondence, and diary entries.

Each chapter is an amalgam. For instance, in Chapter Two, the Johnson section is from an unfinished manuscript, "The LBJ Brand," on which Smith was working at the time of his death. The Eisenhower-Nixon material is from notes and from *Meet Mr. Eisenhower* (Harper & Bros., 1954). The Kennedy passage is taken largely from an article which appeared in the *New York Times Magazine*, and the Roosevelt and Truman descriptions are from *Thank You, Mr. President* (Harper & Bros., 1946).

The Epilogue is taken almost entirely from parts of three speeches: to the White House Fellows, to the University of Missouri School of Journalism, and to the American Newspaper Publishers Association. Other chapters draw more heavily on personal reminiscence, much of which Smith luckily left in note form.

In many cases, we have had to add transitionary sentences and thoughts to keep the narrative moving and to arrange the material into chapter form. In so doing, we have run the risk of misinterpreting Merriman Smith, but trust any distortion has been kept to a minimum. One fortunate circumstance in this regard is that all who have worked on the book knew him and many of his stories and opinions well.

Acknowledgments

Any errors, indiscretions, or oversights are my own responsibility as compiler of the book, but many individuals have contributed mightly to its birth and growth and should be acknowledged for their efforts. Smith's wife, Gailey (now Mrs. Herbert J. McChrystal, Jr.), made available his collected papers which were the raw material for the book. His employers of over thirty years, United Press International, helped at every step. UPI's president, Mims Thomason; Washington bureau chief, Julius Frandsen; New York executive (and Smith's long-time close friend) C. Edmonds Allen: Washington editor, Louis Cassels; and European news editor, Richard Growald, were special sources of aid, advice, and moral support.

The bulk of the manuscript was put together over a period of year and a half at New College, Oxford, where the editor studied with the assistance of the Keasbey Memorial Foundation. Additional hospitality and shelter during the writing of the manuscript were provided by NBC's London correspondent, Ray Scherer and his wife, Barbara; CBS Washington correspondent, George Herman and his wife, Patty; the Edmund H. Katenkamp family of Santa Barbara, California; and the Paul Murray clan of County Dublin, Ireland.

Personal aid and advice during this period were also generously given by Ann C. Whitman, Mr. and Mrs. Thomas E. Stephens, William H. Lawrence, Mr. and Mrs. Morton L. Mandel, Sturgis Warner, Professors David Adamany (Wesleyan) and H. G. Nicholas (Oxford), J. Tyson Stokes, and Nancy Towell.

Finally, an incalculable debt is owed to Evan W. Thomas of W. W. Norton & Company, and to Robert J. Donovan of the *Los Angeles Times* for their leaps of faith. They believed that a book could and should be done from the twenty-six packing crates full of Merriman Smith's memories and records and lent their considerable professional talents to seeing the project through.

T. G. S.
New College, Oxford
England
September, 1971

Foreword
by Robert J. Donovan

ON THE DAY AFTER his election in 1960 John F. Kennedy put his finger on what was unique and important about Merriman Smith, by trade a reporter. Espying him waiting with other reporters at the Hyannis Armory, Kennedy said, "If you're here, Smitty, I guess I've really been elected." For a president, in other words, Merriman Smith came with the job.

What was unique about Smith was that through skill, opportunity, prodigal exertion, gall, aggressiveness, and showmanship he made himself all but an unofficial appurtenance of the presidency through parts of six administrations: those of Franklin D. Roosevelt, Harry S Truman, Dwight D. Eisenhower, John F. Kennedy, Lyndon B. Johnson, and Richard M. Nixon.

Such was his standing and the professional respect in which he was held that at Smith's death on April 13, 1970, President Nixon directed that the flag over the White House be lowered to half-staff.

For nearly thirty years Smith was the White House correspondent of the United Press—or United Press International, as it was later called.

His work on the side as an author, lecturer, and magazine writer and his twice-a-week column, "Backstairs at the White House," were their own proof of his journalistic versatility.

The nature of his work as a wire-service reporter covering the president was, however, more rudimentary: to report what was happening *now*, and to report it rapidly, completely, objectively, fairly, and excitingly. Because of the exigencies of deadlines, he more often than not dictated stories to his office directly from scrawled notes by telephone or on occasion by hand radio.

In his daily coverage of the president he was, in the idiom of the trade, a straight news reporter. In this era of so-called new journalism, team reporting, in-depth coverage, analysis and all that, straight news reporting sounds old-fashioned. Even so, it is still the heart of journalism, and quite possibly Merriman Smith was the pre-eminent straight news reporter of his time, an achievement recognized by, among other things, the award of a Pulitzer Prize for his coverage of the Kennedy assassination.

Smith was also one of the most famous reporters of his generation, owing partly to the institution of the televised presidential press conference. For years millions of viewers watched him exercise the prerogative of the senior wire-service reporter on the White House beat by terminating the conferences with "Thank You, Mr. President."

Merriman Smith covered the White House in the very years when presidents came to dominate the government and continually monopolized the news in this country and around the world.

Hot on six presidents' heels night and day, month in and month out, year in and year out, in the White House, on the road and, indeed, in remote corners of the world, he had a remarkable view of unfolding history. Conceivably no other man has ever been a witness to so many momentous events as he.

Fortunately, as will appear in this book, he had an immense capacity for soaking up and preserving details and anecdotes.

His exposure to presidents and to the operations of the White House was profuse, and his straightforward accounts of what he saw, what he heard and what presidents said to him must be put down as a valuable contribution to the history of the presidency.

A colleague once wrote that Smith was "there, always there." Where? Well, for example, at the White House on December 7, 1941, and with Roosevelt through the war years on secret rail tours to defense plants and military camps and on the trip to meet Stalin and Churchill at Yalta. He was at Warm Springs, Georgia, when Roosevelt died and at Hyde Park, New York, for the funeral.

Soon he was off to the Potsdam Conference in Germany with President Truman and was in Truman's presence when he announced en route home aboard the cruiser *Augusta* that the first atomic bomb had been dropped on Hiroshima. As time passed, he covered the famous Truman "whistle-stop" campaign in 1948 and Truman's meeting with Gen. Douglas MacArthur on Wake Island.

He was one of only three reporters who accompanied General Eisenhower when, as president-elect, he visited the Korean battlefields in 1952. When Eisenhower confronted Nikita S. Khrushchev at the disastrous Paris summit conference of 1960, Smith was there, as he had been at Denver the day of Eisenhower's heart attack in 1955 and later at Gettysburg during the long convalescence.

He covered President Kennedy at the White House during the Cuban missile crisis of 1962. He was riding behind him in the motorcade in Dallas when Lee Harvey Oswald pulled the trigger and was outside the room in Parkland Hospital when Kennedy died. A short time later he stood in the cabin of Air Force One as Lyndon Johnson was sworn in as president.

Smith was at the National Guard Armory in Washington in 1952 when Truman made his unexpected announcement that he would not seek another term and in the East Room of the White House in 1968 when Johnson made his far more astounding statement that he would not run again.

That same year he saw the Democratic National Convention explode in Chicago and the Republican National Convention put Nixon back in the picture in Miami. The next year he accompanied President Nixon on his trip around the world, with a stop aboard the aircraft carrier Hornet in the Pacific to welcome the astronauts back from man's first landing on the moon.

As far as I could tell, Smith never became jaded by years of exposure to great events. His appetite for the big story was unquenchable. Indeed, his unflagging instinct was to make the big story bigger than it was. Although he was the embodiment of the tough, realistic, hard-bitten reporter, the romance of newspaper work, a perishable commodity for many of us, remained with him remarkably. He not only was a superior reporter, but he was forever playing the game of being a reporter, as if he were a character out of *The Front Page*—which he just about was.

Nobody ever understood as well as he how, with a proper knack for showmanship, a reporter might use the glare and glamor of the White House to project himself into the limelight.

That was a knack he had and nourished. It was characteristic of him that at almost every opportunity he would go to New York to hang around Broadway and shoot the breeze with Broadway stars. He had no trouble talking the lingo of actors and actresses, and such were his own garrulous talents that for years he was a frequent performer on either the Jack Paar or Johnny Carson or Merv Griffin television shows.

Because of the spotlight that bathes presidents, White House reporters are inevitably more conspicuous than reporters on other beats. Recognizing this early in the game, Smith was particularly skillful at dramatizing his own role, whether by standing closest to the president in public or sitting in the front row or brandishing a walkie-talkie or defying any guard who might impede his movement around a president.

If a situation required a quick call to the office, Smith was not content to hasten to the telephone, as most others do. He stormed, thundered, bolted. I once made the mistake of standing behind him at a moment when dramatic news was breaking. It was in 1948 in the Dewey election headquarters at the Roosevelt Hotel in New York an hour after midnight when the tense, close election returns were pouring in.

Herbert Brownell, Dewey's campaign manager, suddenly entered the press room, climbed on a chair and announced: "We now know that Governor Dewey will carry New York State by fifty thousand votes and will be the next president of the United States." Before I could move I was sent sprawling by Smith on his familiar broken-field dash to the telephone.

I first met or, rather, encountered Smitty, as he was called by his friends, in the summer of 1947 when, as a new reporter in town, I was assigned to cover a speech President Truman was to give in one of the hotels. The reporters would accompany him in their own rented limousines, which were waiting outside the White House press room. When I arrived I slid quietly into the front seat of one of them, but things did not stay quiet long.

Smith suddenly barged out and demanded that I move to the rear seat, all the time behaving in the manner of an eminently important figure around the White House. The front seat, he gave me to understand, was his by absolute right of something or other—seniority, I suppose.

Since I had no intention of being ordered around, he staged a great scene that went on until there was a danger the president would get away without us. By then I knew I was in a silly situation, and when a Secret Service agent politely asked me to move to a rear seat, I surrendered the front to Smith.

In another sense, however, it was not a silly situation. As I was to learn in subsequent years when I regularly covered the White House myself for the old *New York Herald Tribune,* the showdown at the limousine was a typical case of Smith's being a tough competitor, which indeed he was. And the weaker and less competent a rival might be, the tougher Smith was, too.

Another thing about that limousine scene. Smith was relentlessly alert. He never forgot that by being in the front seat he would be closer to any sudden incident involving the president than the reporters in the rear seat. Therefore, he insisted on his place in the front seat year after year, with results that were to pay off handsomely.

When the motorcade set out in Dallas on November 22, 1963, the press pool car was third in line, two behind the president's. Exercising his seniority, as usual, Smith sat in the front seat between the driver and Malcolm Kilduff, an assistant White House press secretary. I shall let William Manchester tell the rest of the story in his *The Death of a President:*

> As the senior White House correspondent Smith always rode in
> the middle. Thus he was the newspaperman closest to the radio-

telephone on the transmission hump under the dashboard. Jack
Bell of the Associated Press, (Robert) Baskin of the Dallas *News*
and Bob Clark of the American Broadcasting Company were in
the back. In a crisis they could report nothing from this car unless
Smith surrendered the phone, and Smith, with his hard, pocked
face, was one of the most competitive men in journalism. . . .

There was a sudden, sharp, shattering sound. . . .

Of the driver's five passengers (in the pool car) Kilduff, Baskin,
and Clark could do nothing until the car stopped. Smith and Jack
Bell of AP were a different breed. They were wire service reporters; they dealt in seconds.

Smith's seniority had given him a clear beat, the greatest in his
career, and the longer he could keep Bell out of touch with an
AP operator the longer that lead would be. So he continued to
talk. He dictated one take, two takes, three, four. Indignant, Bell
rose up from the center of the rear seat and demanded the
phone. Smith stalled. He insisted that his Dallas operator read
back the dictation. The wires overhead, he argued, might have
interfered with his transmission.

No one was deceived by that. Everyone in the car could hear
the crackling of the UPI operator's voice. The relay was perfect.
Bell, red-faced and screaming, tried to wrest the radiophone from
him; Smith thrust it between his knees and crouched under the
dash, and Bell, flailing wildly, was hitting both the driver and
Kilduff.

From my own long experience with him on the beat I am
convinced that Smith had been readying himself for Dallas from
the day he took over the White House assignment twenty-two
years earlier.

What was the most gripping story that could possibly fall into
the lap of a White House correspondent? Anyone who was as
romantic about reporting as Smith knew the answer: the assassination of the president. I am sure this worried him and spurred
him to keep the president in view whenever he could. Wherever
he went with presidents, unless I am greatly mistaken, he had a
vision of what would happen at the "sudden, sharp, shattering
sound." Why else would the front seat have been worth the fuss?

Merriman Smith was born in Savannah, Georgia, on February

10, 1913. At the age of eleven he was reporting on the activities of his Boy Scout troop. In Savannah High School he edited the school paper and found himself suspended from school for a week for writing an editorial calling the school building a firetrap.

He went on to Oglethorpe University but dropped out to become a sports writer for the *Atlanta Georgia-American*. Then he wrote features for the Sunday magazine of the *Atlanta Journal*. He managed to interview Max Schmeling before a championship prize fight and Clark Gable before the premier of *Gone with the Wind* in Atlanta.

At twenty-two he became managing editor of the *Athens* (Georgia) *Daily Times*. The next year, 1936, he was hired by the United Press and began by covering the Georgia and Florida legislatures and writing features about tobacco auctioneers, rainmakers, a one-hundred-and-thirty-one-year-old woman, gold fever in the hill country of northern Georgia, and a Christmas Eve meeting of an ex-slave association. Once he witnessed a lynching and took a photograph to go with the story. Another assignment took him to a prison. The lead on his story was:

> Six Negro men in the death house atop Georgia's Tuttnall Prison started singing early this morning but by lunchtime their song was ended.
> "Oh you sinners, better get ready, God is comin'," they chorused loudly, hour after hour, until the electric chair had claimed every one of them in the largest mass execution in state history.

His first year with UP he was involved in a million-dollar libel suit. It was brought by the mayor and council of Miami after a story Smith had written saying that the city had the highest venereal disease rate in the country. The suit was dropped when Smith produced a congressional report supporting his facts.

One day, as I understand, Smith was covering the aftermath of a tornado in Gainesville, Georgia, when the presidential special came through carrying FDR to his retreat at Warm Springs. The excitement and the well-dressed, well-fed, comfortable appearance of the reporters aboard, particularly in contrast to Smith who had to file his story by climbing a telegraph pole because of damage done by the storm, aroused his envy. He decided he wanted to cover the White House, too. In 1941 his wish came true just one year after the UP had transferred him from the South to Washington.

Thirty years of covering the White House is hard to imagine. If it is sometimes glamorous, it is also for long stretches very boring and tiring. Particularly when working for a wire service, a reporter is pinned down where the president is, whether it be in the White House or Gettysburg or Austin. The hours are long. Night assignments are frequent. Week ends at the White House are often as busy as weekdays. Or, if the reporter is not working in Washington, he is apt to be sitting around hotels or motels on Saturdays and Sundays in Augusta or Hyde Park or Hyannis Port. It's the same on Christmas and New Year's.

For Smith, covering the White House meant endless train rides in the Roosevelt days and then off and on airplanes a thousand times as presidents changed their mode of travel. With the coming of the jet, a president could visit three continents in a single day, as has happened. When the president finally retires after a hard day the reporter starts writing and is often lucky to get any sleep at all before the next day's grind.

For every news flash and exciting bulletin there is a ton of dull copy about the president's day, his family's doings, the budget, legislation, presidential commission reports, distinguished visitors, and all the rest of the White House routine.

Struggling with crowds, arguing with press secretaries, fretting over luggage are all part of what can be, over a long period, a very wearing assignment.

Smith's persistence and patience through the years were extraordinary. I remember the countless times I saw him at night waiting for the president in a hotel lobby or outside a cabinet member's house or, even once, on a farm while reporters for the newspapers were home in bed. He did not get any big stories out of these long vigils, which his particular job necessitated, but he did get the little details and snatches and vignettes that made up his mosaic of the presidency.

Smith's inexhaustible curiosity about presidents must have

supplied the energy that kept him crowding in on his assignment, as it were. He was forever pushing and shoving, was always after more. He looked for news where many other reporters never even thought of looking. James C. Hagerty, press secretary to President Eisenhower, has remarked upon Smith's miscellaneous and unusual news sources in the White House establishment.

"Reporters sometimes complained about Smitty's 'sixth sense' about the White House," Hagerty once said.

> They felt he could predict almost intuitively when the president was going to make a trip or announce an appointment or when he wasn't feeling well. Part of it was intuition, part his long experience.
>
> But another part involved his friendships with all levels of White House personnel, right down to the ground-keepers.
>
> It was one of these sources, I'm almost certain, that let Smitty know about the abortive attempt to get rid of some squirrels that were burying nuts in President Eisenhower's putting green on the South Lawn. They were being trapped and then released in Rock Creek Park.
>
> I'm convinced that Smitty got this story—which caused such a reaction that the squirrel-trapping was stopped—from one of his friends on the gardener's staff.

Smith's essential talent was as a storyteller. As with others in this loquacious brotherhood, he tended in conversation to be such an exaggerator that it was sometimes difficult to know where fact ended and fancy began in accounts of his own exploits. On the other hand he was capable of such bizarre conduct that it was foolish to doubt any of his acts simply because they were bizarre.

Thus I don't know whether to believe that he got into the Elysée Palace during an Eisenhower-de Gaulle meeting by flashing a Gettysburg Volunteer Fire Department pin, but I don't altogether disbelieve it.

"He is," Hugh Sidey of *Time* once wrote, "a man of many skills, being able to repair a walkie-talkie on a dogtrot, to find a telephone in the remotest wilderness, to navigate a boat on Narragansett Bay, to develop a wardrobe that boasts a suit that looks

like a tuxedo or a tuxedo that looks like a suit in case of an unexpected change in plans."

"With Smith," said Ray Scherer, for many years the NBC man
on the White House, "the story of getting the story was often as
fantastic as the news itself."

In the days when Lyndon Johnson made a secret even of his
intentions to go to Texas, Smith divined that he could get a sure
clue by ascertaining from some obscure source whether the president's dogs were being readied for a trip. In San Clemente, too,
I have heard, Smith learned when Nixon planned to leave his
house by cultivating a nearby gasoline station attendant who
fueled the White House cars.

Smith once wrote a book called *A President Is Many Men*. He
was, himself, a man of many sides at least. He was a gruff fellow
who could be kind-hearted, an aggressive type who could yet win
many friends. Once one differentiated between bark and bite,
he was an easy person to like. Despite his characteristically dour
look, heightened by dark eyes, dark hair, dark mustache, and a
long, coarse, nervous face, he could be very amusing.

A reporter I know still believes Smith kept him from freezing
to death in the long hours outside President-elect Kennedy's
Georgetown house in the snow with laughter over Smith's pan-
tomimes of scenes in the forthcoming Kennedy administration, as
he envisioned them. The *pièce de résistance*, it seems, was Smith's
version of a Secret Service agent guarding the new president on
horseback at a foxhunt, managing the reins while still carrying a
walkie-talkie in one hand and a revolver in the other.

Also Smith was fascinated by gadgets and had odd hobbies like
skeet shooting and cooking. The *Hartford Courant* once carried
his recipe for Roast Pork Nanking à la Merriman, which called
for kumquats.

Once when Smith was covering Eisenhower at Augusta he
spirited away (for three hundred dollars, he said) a bloodhound
from a Georgia prison camp and installed the dog first in the
Bon Air Hotel, where the reporters were put up, and then on the
press plane back to Washington. He first named the dog Harold
E. Stassen, perhaps hoping it would run for president, but then

24

changed the name to Harold E. Titus. One story was that he got the name out of the Augusta telephone directory, another was that the dog was renamed for a Harold E. Titus, who was said to have been connected with a plot to burn down the British Parliament. Either way, his wife made him get rid of the beast after it smashed through a screen door at home while chasing another dog.

Beneath such droll layers was a very solid journalist, although this does not tell the whole story about him either. While strikingly gregarious, he was also lonely. Personal troubles accumulated. It was a grievous sorrow for him when one of his sons, Capt. Merriman Smith, Jr., was killed piloting a helicopter in Vietnam. President Johnson attended the funeral at Arlington.

Also, the years of the White House grind chewed Smith up physically. It was simply not the kind of life in which a man took good care of himself. He had a drinking problem, which exacted its toll as he grew older. Evidently, it led to spells of depression, and Smith may have been in the grip of one when he committed suicide with a pistol in his home in 1970 at the age of fifty-seven.

Until then, Merriman Smith had led the kind of exorbitant life that most men can scarcely imagine. In doing so he made his mark upon a profession in which it is particularly hard to leave a mark because it forever deals with men and events that come and go.

Merriman Smith's Book of Presidents
A White House Memoir

CHAPTER ONE

President-watching: The Trouble with Images

Merriman Smith once began a comparison of the presidents he had covered by noting:

Our Presidents—at least the ones I have known personally—are seldom what they seem. Their images tend to become quite distorted by high-speed journalism, carefully prepared television appearance, prejudicial writers and, of course, by the Presidents themselves.

As a result, he felt, most people tend to focus on caricature rather than complexity in presidents, to become part of an audience for presidential performance rather than dispassionate observers of presidents as they are, and to miss distinctions between the public figure and the private personality in the White House.

The material in this chapter is from a broad variety of Smith's writings, but is arranged according to this central

*theme of the "frailty of presidential image" as a sort of
catalogue of the pitfalls of president-watching.*

FRANKLIN ROOSEVELT would have been a wonderful
actor. He probably would have been a Shakespearean
star who wore fur-collared overcoats, carried a gold-headed cane
and lorded it over the rest of the troupe.

It was this dramatic sense, plus bullheaded determination, that
helped him overcome the incredible handicap of infantile
paralysis. He was virtually a hopeless cripple, but the public
at large did not realize it until his death.

Not in his entire time in the White House could he stand
unsupported. Yet, few people outside of Washington realized
this. He always had to rely on heavy steel leg braces, canes, and,
more often, the support of someone's arm. His legs were literally
lifeless. He walked on his braces and with support only by tremendous effort which often made perspiration pop from his
forehead on a cold day.

But when appearing in public, he was the champion, the
colorful leader with his chin arched upward and his big hand in
the air. He knew he could thrill a crowded stadium by just this
simple wave of a hand, or his brown felt hat. That was all it
took to jerk a hundred thousand people to their feet in a screaming frenzy.

President Eisenhower was considered by many to be naïve
about such matters, a political amateur, but he had a great deal
more sophistication than came through. He knew exactly what
he was doing when he went out to turn on the crowds. I remember being with him while he was waiting to go out into a town
square in Latin America. Somebody came in and said, "Mr. President, the crowd is just about ready for you."

He took a deep breath and said, lifting his arms into the
familiar pose, "Okay, let's go give them VE-Day." Here was the
gesture that everybody regarded as almost holy, yet Ike knew
it for what it was—a very effective dramatic technique.

Every political skill involves, at least to some extent, just plain
acting. Besides his crowd-rousing talents and the way he hid his

physical infirmity, another of President Roosevelt's great talents was his ability to put over sheer, unadulterated hokum. This ability made it possible for him literally to charm people he detested.

"Bring in the old bore and let's get it over with," he would say to his secretary just before an appointment. The secretary would then usher in the person in question.

"Well, well," Mr. Roosevelt would boom, "how in the world are you, Bill? And why has it been so long since you came to see me?"

If the caller had some topic to discuss which the President wanted to avoid, the poor man probably never got a chance to open his mouth. Mr. Roosevelt would start in immediately on some utterly unrelated subject and literally filibuster.

There was once a Governor of Alabama, Chauncey Sparks, who tried for an hour and a half to talk politics with the President while they were touring an Army Air Base at Montgomery, Alabama. Mr. Roosevelt had advance knowledge of the Governor's desires and, for a particular reason, did not want to discuss the matter. Every time Sparks started to open his mouth, Mr. Roosevelt would tell him about the great progress being made by the Marines at Parris Island, South Carolina, in rehabilitating mental patients. And then when FDR exhausted that subject, he started in on Sparks about wild life and how he would, so much, like to have some quail sent to his train. Sparks got the quail.

In addition to being dazzled by Presidential showmanship, there is another trap in which the way we perceive a President can be distorted. It is simply the very human tendency to view a new President in terms of the old. This twisted the public's view of Lyndon Johnson, for example, for many months. Coming as he did after a product of Choate and Harvard, Mr. Johnson seemed to many the hick, the Texan. This sectional view obscured the fact that he had had much more Washington experience than Kennedy and that, in terms of style, he was in many ways more sedate than his predecessor. Johnson's White House parties, for instance, were awfully tame, sometimes somnambulistic. It was the Kennedy parties with cigarettes crushed on the priceless bread and butter plates and an occasional roll being tossed across the room that made veteran butlers cringe and recall the days of Andrew Jackson's revels.

The Truman transition was another difficult case for President-watchers. He was not, like FDR, a great thespian or manipulator or regal figure. He often said that he did not want to be President; he referred to the White House as a "prison." And he described his reaction to becoming President by telling friends, "I felt like the barn fell in on me." Truman seemed a pathetic figure when compared to FDR.

Mr. Roosevelt *wanted* to be President. He loved the pomp and circumstance. Mr. Truman was a bit shy and puzzled at first about such things as whether to salute, stand still or shake hands when a band played: "Hail to the Chief." I saw him do all three.

The press and the public, too, were at a loss to peg the new President. He lacked an image. Roosevelt had fed the American people a straight diet of color and drama for twelve years and the new man seemed a blank slate by comparison. For this reason, I think we latched on to the stories of Truman's love for bourbon and preoccupation with poker and blew them out of realistic proportions.

In fact, he was a light drinker and preferred scotch to bourbon. Poker was one hobby, but he also had a large collection of history books, with a particularly good section on the Civil War, to which he devoted more time than to his Bicycle deck.

What could not be immediately grasped after the drama of FDR was that Mr. Truman was exactly as he appeared at first glance, a typical American without pretense of being anything more. Edward T. Folliard of the *Washington Post* was among the first to catch the real essence of the Truman personality when he wrote: "This man's color lies in his utter lack of color. He's Mr. Average. You see him on your bus or streetcar. He sits next to you at the drug store soda fountain. There must be millions like him."

I remember an incident that occurred about a month after he took office. He was still paying off a mortgage when he became

President and he was accustomed to making the monthly payment in person at a bank in the heart of the Washington business district. So, with little warning to anyone, he called for his automobile and set out for the Hamilton National Bank at Fourteenth and G Streets in Washington. He decided to do this right at the lunch hour.

The Secret Service had hurriedly ordered escort cars and notified the District of Columbia police. When the entourage stopped in front of the bank, traffic was tied up during the busy lunch hour for blocks in four directions.

When the President came out of the bank and found a cheering crowd waiting for him, he was highly embarrassed. He waved his Western style hat at the people in sort of an apologetic way, and then literally leaped into the car.

Truman had a type of color and style and identification with the little man that was all his own. It was, indeed, a key political asset, as demonstrated by the give-'em-hell 1948 campaign. But this side of Truman was something the public missed for some time while continuing to look at him against a Rooseveltian background.

There has been one problem of Presidential image distortion that has been, I think, peculiar to the "blue-blood" Presidents, Roosevelt and Kennedy, to take the ones I personally covered. Both were seen as men who brought aristocratic and refined tastes to the Presidency after periods of cultural drought. It is true that both men brought young intellectuals into government in large quantities and perhaps these people gave the impression of new cultural tastes, but neither President jibed in fact with the image of the culture aficionado.

FDR's favorite bedtime reading consisted of mystery books and cheap detective stories. He cared nothing for classical music. His attitude toward modern art was mystified rejection. Mr. Kennedy was known as the man who brought Pablo Casals and a French chef to the White House. In truth, Pablo Casals came dangerously close to putting the President to sleep, and, as for his gourmet tastes, he used to carry a thermos bucket of New

33

England clam chowder with him nearly everywhere he went. Two of his other favorites were hot dogs served with a covering of chili and tomato soup laced with whipped cream.

Actually, much of President Kennedy's image was attributable more to his family or the people close to him than to himself. He epitomized vigor and the spirit of the 50-mile hike, yet he could not hike at all because of a very bad back. He was seen as a tough fighter, but this was more Bobby than Jack. He was introspective, ironic, philosophic—the gentlest of the Kennedys— and often had to restrain those around him from quixotic charges against their foes.

His opponents and detractors made much of President Kennedy's wealth, estimated at around $10 million at the time he took office in 1961. Yet this was a man who found no greater pleasure than in strolling the dunes of Cape Cod in a faded blue cotton pullover shirt and khaki pants that had definitely seen better days.

Other Presidents of recent years seldom would appear in public, or for that matter, in private, in anything but valet-creased trousers, mirror-bright shoes and otherwise exceedingly proper attire. Even Harry Truman's wild sport shirts in which he flapped around Key West, Florida, usually were brand new, his trousers faultlessly pressed. Only Roosevelt is really comparable, campaigning in an outrageously beat-up old felt hat and, at Hyde Park or Warm Springs, doting on a greenish tweed suit handed down from his grandfather.

It seems, contrary to the images involved, that it is our "log cabin" Presidents that have the more expensive personal tastes. Lyndon Johnson was a good example. President Johnson was quite sincere about his economy drive in government and some explained his attitude by pointing out his impecunious boyhood. This very well may have been the case, but Johnson, himself, was a man who loved the feel of personal opulence.

He once spent an entire Sunday afternoon prowling the basement floor of the old Executive Office Building next door to the White House, peeking in offices, toilets, closets and even an old bowling alley (circa Truman) to see if anyone had left lights burning over the weekend. But it always seemed somewhat ironic to me that he was dressed on this economy mission in a suit that cost over $300, alligator shoes that sold for between $150 and $200, and wearing a wristwatch worth over $1,500.

He always carried a wad of big bills and could peel off hundreds without making a big dent, while Kennedy often had to borrow a quarter if he wanted to buy an ice-cream cone. I make these observations not to construct some sociological theory of wealth and behavior, but to show that the single factor explanation of social background is yet another way that a President's image can be deceptive.

The further difficulty with the LBJ image was simply that he was so much more complex than people supposed. In fact, without a doubt, he was the most intriguing, frightening, contradictory and complicated President I've ever covered.

Capturing Johnson is akin to picking up a drop of mercury. He splashes and subdivides with such irritating frequency. He could summon almost flawless dignity when some secret, inner signal told him that dignity was called for. But this was also the man that before cameras and spectators could claw into his shirttails to expose for worldwide viewing the long, angry stripe of a still healing abdominal incision.

Gregarious to a fault, he also was silent, evasive and seemingly mistrustful of others when it came to disclosing trivial, as well as important, decisions. Regarded as one of the toughest politicians to come along in years, he was easily moved to tears. He actually cried to the point of his eyes filling and tears escaping down his cheeks when he was with someone he trusted deeply.

Within a space of minutes, he could invoke divine guidance, ask others to pray for him and then suddenly switch to blistering profanity interlaced with extremely funny sexual allegories applied to a political figure, the world scene or any particularly upsetting problem at hand. At the same meal, his table manners could range from the most impeccable to a ripping belch.

By breeding, rearing, and taste, he was a Southerner. There was nothing phony about his drawl and sometimes, in private and when speaking excitedly, his speech could become strictly ranch-hand and grammatically shuddering. Yet he could sit down and compose the most classically simple, perfectly grammatical and moving statement for equal rights. (Witness his Voting Rights speech or his blast at the Ku Klux Klan over television in the spring of 1965.) He held strong convictions on gut matters like civil rights, education, and health, but hypnosis, mind reading and truth serum probably could not have separated political motive from deep concern.

At times, he could appear almost unbelievably arrogant. Once I asked him what I thought was the innocuous question of how things were going. He patted me on the knee, then poked one of his massive fingers into my shoulder. He hunched forward in his rocker and reached into the folds of his black silk suit and from an inner jacket pocket pulled out a folded, printed paper. The President's eyes crinkled at the edges and across his face spread the "I've-got-you-nailed-to-the-table" smile of a poker player with a rock-crushing hand.

In that soft, but hard voice, he purred, "I'll tell you how things are going—the people are for me."

I had assumed as much and was somewhat surprised that LBJ needed to state such an obvious case.

"This paper," the President said, tapping my knee again for emphasis as he spoke, "has the latest Gallup figures and I now rate higher than Jack Kennedy *ever* did."

On another occasion shortly after he became President, Johnson with no warning to anyone, walked onto the columned porch beside his oval office and told the Secret Service man on duty that he wanted to leave immediately for a party being given at a nearby hotel in honor of one of his former colleagues in Congress.

The agent said he would send for cars immediately, requiring only a few minutes. Johnson was quite irate.

"Do you mean to tell me that the President of the United States must stand here and await the pleasure of drivers and agents?" he exploded at the startled agent.

Was he an arrogant man, then? Certainly at times, but, again, he was too complex to capsulize by such a facile generalization. For every Johnson watcher who dismissed him as arrogant, there were others who insisted that, far from being lacking in depth or simply vain, he fought a constant battle against insecurity.

They cited the wad of bills, the anger he sometimes displayed when photographed from an unflattering angle. And one could point to further evidence—his almost obsessive drive to return as often as possible to his native Texas hill country when refuges and resorts far more comfortable and aesthetic were his for the asking, and his enormous need for affection. Indeed, not in memory had there been such a kissy, huggy family in residence at the White House. There was the way he talked over the direst sort of problems in times of crisis with casual acquaintances and, sometimes, total strangers. It was as though he wanted the whole world to know the gravity of his tussle with decision.

LBJ was a perfect example of the frailty of image. He was the sort of person whom a hundred psychiatrists could not have figured out, whom a thousand PR men could not have produced or changed, yet he was perhaps the most typecast personality to occupy the White House since Truman. He was a lot of different things, but the one thing he definitely was not was a dumb cowboy.

One final way we misread certain Presidents, I think, is by tagging them as "stuffy" or "aloof" when what is really the case is that they observe a much sharper division between Presidential business and personal life than did their predecessors. President Eisenhower was a good example. To be sure, he was not the hair-down, shoes-off, buddy-type that Harry Truman had been, not by the distance from the National Guard drill ground at Independence, Mo., to the brass buttons and great halls of West Point. Nor did he have the easy-to-write-about flamboyance of Franklin Roosevelt.

His long years as a professional soldier taught him stoicism and reserve. He would lapse into icy formality when bored, puzzled or confronted with what he regarded as an undignified situation.

There was no more human President, though, than the Eisenhower who would squirm like a boy when they patted on his television makeup, or who could take an hour to show a child he never saw before in his life the intricacies of a spinning reel, or who got red in the face when fighting exasperation and anger under the lash of a razor-edged press conference question.

One reason the human side of President Eisenhower did not come through as it might have was that, in sharp contrast to the two charmers who preceded him, he had just about no personal relations with reporters. Some correspondents complained bitterly.

What the critics of Eisenhower's press relations forgot was one simple truth: the outside or so-called personal relationship between President Eisenhower and newsmen was just about what it was with virtually all members of his staff, his administration and Congress.

Dwight Eisenhower, after his career in the relatively formal and structured environment of the military, had developed a strong sense of orderliness in his life, almost a form of emotional compartmentalization. He observed a sharp dividing line between business and his private, personal life.

Reporters were justified when they deplored his lack of after-hours or social contact with them. It is true that stories are more interesting, more revealing when reporters can see a President off duty.

But Ike just wasn't that sort of fellow. His circle of friends was quite small when it came to the people he picked to golf, fish, or play bridge with him. Not even Sherman Adams, who had the reputation of being the closest person in the entire administration to Eisenhower, was on a golf or let's-have-lunch-together basis with the President.

Some of the complaining newsmen had gone on walks with Truman. Others could recall going to the White House on some Sunday nights for scrambled eggs with the Roosevelt family. But Eisenhower didn't even say hello to the reporters when he alighted from his plane in Augusta or Newport.

This was not a matter of manners. Nor did it reflect any particular dislike for members of the fourth estate. It meant simply that in his mind, the reporters were on the scene just as the Air Police honor guard, the Secret Service agents, the communications staff—to do their jobs. And he certainly wouldn't say hello to any of them. Reporters, just as government administrators, were business to President Eisenhower. And business you took up in the office, when you had any.

In a sense this stance was "aloof," and it probably did contribute to an image of heavy formality, but, on another level, it was simply professional and mature and actually less condescending or hypocritical than the "Hiya-boys" attitude adopted by many politicians.

President Nixon strikes me as being in a similar image situation as Eisenhower, but for slightly different reasons. Although he does not have President Eisenhower's long military background, there is undoubtedly an element of formality and reserve in his personality. Persons who have known him off and on since childhood say even as a small boy, he was serious and rather dignified. But, like Ike, he has another side to his personality which, in his case, the image-makers seem curiously unable to get across.

He swears, he takes a drink, he likes movies and occasionally eating out at carry-out tacos joints when he's in California. He enjoys walking along the surf and playing with the dogs—even without photographers present. To see Mr. Nixon and hear him under informal circumstances is a very pleasant experience when measured against his glass-slick, pre-programmed and ultra-dignified performance in public.

Nixon—and he knows it—is coming across as the kind of person who goes swimming in a vest. In truth, he is the sort who, while watching a football game on TV in the White House, sprawls with one leg hung over the arm of his chair, holds a margarita in his hand, and, when the action on the screen gets hot, comes roaring out of his seat waving his arms like any other fan.

The trouble in conveying this seems to lie in President Nixon's reliance on his image-makers. Rather than open his private, at-home personality to direct public view, he prefers to use professional go-betweens from the worlds of advertising and public relations in order to present a preconceived picture of what they presume the public wants to see. Ironically enough, what the public probably would like to see most is the unadorned Nixon without intermediating contrivance.

39

CHAPTER TWO

Some White House Styles

White House style, Merriman Smith thought, was influenced by a range of different factors—the president's own personality and view of the presidency, his organizational philosophy, his age and background and family and tastes. And finally, White House style was just a matter of mood—the distinctive feel of 1600 Pennsylvania Avenue under a particular leader.

The following sketches give a sense of the particular ways in which different presidents govern and a candid view of the modern presidency at work.

1.

Lyndon B. Johnson's was, to borrow Hugh Sidey's phrase, a "very personal Presidency." More than other Presidents, he placed his own stamp on nearly every aspect of White House life. More than any President I covered, he immersed himself, totally and completely, in his job. President Eisenhower had a sort of inner pressure gauge which told him when to escape the office routine for a round of golf or a quick trip to Newport or Augusta. President Kennedy enjoyed relaxing at night with an Ian

Fleming book or by watching a movie. Harry Truman played the piano, took his walks, and pursued other hobbies. And each President left as many of the mechanical details of government as possible to subordinates.

President Johnson, though, was different. He wanted to be President for twenty-four hours of each day. If there was a squabble about such administrative minutiae as the assignment of a parking space, he not only wanted to know about it, he wanted to decide it.

He had no hobbies, and few other interests. His musical tastes were confined to Muzak—in the background and softly. He could not have told you who Simon and Garfunkel were, or Joan Sutherland, or Zubin Mehta. He scarcely noticed the food he ate at banquets or state dinners, and his preferences at home were extremely basic. His knowledge of sauces, for example, stopped at catsup.

He read few books that did not concern him or his problems directly. He probably hadn't read a novel since college. Spectator sports bored him profoundly. Like other forms of sit-down entertainment, they involved staying fixed at one point for too long and he despised any situation which required him to remain seated and relatively silent for two or three hours.

His taste in resorts simply did not exist. When he wanted to work away from Washington, he went to his ranch, summer and winter. Camp David, Md., was an exception only because it was so much closer. You could have offered him the finest seashore or mountain accommodations in the world and he would have turned it down. He just wasn't interested. He would not have gone swimming in the surf if waves broke on the White House south grounds. He was amused, even baffled, by what he considered such status symbol sports as fox hunting in Virginia, sailing off Newport, lawn tennis or skiing. And golf took far too much time.

His job and his hobby, too, was being President. He was an almost compulsive worker and wanted you to know this.

"Don't call it a working vacation!" he would bark at reporters when at the ranch. "Just say I'm working."

His Presidency was also personalized by the way he drew out information from others and then held it close for his use only. Before a big decision, he would consult nearly everyone from former President Hoover to the White House gardener, but then would remain secretive and possessive about his thinking on the matter up until the last minute, as if to emphasize that the decision was all his. He frequently told his closest advisors of the content of his final judgment only when the White House was approaching the point of issuing a mimeographed public statement.

There was some mysterious belief in Johnson that he was possessed of an almost metaphysical sense of timing. He preferred to wait until the last possible minute to make personal plans known, to keep his cards close to the vest, as it were. This was another way to keep the Presidency a personal instrument of power, but the result was that no one, not even Lady Bird, could predict with any assurance or appreciably ahead of time which church he would attend the following Sunday, much less what he was going to do about a government appointment. The rallying cry for spur-of-the-moment Johnson excursions became "Where the hell are we going?" as Secret Service agents struggled into topcoats and raced for the White House driveway.

He was a most demanding executive, hoarding people as much as information or plans. His key staff members frequently worked from about 9 a.m. to anywhere from 10 p.m. to midnight. They learned to expect phone calls at any hour from the President, demanding more information or simply searching for someone with whom to talk. Johnson, himself, usually got into bed around 11:30 p.m., but lay propped up on a triangular pillow arrangement for hours, reading reports, phoning all over the country. There were times of tension and worry when Johnson became so wound up that even after he had finally quit work for the night, he would ask a close aide to douse the lights, but remain in the room until he dropped off to sleep. Often he would stay up or ask to be awakened to get the results of specific bombing missions or other events in Vietnam.

He would frequently be up again by 6:30 or 7:00 a.m., reading newspapers and calling staff members, working in bed until 9:30 or 10 a.m. It was as if he sought to defeat his problems by working them into the ground. "I don't know how much longer I can take it" was a typical staff comment, particularly in the early days of his administration. The Walter Jenkins tragedy was clearly a case of strain and exhaustion. And Bill Moyers left for the editorship of *Newsday*, the Long Island newspaper, with no regrets, but bad ulcers.

We often wondered about the strain on Johnson, himself, particularly since he had suffered a heart attack in 1955 of equal magnitude to the serious attack that President Eisenhower had in the same year.

"No," a doctor who had known LBJ for some time said, "this is an unusual man. He felt awfully frustrated politically in 1955 when he had that attack, but it is an entirely different situation with him in the White House. Here, he can act—send out thunder bolts. What *would* concern me, however, is another protracted period of frustration—but no, not in the Presidency."

Actually, it was not so much the hours and amount of work involved that made Johnson such a wearing executive on his staff. John Kennedy probably demanded as much homework and extra effort from his people and the Nixon staff are certainly not dawdlers, but LBJ had the added compulsion to control every part of White House life. Leaving an office light on could result in a personal dressing-down from the President. Even one's choice of clothes could come in for sharp criticism. Johnson assistants were expected to wear a certain type of dark suit on all business days, and would hear about it if they didn't.

No detail was too small, no subject too pedestrian, no bit of information too unimportant for the Presidential interest. My own experiences with Johnson provide some examples. It should be remembered that I was not a close personal confidant, but rather a working reporter whom he happened to see quite a bit.

For one thing, I was not exempted, nor were other reporters, from Presidential sartorial advice. He once pulled me aside at a meeting of the Latin American Presidents in Punta del Este, Uruguay, and told me in no uncertain terms that I looked ridiculous and unprofessional in white canvas-topped shoes, even with a light tropical suit.

"You've got to get out of those white shoes, Smitty," he said.

On other occasions, he would spot reporters wearing un-matched jackets and trousers to work on a week day. Johnson would point the man out and say to others, "Look at that fellow —doesn't know what day it is." (LBJ thought sport coats were all right on Saturdays.)

At other times, the depth of his personal knowledge about some relatively unimportant person's background could be very surprising. I once asked him privately in an interview on his fifty-eighth birthday how he could enjoy such a day when he had such a painful accumulation of crises—Vietnam, inflation, racial violence.

"You've got to remember," he said, "that a President can con-centrate on his official problems with almost no thought of daily personal detail. Hell, I don't have anything like the troubles you have—you lost your boy in Vietnam when you were going through a divorce from your first wife, behind in your taxes, poor-mouthing me on the Merv Griffin Show to make money for big tuition bills—I've got it a lot better than you have."

I was more than a little startled and taken aback. I don't know to this day whether he had deliberately had a check run on me or whether he had just been asking around. It was not an isolated case, though. He knew vast amounts of trivia about all sorts of people in Washington.

He had used such knowledge to his advantage on Capitol Hill as Senate Majority Leader, flattering, probing for weakness, re-minding of debts, as he exercised his considerable skills of legis-lative salesmanship. This practice carried over to the White House. Again, a personal incident comes to mind.

Flying back from an Asian tour which had included a quick appearance in Vietnam, I mentioned in a group conversation that included some Johnson staff members that the trip reminded me of FDR's 1944 "secret trip to the Pacific for highest war coun-cils with Nimitz and MacArthur" with whom Navy records showed he talked for 55 minutes over five days and nights. On

45

this trip during which FDR accepted the Democratic nomination "with the fighting men at a secret naval base on the west coast"—and which happened to be a very plush railroad car parked on the edge of the Marine base at San Diego—he spent far more time posing for photographs with troops in all manner of fierce array.

At any rate, my less than flattering comparison apparently got back to the President, because on the next leg of the trip I was ushered into the Presidential presence for a discussion of my reporting. It was the classic "Johnson treatment." First, he began by chewing me into ragged, but bite-sized pieces about something I'd written from either Darwin or Korat. Then came the pause, the smile, the friendly punch in the solar plexus— "You lost a son in Vietnam, so you have a pretty big stake here, yourself."

I do not mean to give the impression that Johnson used this as a club with me. In fact, he took a very personal interest in the loss and helped my family and me immeasurably through a difficult period, but this personal involvement and approach was just that part of his style which made his way of running the White House so distinctive.

He probably had less private use for the perquisites of the office than most of the Presidents, but there was not one of his privileges that he would not put to use for political effect or to satisfy his notion of what Presidential power should entail.

Once at the ranch, Johnson stepped from the house and told a staff member that the three men with him were his guests and he wanted them flown back to Austin by helicopter, with cars at the landing pad in town to ferry the passengers to their hotel. The staff member agreed and ran—literally ran—to the trailer to alert the officer in charge of the helicopters.

The officer commanding the three choppers, stationed most of the time at the ranch when the Johnsons were in residence, threw up his arms in dismay. He explained that the President, himself, planned to use two of the choppers within twenty minutes and the third helicopter was committed to another assignment, being in the air at the moment.

46

The President's assistant bit his lip. He had known of no plans for LBJ to leave the ranch that afternoon and here was an airlift set up and ready to go. He called the main house, told another staff member about the situation and asked for orders.

The helicopter dispatcher could hear the President saying with vehemence that could have been measured on a seismograph that he was, to put it mildly, displeased—that he had directed that his guests be returned to Austin by chopper at once and he saw no reason why the order should not be executed as given.

The guests felt quite embarrassed about the whole business and, more immediately, were becoming quite cold standing outside the trailer in a stiff winter wind as they caught wisps of the worried conversation and a lot of cigar smoke drifting from the portable command post.

One of the guests implored the White House personnel, "Listen, take us back by car or just drive us up to the highway and we'll catch the next bus."

"If the Old Man ever heard of that, we would catch even more hell," one staffer replied through the half-opened trailer door.

After considerable telephoning and firing radio bolts into the air, the third helicopter was diverted from its mission, brought back to the ranch landing strip where the guests went aboard and scarcely cleared the field before Johnson and some other friends, accompanying agents, and a few reporters trooped out of the ranch house to board the remaining two 'copters for a brief hop to a nearby ranch where the President liked to go to discuss cattle-raising.

A superficial incident, perhaps, but symptomatic, I think, of Johnson's style and also of his view of the Presidency. They were his helicopters. His staff and his reporters wore suits to work. He was the President ("the only President you have") and it was his White House to mold, his administration to drive to success. The early morning vigils for the return of the planes in Vietnam fit the pattern. He felt responsible for each plane and each crew and, in a sense, he was. They were his and part of his "very personal Presidency."

47

2.

I used to travel to Gettysburg once or twice a year after President Eisenhower left the White House, just to chat and get his views on how the new President was doing. Often, I would get a story, but sometimes we just talked.

When I went to the farm in the spring of 1965, we fell into a discussion of Lyndon Johnson. I was telling General Eisenhower that, yes, it was true that Johnson was often awake at 3 a.m. on many mornings, calling Saigon and receiving the latest possible word from the Pentagon on results of specific air strikes and company-sized ground operations against the Viet Cong.

Ike had been leaning back in a comfortable chair, but bolted upright and seemed genuinely upset.

"Oh, he can't do that and possibly maintain the proper posture or frame of mind for basic decisions. I'm to have dinner with him soon and I intend to give him a real Dutch uncle talking-to."

On my next visit in the fall on the occasion of his 75th birthday, I asked Eisenhower if he had given the President his Dutch-uncle talk.

"Yes, I told him what I thought, although you can't be as blunt as you might be when talking to the President. I told him that when I was operations officer at the War Department, I moved whole divisions in and out of the country and I reported to General Marshall about it only when I saw him on Saturday mornings for our review of the week, and this is the way he wanted it.

"A man with responsibilities of President simply should not allow himself to become bogged down in detail. For one thing, in a war or combat situation, this can be upsetting emotionally and throw off judgment.

"The President's job is to know exactly what the problem is that he should solve and then decide how to solve it. Then he's got to find his lieutenants, his proconsuls, and then trust the men he himself picks and say, 'now you must do this, within the limits I give you.'

48

"Do you go, do you send troops to, say, Lebanon or don't you?
Now, it's up to somebody else to find where are the troops,
exactly what kind, what's the date they're going in and so forth.
The President of the United States must not burden himself with
all of those things."

These words made quite an impression on me, I remember,
coming as they did in the middle of the hectic Johnson years.
Eisenhower's opinion reflected a totally different White House
style—the posture of command—and recalled an era when
organization-chart efficiency and delegation was the norm.

The philosophy was to appear again in the Nixon administration. President Nixon feels that he should reserve himself for the
"big decisions" and should take the "long view" of problems,
instead of just bouncing from crisis to crisis. He thought, for
instance, that President Johnson reacted in the Dominican Re-
public episode largely on the basis of incomplete and exaggerated
information—a mistake he could have avoided by taking a more
detached and systematic view.

The whole idea of keeping a President above the fray for only
key decisions can be traced in recent times to Sherman Adams,
President Eisenhower's assistant. In the early days of the administration, Adams envisioned a White House office so well organized
that the President would have to make only five or six basic
decisions a year. In Adams' administrative dream, expert staff
organization would keep the President free from minor administrative detail, from Miss Wisconsin Cheeses and state-level Republicans wanting a federal job for Uncle Jasper.

Unfortunately, the plan—at least as conceived in ideal terms
by Adams—was doomed from the start. There was no way that
the President could spend much of his time in some antiseptic
aerie, contemplating a never-ending flow of memoranda and
emerging only for regular meetings with the Congressional
leaders, the Cabinet and the National Security Council.

Notes from Senators had to be answered, frantic pleas from
the National Committee dealt with, emergency cables evaluated,
and ceremonial obligations fulfilled. So the system was gradually
loosened, although Eisenhower, himself, always endorsed Adams'

49

principle. The ex-General's desire for patness, consistency and regularity continued to be reflected in other ways. He had the greatest number of fixed weekly conferences, for instance, of any recent President.

The ceremonial demands were among the most vexing to Eisenhower. He thought, for example, that it was an outmoded 19th-century mystique that required that state visits from foreign leaders last three days each with three full-scale dinners, two involving the President. He said that ninety per cent of this business could be taken care of by the Secretary of State, were it not for binding precedent.

President Kennedy felt very much the same way about ceremonial duties. I remember one Monday morning when he was just returning from a weekend at Cape Cod. He had alighted from his helicopter on the south lawn and was walking toward his military aide, Major General Chester Clifton, who was waiting beside the grass with a portfolio of new trouble overseas. JFK glanced up at the grassy bank outside the President's office and was surprised to find a covey of beauty queens steered to the White House by a benevolent member of Congress.

Kennedy looked quite displeased, gave the girls a wide berth and hustled into his office. He later groaned, "More beauty queens—Eisenhower was right!"

Eisenhower was not so unusual in the way he chafed under the ceremonial demands of the office. All Presidents object to mundane obstructions or frivolous constraints on what they consider to be their real job. But it was Eisenhower's conception of just that—what he considered his real job as President—that distinguished him from, say, a Truman or a Roosevelt.

I once asked him, for instance (and this was while he was still President), "Do you regard yourself as a politician?"

He answered with a vehement, "NO!" He said that while he had been in and out of Washington for a long period of years, he had always regarded himself as one thing—an Army officer. He did add that, since he had entered elective office, he had often made better political decisions, he thought, than the professionals. He said he felt this was because he instinctively took a longer, broader view of a political situation than most professionals who, too often, had fairly restricted vision and could look at a situation only in terms of immediate political benefit.

But he completely rejected "practical politics . . . as this phrase is usually employed." He said, for example, that the President's role in the field of patronage was far too extensive. He regarded as an undesirable example of practical politics the practice of checking on a prospective federal appointee's campaign contributions before considering his other qualities.

Harry Truman, on the other hand, would have been shocked at even the suggestion that the dispensing of patronage and active leadership of his party was an unimportant or unworthy task for a President. He spent hours on political problems and the patronage questions, down to a postmastership in some rural backwater.

The difference in attitudes between Presidents Eisenhower and Truman can, of course, be largely attributed to their contrasting backgrounds. The time Mr. Truman spent studying the lower levels of politics as a precinct boss was spent by his successor at West Point and the Army War College, following a professional soldier's career. There is, to be sure, a lot of politics in the Army, but not the kind Mr. Truman learned from the Pendergasts in Missouri. Hence, it was rather painful for Mr. Eisenhower to start, on the far side of middle age, learning what to him was a new profession.

As a result, Eisenhower left many of the strictly political decisions to party officials. Such delegation freed his time, he felt, for other more important matters, including simply the time for relaxation which he thought was essential for keeping a clear mind and sound judgment.

This left him open to the charge that he took too much time off, particularly for his golf. It was true that most days he left the office by 4:30 and 5 o'clock in the afternoon, but relative measurements of how hard different Presidents worked are extremely tricky.

A Roosevelt-Nixon comparison is, of course, absurd, since the world has shrunk so in the intervening years and since rapid communications and nuclear weapons have so changed the tenor of decision-making. But even a Truman-Eisenhower comparison on something like "amount of work done" is like comparing apples and oranges. They did different things.

Mr. Truman might have used the better part of a day to fill a dozen patronage jobs, pouring over the political background and party recommendations involved in each case, while Mr. Eisenhower would take only a few seconds to sign appointment papers approved by others. Comparisons cannot be so systematic.

There was no mistaking a change in the winds, however, when John Kennedy entered the White House in January 1961. His White House style was nearly the opposite of the Eisenhower format. In came a man of frenetic pace, a mocker of protocol and formality—a President whose administration when contrasted with his predecessor's seemed almost helter-skelter. A man once wrote a book dividing chief executives into "Presidents of action" and "Presidents of restraint" and I never really thought it could be done, but here perhaps was a pair that provided a laboratory case.

The danger came in equating action with "good" and restraint with "bad," and, indeed, it was difficult at first to report on the manner in which President Kennedy was conducting business without being editorial or seeming to imply criticism of the former President Eisenhower.

Ike was a calm, deliberate and unruffled figure of an elder leader who had seen just about every kind of crisis the world could produce. It took a lot to produce anything approaching frenzy in the man, and only impending doom would have kept him in the office past the dinner hour. He was not only running the Presidency as a general, but as a *retired* general, closely questioning his staff about decisions, but leaving to them the bulk of the day-to-day problems. As he pointed out, himself, he had already made his place in history before entering the White House.

Kennedy, on the other hand, was almost painfully aware of his youth, his very slim margin of victory and felt the need to prove himself. In addition, he was met in short order with a series of crises upon taking office—the Bay of Pigs, Laos, Berlin, the Cuban missile crisis, Birmingham—that left him little time for contemplation. The result was that Kennedy and his staff seemed to be performing with the elbow-swinging fervor of roofers who've been told to expect rain tomorrow.

Even as he crossed the office threshold in the morning, he would call out instructions to various staff members. He wanted information, all they could get, on a certain situation in government and he wanted it in a hurry; by day's end at least. This, to some veteran administrators, was quite a shock. During the past administration, they frequently had more time on comparable assignment. But what surprised these men even more was that Kennedy often was waiting in his office at 7 or 8 o'clock at night when the requested report arrived.

Gone was the precisionary, always-on-time and tidily compartmented chain-of-command system. The new President insisted on maintaining a clear channel of communication and direct contact with his Cabinet officers. Under the Kennedy system, it was a most unusual day when several members of the Cabinet were not at the White House on missions of their own or at the behest of the President. They arrived and departed with such suddenness that their names frequently did not appear on the Chief Executive's list of appointments, but their limousines could be seen parked along West Executive Avenue, sometimes until late evening.

Staff business became the President's business. Work assignments were made on an informal basis, particularly after the Bay of Pigs disaster undermined Kennedy's confidence in such formal structures as the National Security Council and specialist advisory groups like the Joint Chiefs of Staff. Kennedy also employed a technique which had been used quite frequently by President Roosevelt in staff administration. He would give a problem to two people whose views he knew clashed on a subject, figuring that out of the adversary approach, he would get the best appraisal of the issue.

His system required great flexibility and the ability to shift directions. He set out basic goals and did not hesitate to change his avenue of approach, if it seemed advisable. If there was one word to typify his operations, it would seem to be "changeable."

53

He changed speech texts right down to the second he began delivery. He scrawled changes in letters ready for signature. He changed the schedules of his trips on the way to the airport.

All this was not done without cost. The last-minute fiddling with speeches caused much of what he finally *did* to miss print. Perfectionism and late-hour rearrangement delayed messages to Congress, in some cases for two or three days. The Republicans decried this as indecision, of course, while the Democrats hailed it as an admirable attack on cumbersome formalism.

Another change from the Eisenhower days was Kennedy's personal contact with reporters. For one thing, he could "talk shop" with newsmen. More than any other modern President, Mr. Kennedy had a realistic understanding of professional news operations. He genuinely liked quite a few reporters above and beyond the call of political expediency. He sometimes asked one reporter or another for advice and, in so doing, was not just attempting flattery. He genuinely wanted to know what the man thought.

Kennedy, himself, had a passion for reading, which further elevated his standing with many journalists. He could routinely quote from six or seven daily newspapers, as well as from such assorted esoterica as the *Army, Navy and Air Force Journal, The Economist,* and *Problems of Communism.* Where Eisenhower— or Sherman Adams, for him—would turn away a long report and ask for a synopsis, Kennedy would shun the précis and ask for the full edition—with footnotes and appendices. All of which he would voraciously devour at well over a thousand words per minute.

One's reading speed, in fact, became a new badge of honor in the Executive Branch. How many push-ups could you do? A nap!? The new organization of the White House, its young look and its new pace all combined in a Kennedy style that was characterized by nothing so much as activity, activity which the Eisenhower method of organization might have seen as largely wasted motion and useless in itself, but motion nonetheless— kinetic energy as a principle of government.

3.

The aura of the FDR years was one of grandeur. Mr. Roosevelt was good and he knew it. He was superbly confident that he was the best political strategist known in American history. He knew for a fact that he could outguess and outmaneuver his opponents. As he did, time and again. He lost specific battles on occasion, but he won the wars.

To many, he was a fabulous monarch, a dramatic king. He could be and usually was socially democratic, but always with a regal air that never let you doubt that he was in full command of the situation.

Probably from childhood there was never a gathering that he did not dominate.

The Truman White House style changed one's whole perception of the Presidency. Following the exalted statesman came a plain-talking, middle-class, average-looking ordinary fellow. Franklin D. Roosevelt was *for* the people all right, but Harry S Truman was *of* the people. It took a while to sink in, but this man was one of us.

There were many sorts of changes at the White House when Truman became President, of course. One was a simple matter of mobility. Secret Service agents had to get used to the idea of a President who moved about easily, and Mr. Truman certainly could, darting off on his walks at 120 paces a minute. But the big change in the White House mood was the new identification of the Presidency with the so-called little man.

When Mr. Roosevelt died, Mr. Truman thought as an average American would: when you move into a new house that has been occupied by other people, the place could stand a coat of paint and general freshening.

While this was being done, the President and his family moved out of their $100 a month apartment and into Blair House, the government's guest house for visiting dignitaries just across Pennsylvania Avenue from the White House and what was then the State Department.

55

Mr. Roosevelt used to start work about ten or ten-thirty, but Mr. Truman gave people quite a shock. The first morning, he turned up for work about eight o'clock, walking across from Blair House in the middle of a group of Secret Service agents.

About the second or third morning, the President noticed a small group of White House reporters waiting to walk over with him. They were men in plainly apparent early morning suffering.

"What's the matter, boys?" the President asked. "You all look sleepy."

"Oh, everything's fine," one of the newspapermen answered. "It's just that we didn't know when you became President that we would have to begin working in the middle of the night."

Truman laughed.

"Stick with me and I'll make men of you yet. Just wait until I get organized and start coming to work on time."

Several other examples of his direct manner and plain speech stick out in my memory. Curiously, they all seem to recall President Truman when he was away from the White House. He did tend to feel penned in by the physical confines of the White House, and liked to escape whenever possible, if only for an hour or so.

Not long after Mr. Truman assumed office, Washington newspapermen planned a cocktail party and buffet supper for Presidential assistant Steve Early who was preparing to leave the White House for a vice-presidency with Pullman, Inc.

The President was told about the party and he said he would like to come and join in paying tribute to Steve. Truman came early and strolled around the big Presidential Room at the Statler Hotel, greeting friends and in general having a fine time.

Graham Jackson, the Negro musician from Georgia, was there, playing alternately at the piano, and then at an electric organ. Graham wanted to play something special for the President and Mr. Truman sent word he'd like to hear the Chopin Polonaise.

Jackson, whose greatest talent was boogie-woogie, but who prided himself on knowing from memory about every musical composition ever written, started in. He gave Chopin some new, hot touches and Mr. Truman smiled broadly throughout the number.

He applauded Graham enthusiastically when the music was done, remarking to a reporter standing by him, "Well, that might not be Chopin, but it was plenty loud."

A waiter brought the President a bountiful plate from the buffet and Mr. Truman sat at a table with Steve Early and some friends. Everybody was hungry and started eating immediately. Truman toyed with his food. He looked at his watch several times.

"Mister President, can we get you something else?"

"No, Smitty," he said a little sadly. "I'll eat a little here and then I've got to go back to the White House and eat some more. We've got company for dinner and I just have to go back."

The President thought a moment and ate a shrimp.

"It seems," he said more to himself than to his companions, "that there's somebody for supper every night."

There wasn't an ounce of pretense in Mr. Truman. He abhorred sham.

This was demonstrated on the European trip aboard the USS *Augusta*.* The first afternoon at sea the President wanted a breath of fresh air, so he told his staff and some of the *Augusta's* officers that he wanted to go out on "the front porch for a while."

The regular Navy officers arched their eyebrows at the completely unnautical term "front porch." But his own Naval Aide smiled knowingly and escorted the President to the forecastle deck.

We later kidded the President about the term, and for saying upstairs and downstairs instead of above and below.

He had a very logical explanation.

"The only time I was ever at sea before was going to France and back in the last war. Now, wouldn't it be silly for me to try to ape the language of men whose business is ships?"

When Truman first began his famous early morning walks

---

* The trip to Germany for the Potsdam Conference in 1945.

around Washington, my first reaction was that this amounted to small-town exhibitionism. But after I walked with him a few times, I realized how deeply and quickly he felt the imprisoning nature of life in the White House.

One morning with no photographers around, Truman was swinging down K Street not far from the White House when he spotted a half dozen people lined up at a bus stop. Unobtrusively, he got at the end of the line and stood still. First a man, then a woman looked around at him. Then they seemed to shrug and resume their newspaper reading. One woman turned around several times and shook her head.

This sent the President into chuckles. He could contain himself no longer as he watched the doubletakes. He bade the startled bus line a friendly good morning and went his way, thoroughly pleased with himself.

Another morning, I was with him in St. Louis. He came out of the hotel shortly after daybreak.

"Come on," he said to the small group of reporters and photographers. "We're going down to the river and spit."

He must have sensed my confusion.

"Don't they go down to the river and spit where you come from?" he said. "I do every time I come to St. Louis."

We were with him in Olympia, Washington, not long after he took office. The war was still on and Truman was to go to San Francisco for the windup of the first UN organizational meeting. The meeting got off schedule and rather than arrive prematurely, Truman decided to wait in Olympia with his old Senate pal, Governor Mon Walgren.

The party went fishing one day in Puget Sound. Photographers were clamoring for a picture. The Governor talked Truman into putting on a heavy Indian sweater and posing for pictures while reeling in a big kingfish caught by other fishermen much earlier. The fish was thoroughly dead and came out of the water as a motionless slab.

A newsreel cameraman, Hugo Johnson, suddenly yelled, "Hold it." He pulled his skiff to the side of the yacht and said to the President, "Don't pose for motion pictures with a dead fish—remember what they did to Cal Coolidge for the same thing?" Truman quietly handed the rod to someone beside him. In the ensuing years that Truman was in office, he never forgot Hugo Johnson for the favor. When Truman went to the Potsdam Big Three meeting, only one newsreel cameraman was allowed on the trip—Hugo.

It was on the same trip to the first meeting of the United Nations, the State Department told President Truman he should give a reception for the Chiefs of Mission and he agreed.

After receiving the Foreign Ministers and Ambassadors, Truman looked around the room and saw that for refreshments, the State Department had provided a flowing bowl of rusty-looking liquid which protocol men told the President was champagne punch.

"Hell, that stuff will rust your pipes," he declared to one and all. "Come on up to my suite, gentlemen, and I'll pour you a real drink."

The diplomats first were shocked, then broke into broad smiles as HST led a line of distinguished world figures toward the elevators.

Because Truman identified so thoroughly with the little man, the little man returned the favor and kept him abreast of many matters which ordinarily escape a President.

On one occasion he traveled to Bolivar, Missouri, for an open-air speech in incredibly hot weather. It was a long, tedious ceremony in broiling sun which sent several members of his entourage scurrying to cooler places.

As his train pulled out of Bolivar, Truman strolled into the diner and stood beside a table where four heat-frazzled friends were trying to recoup on long, cool gin drinks.

"Heh-heh, how did you fellows like the basement of our City Hall?" he said with a chuckle.

The four men were flabbergasted. Indeed, they had left the speaking, sought out the nearby City Hall and gone into the cool basement where one of them produced several miniatures of Scotch which he passed around. How did Truman know?

"I'll tell you one thing, gentlemen," Truman said as he started to walk away. "Bolivar, Missouri, in the summer time is no place to be sipping Scotch in the middle of the day—not even in the City Hall basement."

He knew when a stenographer's baby caught a cold; when a White House servant lost a relative. He thought it was hilarious when Leroy, the White House leaf-raker whom he knew and liked, fobbed himself off as an important official and was shown to a box at Hialeah (Florida) racetrack.

The knowledge, and indeed pride, that he was a fairly typical fellow with no pretensions of being superior gave him, I think, a certain equanimity about his fate that other Presidents have lacked. The famous 1948 campaign is a good example. He was seeking election to the Presidency for the first time in his own right and literally every published expert in the field said it could not be done. Today it is difficult to imagine how thoroughly defeated Truman was in advance. (Or to imagine the magnitude of the upset. Compare the margin of John Kennedy, who was supposed to win, of a little over 100,000 with the margin of Truman, the decided underdog, of over 2 million votes.)

He never thought so, himself. In fact, he did not wait up for the election returns, choosing to go to a definitely middle-class resort outside Kansas City where he went to bed with the birds. One of his chief Secret Service agents shortly before dawn could not stand the excitement any longer and awakened the President to give him the wonderful news.

"You should have gotten some sleep like I did," Truman said, sitting up in bed, rumpled, drowsy and reaching for his glasses. He looked up at the exuberant agent and chided softly, "What did you expect anyway? I've been telling you this all along."

My final memory of him as President recalls that his peace of mind and way of putting things bluntly was not dimmed by his years as Chief Executive. I had been granted a final interview on his last day in office and asked whether he thought he would need protection after he left the White House. He snorted and said, "If any nut tries to shoot me, I'll take the pistol away from him, ram it down his throat and pull the trigger!"

4.

Aspects of a President's White House style come across in his press conferences. This was especially true in the days of the Roosevelt administration before these meetings were sanitized by the glare of television exposure. Press conferences then were dueling matches where the President and reporters truly crossed swords. Exchanges could become angry, as when FDR told a reporter to "go stand in the corner" for asking a stupid question, and bizarre occurrences could happen, as when a haranguing woman, posing as a journalist, had to be bodily removed from one of the meetings in the President's office. She looked, remarked Roosevelt later to his secretary, like "something out of the procession in 'Aïda'" as Secret Service agents simply lifted the lady, chair and all, and carried her into another room.

Roosevelt's press conferences showed his flamboyance, his wit, and his lordly self-assurance. He loved, for example, to tell parables to the press. And after he told them a few times, he was dead certain that they were true. During the early stages of the war when inflationary trends were first showing themselves in force, he told a press conference a story. He swore it was true.

It seems a garage mechanic friend of his "dropped in" for a chat. Now, how in the world a mechanic ever dropped in on Mr. Roosevelt was beyond explanation. He claimed a lot of friends in comparatively low stations of life. I regarded them as his imaginary playmates because I doubted seriously one of them ever existed. He told often of a Chinese laundryman he knew, a baseball player, a small dirt farmer, a garage man. This mechanic, he said, had come to him complaining about the high price of strawberries in February. His "missus," the mechanic was alleged to have told the President, was having to pay a God-awful price for strawberries.

The President said he lectured his mechanic friend sharply. Since when could mechanics afford strawberries out of season? Why didn't they eat something else? Why throw away their defense plant wages in such a foolish fashion? The President used this to prove that the price line actually was being held, but that too many people were spending their money on unnecessary luxuries.

About six months later, the inflation question came up again in a press conference. Someone wanted to know whether the President really thought the price line was being held, and how much longer would it last. The President declined to comment directly. He thought for a moment and added that there were too many people like a master mechanic he knew.

This man, he said, had dropped in "to chat" and complain about the high price of asparagus. And since when, the President said he told the mechanic, did he find it necessary to have asparagus, out of season, on his menu? Why didn't they eat something else? Why contribute to inflation by wasting their defense plant wages on unnecessary luxury items?

I could not resist it. I knew it was presumptuous and bordered on the disrespectful, but I had to ask the question.

"Mr. President," I said, "is that the same mechanic who came in a few months back complaining about the high price of strawberries?"

The press conference exploded into roars of laughter. Mr. Roosevelt turned a little pink and shouted over the guffaws:

"My God, Merriman. It's true. It *is* true. It was the same man."

But he could hardly finish the sentence because he was laughing too hard himself.

On the other hand, no President was ever feared so much in a press conference as Mr. Roosevelt. He could be as rough and tough as a Tenth Avenue blackjack artist. And he could be utterly charming, disarming and thoroughly likeable. It just depended on the question, who asked it and how Mr. Roosevelt felt when he got up that morning.

The fear was understandable. It plainly is not a pleasant experience to be taken to task, publicly and face-to-face, by any President of the country. A reporter cannot argue back unless he is a columnist or editorial writer, and even then it cannot be done in the President's office, but only in print.

There were repeated attempts to argue with Mr. Roosevelt in

a press conference, but there was never a clear-cut victory for a reporter. Jim Wright, then the veteran correspondent for the Buffalo *Evening News,* once won a draw with Mr. Roosevelt who had been hypercritical of some people—mostly newspaper bosses—who were attempting as he put it, to hamstring the administration's conduct of the war.

Wright—not one of those in the President's mind—interjected that he wanted to know who these people were.

"Oh, Jim," said the President rather disgustedly, "of course you know who they are."

"No, I don't, Mr. President," Wright answered firmly.

"Sure you do," Mr. Roosevelt came back.

"No sir, I honestly don't know and I'd like to know," Wright persisted.

The President's face colored and his half-smile faded into a set, stern impression.

"You know, and everybody in this room knows whom I'm talking about," the President said sharply.

And that ended the matter.

Publicly, Mr. Roosevelt forgave the working reporters because they knew not what they did. He claimed repeatedly that the reporters "slanted" stories only on orders from their rich, greedy bosses. To hazard a percentage, Mr. Roosevelt was wrong more than 90 per cent about story slanting.

He once accused me of asking a question on orders from some mystic power above me. In fact he told a press conference he *knew* that I did not want to ask the question. I liked Mr. Roosevelt very much. I think he was a great man. But in this particular instance he manufactured a false story purely to suit his purposes, to dodge an issue.

It happened during an aboard-train press conference coming back from the west coast in 1944. The President had just come back from Hawaii and there had been considerable editorial speculation that, just after accepting his fourth term nomination, he had flown to Pearl Harbor to see General MacArthur and Admiral Nimitz purely to emphasize his role as wartime Commander-in-Chief for the benefit of the voters.

Near the end of the conference, I said:

63

"Mr. President, are you aware of the fact that a number of newspapers—and some politicians, too—are inferring that this trip had political motives?"

The President laughed and shrugged his shoulders.

"Then they knew more about it than I do. There was no politics in it. You were there. You saw what I did."

I forgot about it except to include a brief paragraph far down in my story of the conference.

The first full press conference he held after the trip, the question was raised with him again, but by another reporter.

I don't have his exact words, but the sense was this:

"A young man whom we all know (and he nodded toward me) asked me the same thing the other day. Now, he knew better. He knew the answer. But he had to ask the question. He had received orders from his big bosses to ask such a question. He's a fine young man and I respect him. I know he did not want to ask such a question. So I don't blame him. He was on the same spot with a lot of other reporters. Very often they have to take orders and do things they know are not right."

I started to speak up, but realization of the futility of an argument stopped me. If the President had done what he had admonished so many other people to do—to think things through —he never would have said what he did. Certainly, the President must have known that I had not been in direct contact with any of my superiors for over five weeks—even since before he accepted the nomination. The President was the person who ordered us blacked out on communications.

(And I told Mr. Roosevelt later, not to my knowledge have I ever been "ordered" to ask a question or slant a story by any newspaper boss in my life. No editor has ever said, "Here, let's do a job on this guy regardless of the facts." I had roughly the same conversation with Mr. Nixon in 1960. He wanted to know why we were slanting crowd estimates against him and for Kennedy. The reason was that Kennedy was getting bigger crowds.)

Roosevelt had great vision; he thought big. The New Deal programs were a testimony to the scale of his imagination and certainly the broad-brush approach was necessary to resuscitate the nation's economy, but FDR, the pipe-dreamer, was also in evidence in many of his press conferences. He once suggested moving the capital to Denver and, on another occasion, thought out loud that perhaps a tree-growing project for the Sahara would be just the thing to make the Arab world more viable agriculturally.

He had a similar plan for the location and operation of the United Nations. The excerpt below is from a shipboard talk with newsmen on the homeward voyage from the Yalta meeting in 1945.

PRESIDENT:

Three years ago when I was first talking about the United Nations, Winston said to me, "Where will you put it?" I said, "Not Geneva. Geneva's unlucky, has an unlucky record. I don't want to hold it in any one location. I want everybody pleased." Although I don't think I'll get it, I want to get a building like Al Smith's Empire State Building just for the records and the records staff, and then have the conference meet half the time in one of the Azores Islands. I was there once. In front of my house—I knew a Portuguese on San Miguel—had a great big house. He used to like to take me out on the front steps. There, right in front of me were royal palms and Norwegian spruce, growing side by side. It's a wonderful climate.

CHAPTER THREE

Backstairs at the White House

. . . the White House press has one duty that is vital and that nobody else can perform. It must report hour by hour where the President is, what he is doing and occasionally what he is thinking. It is surveillance reporting. The President's words, the reaction of his audience, his health, his family—these are the things that perhaps matter most to Americans from hour to hour.

A handful in the White House press does it superbly, some even try to get a glimpse of the backstage play. Others do little but sag in the black leather chairs in the White House lobby and wait for the press secretary to hand them the daily news budget. Few men lick the job of being White House correspondent. Mostly, they go off to New Delhi to become foreign correspondents or are pushed into higher posts back in the office when their legs and stomachs begin to weaken on the White House beat.*

* Hugh Sidey, *John F. Kennedy: President* (New York, 1963).

If Merriman Smith had a specialty as a journalist, it was the "backstage play" of White House life. He wrote a column called "Backstairs at the White House" for UPI, and made, as someone once wrote, "both a profession and a hobby out of the Presidency."

The behind-the-scenes view of White House life—which he had for more than twenty-nine years—gave him some outspoken opinions about not only the office of president, but also of what it is like to live at 1600 Pennsylvania Avenue.

IT IS HARD to understand why a man will deliberately seek the toughest job in the land. Mrs. Warren G. Harding cried out against her husband running for President, expressing the belief that it would kill him. It did. Franklin D. Roosevelt at the end of his third term said everything that was in his soul yearned to return to the family home on the Hudson River. But he ran for the fourth term in which he died. Harry S Truman said repeatedly that he did not want to be President, that his happiest years were in the Senate. Yet he fought for a second term.

The lure of being President knows no equal in this country. Men suffer extreme indignities and even the threat of poverty and assassination to seek the job. The main attraction, of course, is prestige; the impetus, a love of power. A President may be completely hamstrung by an opposition Congress, but he still has unmatched national power, crowds still turn out in city streets to cheer him and he always feels an almost holy sense of responsibility to the nation, whether his fulfillment of that responsibility is bungling or masterful.

Yet the office itself is a bundle of contradictions. The President may ask Congress to pass laws, but he cannot make a law himself. He may direct a theoretically subordinate government agency to take some action, only to find that it delays or subverts his will. The manner in which his Executive Departments administer the laws is always subject to review and interpretation by the Judicial Branch of the Government.

68

The complex nature of the office means that the President should be an excellent actor, a better-than-average financier, have administrative ability superior to that of a big corporation executive and be quite a fair student of the military sciences. He should know some law, geography, medicine and sociology. He ought to know a lot about farming. He should have been an avid student of international affairs before going to the White House.

In other words, he should know something about not only every important phase of American life, but also of the economies and thoughts of the other nations of the world. There have been, and there will be again, Presidents who do not measure up to these requirements, but, in this case, we still expect a Chief Executive to "grow with the office," to learn on the job what he has missed in the struggle to get there.

In addition to all this, we expect Presidents periodically to go to the people—literally, to touch them, often until the President's hand is puffed, scratched and bleeding. What does shaking hands have to do with a man's ability to direct the fate of the world's most powerful nation? Nothing at all. But the Presidency—pinnacle of an American elite—must regularly prove its democratic credentials.

Presidents must be a mix of philosopher and pol with neither element appearing too prominently. A President must store up his political capital, his Gallup Poll ratings, and his "charisma" and save them for creative accomplishment, legislation and reform. Yet he must also deliberately expend this capital when he has to take the necessary, but unpopular, stand.

There are other ironies to the Presidency. The White House staff has grown ten times in less than fifty years. Yet the job has grown even faster, and the isolation of a President with it. And no matter how much the President delegates authority, if a subordinate makes a poor decision, the final blame always rests on "the boss."

Our system gives the President four jobs, all of which could be full-time: Chief of State, Head of Government, Ceremonial Chief of State, and Head of a Political Party. Yet the Washington Senators baseball team expects the Chief Executive to throw out the first ball each Opening Day. And the President is charged by law to issue and sign prize fight regulations for the Panama Canal Zone.

If the Presidency is a contradictory institution, then, certainly, life in the White House is a mirror of its anomalies. Thomas Jefferson sensed this when he referred to his "life of splendid misery" in the White House. The President is surrounded by hundreds of men and women whose every waking hour is dominated by one life: his. Thus, life in the White House reinforces an awareness of the powers of the Presidency. On the other hand, he is also surrounded by a high, black iron fence and the unblinking eye of public scrutiny.

Yet somehow, Presidents survive in this hellish job and somehow the life of the White House acts as a crucible, forging more leaders than it breaks. Just how this process works, day-to-day, has been one of my main interests as a correspondent.

Focusing on everyday White House life has some disadvantages for a reporter. It involves lots of time watching for relatively mundane incidents and details, hours talking to White House policemen and butlers and gardeners, hours which might have been spent some other way—talking to a Cabinet officer, maybe, or studying the *Congressional Record*. But, as columnist David Lawrence wrote in 1927 about the White House, "an item from the backstairs might be more interesting than an item from the grandstairs." And these are the items which lead to some understanding of the "splendid misery."

The "splendid" half of Mr. Jefferson's paradoxical quote is hard to overestimate. President Nixon—in fact any modern American President—leads the sort of personal life that no multimillionaire, no industrial baron, no scion of inherited fortune could possibly match.

For example, there is not an American private fortune large enough or willing to support what amounts to a personal fleet of twelve-passenger turbo-jet helicopters manned around the clock, seven days a week, and available on five minutes' notice. And add to that a constantly available pool of high speed jet transport aircraft with a passenger capacity of more than seventy persons each. This takes care of any transportation problem a

President might have for official or purely personal reasons. No millionaire can make the same claim.

The Air Force plane in which President Nixon cruises the world is an electrical and aerodynamic marvel. Not even an Onassis or a Getty could have one, much less afford one. Air Force One, or AF26000 as it's known to the military, has nine air-to-surface telephones, plus radio-teletype and an assortment of other, secret communications equipment.

When Richard Nixon took office, the plane was overhauled and reconfigured on the inside to his tastes. The bill came to something over $300,000. When he bought the "Western White House" in San Clemente, what was once a rather weedy estate became an attractively gardened fortress, complete with helicopter landing pad. This was done largely through the efforts of the General Services Administration.

Nor is this a new Presidential syndrome. President Kennedy, for example, never went on the road without a special mattress and a very large chair which was his favorite. Not even the President of General Motors tries to travel with a full size mattress and a 200-pound chair.

When President Johnson needed a haircut, the barber came to him wherever he was—in the office, in his bedroom or beside his swimming pool. He did not have to worry about his dogs being fed—someone did that for him. There are no taxis to be paid, no restaurant checks, no tipping for a President.

If a President wants to travel, he never has to worry about his luggage. He never considers such mundane matters as laundry or dry cleaning or whether he's about to run out of razor blades —all this is someone else's duty.

In the area of communications, the richest men in America don't come close to a President who can talk with no personal charge to him to virtually any civilized spot on the globe—and some not so civilized. Furthermore, this incredible communications capability is present wherever the President is—in the air, afloat or speeding along a highway. Somewhere there may be an oil-happy sheikh with a solid gold Cadillac, but it is generally believed that a President rides in this country's most costly car—

a limousine which supposedly cost the Ford Motor Company something over $150,000.

If his wife wants fresh flowers in every room of the White House, she has but to murmur her wish. If they want music at lunch—anything from the classics to rock and roll—all they have to do is call the Marine Band which within its ranks has a jazz combo, a string ensemble and a small symphony.

If there is a star of stage, screen or television whose talents the President would like to observe first hand, all he has to do is express a desire and, within a reasonable time, there can be a command performance in the East Room.

Most of the luxuries—particularly those of the time-saver and nerve-soother variety—are designed, the standard argument runs, to free the President from worry or concern with any minor detail which could distract from his major burdens: the awful problems of a modern, urbanized society; the life-and-death responsibilities as Commander-in-Chief. This is, of course, partially true, but undoubtedly many of the perquisites of the Presidency exist mainly to pay homage to a national figurehead.

Curiously, perhaps, the opulence of Presidential living has never successfully been made a political issue in any campaign. This may be due to occasional symbolic enconomizing gestures— Eisenhower's mothballing of the Presidential yachts, LBJ's dowsing of the White House lights—but, more likely, it has to do with the desires of the American public. Like the answer of the dictator who was asked about his lavish limousines when the people in his country were mostly very poor, it appears in America that "the people want it that way." Like the British, we take pride in our own type of royalty.

We don't seem to worry about the tax dollars so much when we can see a tangible return. And, in the case of the Presidency, we get an ongoing spectacle for our money. The public gradually takes the attitude—and one which is admittedly fostered by aggressive reporters—that they in some sense "own" the President and First Family.

So, some roughly equitable relationship seems—almost by evolution—to have been worked out. Much is given to a President and much is demanded from him and his family.

One result is that the White House is not really a home. True, a First Family moving in will find just about everything needed for modern survival and graceful living—one of the largest and best trained servant staffs of any known residence in the world; several kitchens, the largest of which routinely turns out ten-course dinners for 140 to 190 seated guests; a steam room; a gymnasium; a sewing room, adequate for top name dress designers as well as linen maintenance and repair; a florist shop; and out on the grounds, dog kennels, tennis courts and a golf green. But, partly because of all these amenities, a member of the President's family is never alone, never really free from a goldfish-bowl existence.

Some of this is due to security considerations—the ever-watchful, ever-present Secret Service—and some to the presence of reporters and, to a lesser degree, the public. For example, after the glamor has worn off, teen-age residents of the White House have seemed to find 1600 Pennsylvania Avenue an inhibiting address. Their friends can come and go only with a certain amount of official effort and regimentation, leaving names with the guards, and so on. In general, the natural spontaneity of adolescent life is cramped, if not killed.

To a young child, there is the growing awareness that he is different—special, to be sure, but still different. Photographers crowd around to take his picture, but not his friends. School comes to him instead of the reverse. He probably sees more of Father than when he had other work, but he has him to himself much less. He may see the President walking from one wing to another during the day; the family can, if they want, see him frequently at Rose Garden ceremonies, press conferences in the East Room, at garden parties and numerous receptions. They will see more of him on television than ever before, but if the young boy or girl really wants to talk with him, it may have to be early in the morning or late at night.

The family also operates under the assumption that unconventional behavior or even just sloppy appearance will be noticed and publicized and may even take on political importance. Thus, the teen-age daughter of a President may think twice about wearing some daring new fashion, afraid that it will be held up as an example of declining morals under, say, a liberal administration.

Such fears are not just over-sensitivity or petulant paranoia, but have a firm basis in fact. These Presidential children are often fairly precocious political pros. They know how trivial matters can take on symbolic proportions. Political history is full of examples.

Take something as obscure as President Truman's problem with the name of his plane. Before he ever took office, the plane was known as the "Sacred Cow" because of its large white shape. Some people objected. One faction said it was an insult to the Hindus of India. Others wrote that the use of the word "sacred" was sacrilegious. Special stationery was printed for the plane, calling it "The Flying White House," but still the name persisted.

The family hears Father's press secretary insist that the President visited a friend's "farm" to hunt—not his "plantation"—and they are reminded that they must watch every word. Naturally, they want to help. They know, too, that they can lose votes by a wrong step, a careless word, or an indiscreet disclosure. It's as if their husband or father were a salesman. They would feel terrible if they did something to lose a sale or scare off a customer. The opportunity is compounded in the White House and the stakes are higher, so the concern is intensified. Like the President, members of his family become performers.

While First Families have usually grown pretty stoical about constraints on their lives, Presidents, themselves, have often been quite adamant about guarding family privacy. There is rarely much they can do, but some have gotten quite angry over such matters.

President Truman's sensitivity about the privacy of his daughter, Margaret, was well-known. For example, when a Washington columnist printed that Mr. Truman sent her to their home in Independence, Missouri, for the summer to get her away from Washington parties, the President was furious. The connotation was that Margaret had turned into quite a party-goer, and the President said he regarded the column as an unwarranted lie.

Truman's reaction reminded some press room old-timers of a

74

similar incident involving Woodrow Wilson and his daughter, also named Margaret. President Wilson, shortly after some newspapers had printed an item about his daughter which he found highly annoying, called a conference of correspondents.

"I address you as Woodrow Wilson and not as the President," he said.

He referred to the reports about his daughter and then said sharply, "This must stop . . . The next time, I shall do what any other indignant father would do. I will punch the man who writes it in the nose."

Often, it is a First Family mother who is most zealous in guarding a child's privacy. Jacqueline Kennedy got a well-deserved reputation in this regard. One other very protective figure was Barbara Eisenhower, Ike's attractive daughter-in-law and mother of his beloved grandchildren. I remember one incident where she actually got angry with the President for subjecting one of the children to added publicity.

It was an Easter Sunday at Augusta, Georgia, where the family was vacationing for a few days. At the end of a routine picture session, Barbara went indoors, but the President called to his grandson, David.

"Come over here, David, I want you to show these men something," he said.

David marched over to the President's side as the photographers and reporters crowded around. The youngster's navy blue jacket was carefully buttoned and he was the living picture of a well-scrubbed and combed six-year-old in his Easter best.

The President suddenly clapped his hands loudly.

David tore open his coat, pulled a monster cap model of an old frontier six-shooter from his belt and quickly pulled the trigger.

Flashbulbs exploded all over the lawn. The President and reporters praised David loudly for his quick draw. The cameramen screamed to have it done over again and the President, proud of young David's cap-pistol prowess, repeated the handclapping exercise. With another flare of flashbulbs, the front door of the Augusta National Country Club cottage flew open

75

and Barbara marched down the walk with a grim, determined look on her face.

"Oh-oh," the President said softly.

"Here, David," his mother said, "come on inside. I don't think that is the sort of picture for Easter morning . . ."

David meekly stuck his gun in his belt and headed toward his mother, with a hangdog look of a gunman brought to justice. The President looked toward the golf course and remarked what a wonderful, bright day it was.

Actually, parents who want "normal" childhoods for their off-spring in the White House seem to me to be asking for the impossible. Life there is not normal at all. White House children are simply by definition the center of considerable attention.

It does remain an open question, however, whether this sort of abnormal childhood leaves any permanent, harmful effects. And if you *could* prove that more children who have lived in the White House grow up to have, say, psychological or marital or other personal problems, could you isolate this to the actual White House experience? For example, children of famous figures in general—not just Presidents—have often been argued to have a built-in tendency toward emotional difficulties of adjustment and identity.

In fact, the experience of children in the White House has been rather uneven. When little Diana Hopkins, daughter of FDR aide Harry Hopkins, lived in the White House with her father, she seemed a miserably lonely little girl. She was then the "only child" of the White House and tended a rather pathetic little "victory garden" on the back lawn and kept to herself.

On the other hand, the Kennedy children seemed to lead a fairly unfettered and happy existence in the White House. John, Jr. could turn the President's antique desk into a first-rate secret fort and Caroline once used the ladders of a Navy destroyer as a makeshift jungle gym. But they did, it seemed, suffer more than most children from the frequent separations from their parents.

Sistie and Buzzie, the children of President Roosevelt's daughter, Anna Boettinger, probably came as near as any children to having a truly happy and carefree time in the White House. I remember one winter day when Sistie and Buzzie slipped into the kitchen and purloined two large aluminum serving trays. They spirited the trays out through the old diplomatic reception room and were first discovered sledding on the rolling south lawn of the White House. It probably was not until that moment that anybody in the preoccupied family realized that the little boy and girl did not have sleds.

Over the years, even the plight of animals around the White House has served to illustrate that 1600 Pennsylvania Avenue is not like other homes. Fala, FDR's little Scottie, was nearly denuded several times by people at large receptions who would try to clip some of the famous dog's black hair for souvenirs. And the names of Charlie the Terrier and Tom Kitten used to come up in press briefings in the Kennedy administration. Pierre Salinger, JFK's press secretary, once had to explain why Charlie, Caroline's dog, was being banished to Middleburg, Virginia. It turned out Charlie had been chasing the White House ducks. On another occasion, Salinger had to answer questions about the rumored pregnancy of Tom Kitten.

Wild animals got attention too. The White House now has electronic recordings played on outside speakers to keep starlings from marring the beauty of the grounds and the tranquility of the setting with their screeching. Theoretically, the sounds are of starlings in distress and this is supposed to warn the other birds to stay clear. Starlings, however, still abound.

During the Eisenhower administration, squirrels who had been burying their nuts and acorns in the President's green, were caught in box-traps and exiled to Rock Creek Park. This so upset one suburban gardner that he trapped his own squirrels and released them back through the White House fence, until stopped by police. All these little vignettes got considerable news play; the saga of the squirrels was page one in the *Washington Post*.

So the lesson, if any, that Presidents learn from public reaction to such trival facets of the Presidency as animal life is that they have an unparalleled audience, a unique opportunity in public life to use their personal actions as an example—to teach. They can use the Presidency, as Teddy Roosevelt said, as a "bully pulpit."

John Kennedy attempted to use the glamour value of the office to promote such causes as physical fitness. Even the non-athletic Pierre Salinger got involved in the fifty-mile hike craze until he thought better of its effect on his rotund figure and got the AMA to warn against such treks for the out-of-shape. President Johnson, as mentioned before, really started his turn-off-the-lights campaign as a symbolic gesture. In fact, the electricity bill went *up* during the Johnson years for other reasons, but the point was made.

Just how sensitively attuned the public is to events in the White House and in the lives of its occupants is constantly reinforced to Presidents in a variety of ways. Presidential influence clearly extends beyond the nation's politics.

During the Kennedy administration, furniture companies advertised "JFK Rocking Chairs;" millinery shops displayed "Jackie Pillboxes." When FDR was photographed using a long cigarette holder, the sale of these hitherto effete items skyrocketed. Bow tie sales boomed when Mr. Truman started wearing them.

The White House always resists direct commercialization, as when a flower seed company came out with the "Lady Bird Mum" at the height of Mrs. Johnson's beautification activities. There is usually a staff memo, followed by a directive from the Better Business Bureau, but nothing can be done legally. Businesses thrive on presidentially-inspired fads. A lot of people criticized Mr. Truman for wearing loud sports shirts and eccentric hats, but you never heard a word of that criticism from the sports shirt makers who noticed the new demand. The first time President Kennedy was photographed smoking a cigar, the overjoyed Cigar Institute put out three press releases.

A President finds that objects he has merely touched become things of some importance. Harry Truman left a trail of souvenir coffee cups through his years in office. Occasionally on his famous early morning walks, and particularly in areas outside Washington, Truman would stop at a diner or cafe for coffee. He always paid one dollar per cup and on numerous occasions, the owner framed the dollar and enshrined the unwashed coffee cup.

During the era of Franklin D. Roosevelt, virtually anything he used outside the White House—dinner plates, wine goblets, scratch pads—was target material for souvenir collectors. Signing bad checks was out of the question for they would never be cashed if they were for moderate amounts. So many small checks remained outstanding and, in fact, disappeared, that Roosevelt's secretary gradually took over all check signing.

During the Kennedy administration, the White House had to make a very firm rule against making public any of the food preferences, favorite toys, or precise clothes measurements of the President's children. Shortly after a story appeared that Caroline liked chocolate, the White House was flooded with everything from Hershey Bars to a six-foot, 190-pound chocolate rabbit from Switzerland.

President Truman, for some reason, was probably the greatest attractor of the unsolicited presidential gift. After a story was printed about Mr. Truman playing horseshoes at the White House, the mail room quickly lost count of the numerous horseshoes he received, including one gold-plated shoe mounted on purple velvet.

On another occasion, shortly after he took office, Truman paid a hometown visit to Kansas City, Missouri, and dropped in on his old haberdashery partner, Eddie Jacobson. World War II had ended a short time before and it still was difficult to buy white shirts without a good bit of shopping.

Truman told Jacobson he wanted a half dozen white shirts, size 15½ with a 33-inch sleeve. Jacobson was distraught—he didn't have a shirt that size in stock and expected it would be weeks before he could get them from a manufacturer.

This little snippet of history was duly recorded by reporters trailing along behind the cane-swinging Chief Executive and the news was printed in hundreds of newspapers from coast to coast.

Within two or three days, the dining room of the Presidential suite at the Muehlebach Hotel in Kansas City was overflowing with shirts—white shirts, blue shirts, even some red, white and blue shirts. Estimates of the number of shirts mailed to Truman varied. He was embarrassed and said he received "a few dozen." Actually, the figure was between 1,500 and 2,000.

In one sense, such attention is a tribute to the office and also to the man. But it is also that part of the Presidency which Truman referred to as a "prison." Many observers have noted that the White House life is unreal in its isolation of a President, his removal from everyday concerns. George Reedy's *Twilight of the Presidency* is a recent example. As Reedy put it:

> The trouble with the White House . . . is that when he [the President] picks up a telephone and tells people to do something, they do it. They may sabotage the project, after they have hung up the phone. They may stall, hoping that "the old son of a bitch" will forget about it. They may respond with an avalanche of statistics and briefing papers in which the original purpose will be lost and life will continue as before. But the heel click at the other end of the wire will be audible and the response—however invalid—will be prompt.

Yet, there is a side to living in the White House fish bowl that is probably a healthy condition of democracy. It may be a good thing, for example, for a President to realize his effect on public opinion, tastes and fads. And it is even perhaps best that he feels the constant public eye and feels constraints on whimsical or eccentric behavior. After all, the commander of a nuclear arsenal as powerful as that of the United States should, if nothing else, be reminded of virtues like prudence and restraint. This is all part of the crucible of the Presidency and Jefferson's splendid misery.

One relatively little discussed side of the Presidency is the hangover which the heady experience of living in the White House— with its unmatched trappings of power—may leave for a former President.

Our system makes scant provision for the adjustment Presidents have to make after the inauguration of their successors. The situation has been remedied to a certain extent in recent years. Former Presidents now keep some Secret Service help and usually can get access to government aircraft if needed, but the problem has always been of a deeper nature.

One day, their wish is the command of hundreds of dedicated professionals. Their personal worries are kept to an absolute minimum. A former President has not, for instance, had to think about money problems while in office. His investments and holdings went into the hands of trustees when he entered the White House.

The next day, he is a private citizen. He cannot call for a helicopter nor ring for a limousine. In the days of the Truman-to-Eisenhower transition, transportation home was not even provided the outgoing President. If it weren't for some of Truman's friends who gave him a luncheon party and a little send-off, he would have just driven to Union Station and taken the train home to Missouri.

President Eisenhower's post-White House adjustment was even more interesting, since Ike also had the years of living as an Army five-star General behind him. For one thing, he had to take driving lessons. In the Army and then in the White House, he had always had drivers.

Probably most of all, he missed the Secret Service. Although Eisenhower said at times in the White House that he felt hemmed in by the Secret Service, he had come to rely on them increasingly for service not involved with his protection. They fetched his golf clubs, drove his golf cart, reminded him of hats, gloves and coats. More important, they kept time for him, seeing to it that he arrived and departed on schedule. Many of these were the chores performed for him as an Army General by a retinue of aides.

He missed, he told me once at Gettysburg, the large, protective White House switchboard with its 24-hour staff of super-efficient operators. One of his first adjustments after John Kennedy's Inauguration Day was learning to use a dial telephone. He first tried grasping the entire dial as one might twist a safe combination and understandably got some wrong numbers. Before, all he had to do was pick up the phone and give a name—not even a number.

Strangely enough—even with a salary now up to $200,000 from

the Truman level of $75,000—Presidents rarely save any money from their earnings in the White House. Most of our recent Chief Executives have gone into the hole every month, but fortunately they have been able to afford it.

The only President since Calvin Coolidge who has had to live within his federal income was Harry Truman. It was possible for Truman to save some money during his White House years, largely because he was able to cut down sharply on entertaining when he lived in Blair House from 1948 until shortly before the end of his term in 1952. The White House, itself, was undergoing internal reconstruction during those four years.

The Presidency, however, did cost the next three Chief Executives money from their private funds—Eisenhower, Kennedy and Johnson. This can come about in many ways. For example, a President and his wife have to send out an incredible number of wedding presents. During the Johnson years, the President and his wife, Lady Bird, averaged something over five wedding presents a week and the cost out of their private funds ran between $50 and $100 per present. This comes to something between $12,000 and $25,000 a year. Also, the First Family must pay for its own food and for meals served to personal guests. And, there are higher clothing costs, particularly for the ladies of the family. So, not even the evident lavishness of White House life is free from another contradictory side of the coin.

Monetary costs, emotional costs, costs to family happiness and to health, vilification, the threats of assassination—why do men risk everything for a chance at this job? Perhaps because it's the ultimate fulfillment for a man in public life. President Kennedy said he chose politics as a career because it was the greatest challenge. It called on more of a man's faculties—intelligence, courage, perception, judgment, humor, physical stamina, persuasive powers, etc.—than any other.

And within the profession of politics, the Presidency is the one job that demands and uses the most of a man. Also, of course, it offers the greatest rewards: a form of immortality, since *ex officio* the President becomes a figure in history; an unequalled sense of the raw personal power which is—not just money, as has been suggested—the real "mother's milk" of politics; a chance to build things, change things, mold them.

So we're back to the paradox of the office. If power is defined simply as the likelihood of what you want to happen *actually* happening, then the Presidency is at once powerful and impotent, a place of fulfillment and a place of frustration. But this is its fascination, one aspect of which might best be viewed from backstairs at the White House.

CHAPTER FOUR

People around the Presidents: Cronies, the Hired Help, and VIP's

The "people around the presidents" were Merriman Smith's news sources, traveling companions, professional associates and quite often his friends. They ranged from top advisers to the White House policemen and butlers. They included foreign monarchs and presidential golfing partners; friends of the presidents and hangers-on.

These people were a source of both information and entertainment to Smith and so this chapter draws on both analysis and anecdotes from his writing.

PRESIDENTS, much more than Americans of lesser station, have difficulty in making and keeping close friends. As Henry Adams wrote, "A friend in power is a friend lost."

Too frequently this is not the fault of the person in power, but of his friends. Also, this is why Presidents frequently do not add appreciably to their circle of close friends while they are in office.

Staff members and official associates of the President will be dealt with later in this chapter. For the most part, they cannot be described as personal friends of the President because the nature of their work encourages an arm's length or boss-and-employee relationship with the Chief Executive. With few exceptions, the people who work with a President are not his closest friends in his personal and off-guard moments.

Most Presidents have found that within minutes after their election, the country springs up with all kinds of old friends—boyhood, school, business, political. Many of these are nothing more than publicity seekers and opportunists whose claim to friendship with the Chief Executive is thin, sometimes non-existent, and often exaggerated for reasons of self-advancement.

The knowledge of this is disillusioning and tends to make Chief Executives cling tenaciously to their pre-White House friends and make new friends stand an inordinately long test of time. The fear of being used and exploited by so-called friends has driven some Presidents to spend many of their hours of personal companionship with relatives.

For many years, FDR's favorite traveling companions were two Dutchess County cousins, Laura Delano and Margaret Suckley, and his law partner of the 1920's, Harry Hooker. They went all over the country with him time after time. They were his principal companions and conversationalists aboard his special train at night after the crowds of the day were behind him and he could stretch out in his private lounge. He could have a toddy and speak his mind with complete freedom, knowing that his words would never leave the room.

Although FDR was a famous man as Governor of New York long before he became Chief Executive, his elevation to the Presidency brought about the quick transformation of hundreds of men and women he had known casually. The late Marvin McIntyre, FDR's famous secretary and adviser, once said that almost overnight Mr. Roosevelt's slightest acquaintances became

"Franklin and Me." Mac estimated that the self-styled "school-mates" and "classmates" of FDR would have filled all the public school buildings of New York City.

Battery D, 129th Field Artillery, 35th Division, United States Army, also grew by the thousand after Harry Truman became President. Mr. Truman commanded this battery during World War I and by the time he had served a few months in the White House, Battery D men seemed to come to life in almost every city, town and village of the country. A few score men suddenly became thousands.

And, although Robert J. Donovan pretty well fixed the identi-ties of John Kennedy's crew in his book, *PT-109*, the White House in the early 1960's still frequently heard from men who had "been with Jack in the Pacific." Staff members could not automatically dismiss such claims. In fact, they lived in dread of sending the standard form letter ("The President has asked me to acknowledge . . .") to someone who truly was an old pal.

Members of the Eisenhower staff were amazed one night in 1954 to see one of Ike's golf partners on a commercially-sponsored television show, describing in some detail how he had played with the Chief Executive a few days before. The name of the show was "I've Got a Secret," and to authenticate his story the proud golfer displayed his scorecard. The game he described had been the first time Ike had met the man. And they didn't see too much of each other thereafter.

Presidents, as a result of such kiss-and-tell experiences, usually insulate themselves with cronies of whom they are absolutely sure. These persons usually live up to Ralph Waldo Emerson's definition: "A friend is a person with whom I may be sincere. Before him, I may think aloud."

All Presidents seem to have at least one essentially non-intellec-tual friend, a pleasant fellow with money who can afford to hang around in volunteer service as personal errand runner, punching bag, laughing boy, confidant and companion. These men usually aren't the type to tell the President hard truths or unpleasant news. Often, in fact, they are emotional chameleons. If the Presi-dent feels fine, the friend does push-ups. If the President feels low, they are acutely depressed. If the President says, "It looks like rain," the friend says, "We're in for a helluva storm."

By so doing, these cronies add to the peace of mind and relaxation of Presidents, but they probably also add to the isolation of the office. There is actually not much that can be done about this. Ideally, a President's contacts would come from the broadest possible cross-section of the nation, but this ideal has to take into consideration a simple preference for certain types of people, the human inclination to listen with a greater degree of interest to those who come closest to meshing with his own viewpoints.

Charles G. ("Bebe") Rebozo has been portrayed by some Nixon critics as a mysterious, somewhat ominous presence behind the throne. Such critics forget that nearly every modern President has had at least one such friend.

Lyndon Johnson talked over all sorts of subjects and problems —even key government issues—with a close Texas pal, Judge A. W. Moursund. John Kennedy enjoyed the constant attendance of an old schoolmate and New York advertising man, L. K. "Lem" Billings. And Franklin Roosevelt had several of his buddies actually living at the White House at one time.

Washington businessman George E. Allen was a close friend of three Presidents: Roosevelt, Truman, and Eisenhower. The feat of crossing party lines gives him a unique record in the annals of Presidential friends. There were basically three reasons for Allen's success:

1. George worked at being liked. He was a shrewd judge of other people and highly successful in anticipating the moods and wishes of a President.

2. Normally he was a clam about his relationship with any President. He talked about everything else on earth (so much that he was once dubbed "the rich man's Hubert Humphrey") and he wasn't above occasional name-dropping, but Allen did not engage in gossip, such as "the President told me . . ."

3. He was very well-informed on politics, operations of the federal government and world affairs. He had a happy faculty for summing up a complicated or tense situation in simple and frequently entertaining language ("if old de Gaulle runs a good test

out there in the Sahara, they'll have to enlarge the locker room at the Bomb Club").

Also, because Allen and other close personal friends of Presidents do not want anything—in fact, most of this type make clear they *won't* accept any appointment or favors—because they are not likely to cause embarrassment through conflict of interest, they are often in a position to do substantial personal favors for Presidents. George Allen, for instance, looked after Eisenhower's cattle-raising interests at the Gettysburg farm. Some close Orange County friends of President Nixon put in a practice six-hole golf layout beside his home at San Clemente.

Richard Nixon's closest friends seem to reflect his own background. They are, and have been throughout his political career, mostly Horatio Alger types—self-made, but highly successful men.

One of his close friends, Don Kendall, President of Pepsi-Cola, began as a salesman in Pepsi's syrup department. Another old friend, millionaire pharmaceutical magnate, Elmer H. Bobst, rose from humble beginnings in Clear Springs, Maryland.

There was a side to President Eisenhower's taste in people that resembled Franklin D. Roosevelt, who had a penchant for royalty. Mr. Roosevelt liked to associate with the ruling families of Europe. He delighted in calling kings and princes by their first names. Mr. Eisenhower had some measure of the same attitude toward giants of American industry and finance. There were few peasants among his social companions. It is quite likely that his interest in a man was more in his achievement than his wealth, but it seemed that in many instances wealth and achievement were combined in Ike's social selections.

Actually, of course, Presidents spend the majority of their time with their staffs, not friends or social acquaintances. But staff members, too, reflect the tastes and style of a particular President. In turn, there is undoubtedly a sort of self-selection process which leads certain types of men and women to tie their destinies to a certain man. Presidential staffs are uniformly hardworking, conscientious, but, most of all, fiercely loyal. The result is that, like the cronies and personal friends, a President's staff and official associates are often chameleon-like, too.

If the President bawls hell out of someone in the morning, people on successively lower echelons catch hell throughout the day. If the President is tense, his staff shows signs of tension.

If a President says to his top staff in the morning, "Things are going swell," the assistants go around wreathed in smiles for the rest of the day. And if a President drops a hint to an adviser that he thinks Administrator Doakes is not too bright, it is only a matter of hours before lesser staff members are gossiping by the water cooler, "Old Doakes, the fool, is on the way out."

Staff members become quite sensitive to subtle indicators of the President's mood. Eisenhower assistants—not entirely jokingly—associated a particular brown suit of the President's with a sour mood. And the Johnson staff was constantly looking for the personal reactions of its boss. He could communicate displeasure with an associate simply by looking over the man's shoulder while shaking hands with him. Or, he could confer one of the higher LBJ accolades by addressing another associate in a kidding, intimate manner.

The Johnson personality also shared one quirk with several other Presidents in my memory—particularly Eisenhower and Truman. In times of crisis, he would become—or appear to become—more relaxed than usual, and even talkative. He might talk around a problem with dozens of people hour after hour, day after day, before reaching a point of decision. Once he had made up his mind, the pent-up desire to talk out the problem seemed to subside and he often showed his relief in some other way—in doing something physical and non-cerebral like taking walks with his dogs around the White House driveway.

Most Presidential staffs seem to worry most when the boss gets silent or distant. This is usually a sign of anger or displeasure. President Eisenhower was supposed to have had quite a temper in his Army days. In fact, Mamie Eisenhower once told some friends that Ike tried to learn tennis in his earlier days, but became so angry at his ineptitude on the courts that he would butt his head against the nearest tree. He learned, for the most part, to control his temper, but he did so by bottling anger inside —at least temporarily. Silence, plus a gradual reddening of the face, caused secretaries to find files to check and assistants to leave for a vacant spot to telephone.

President Kennedy—and, now also President Nixon, I think—knew how to employ silence, and even anger, as administrative tools. Particularly in crisis, Kennedy would refrain from talking much about the problem at hand and particularly from "thinking out loud" at staff meetings. His theory—and it appears to be shared by Mr. Nixon in his searches for "options"—was that any expression of his thinking or general approach might influence his subordinates toward telling him what they thought he wanted to hear, instead of the truth or the most effective solution to a problem.

Also, Kennedy, I always thought, used to "lose" his temper strategically. Much like a coach who knows that some players or situations call for coddling and others for tongue-lashing, Kennedy seemed selective in his anger. Once employed, however, subordinates would go to nearly any lengths to avoid it a second time.

Consciously or not, Presidents often have at least one staff member around whose principal job is to keep the Chief Executive in a good mood, his spirits high, and when possible, to make him laugh. Dave Powers, an amiable Massachusetts Irishman, fulfilled this function for President Kennedy. He knew a thousand political stories, many Irish songs, and had a fantastic knowledge of sports, particularly baseball trivia.

I think the all-time champion in this field was Major General Edwin M. "Pa" Watson who served in theory as a military aide to FDR.

Pa was a rotund Alabamian with a heavy Eufala accent and a store of jokes that was inexhaustible. Pa was with Roosevelt a lot and while he definitely was not a New Deal liberal or a high-brow of any description, he had a wonderful ability to josh Roosevelt into good spirits.

Watson was a man of no particular political judgment. His principal talent lay in his good nature which he never seemed to lose—in public, at least. FDR liked to have him around as a sort of high-salaried mascot.

There was rarely a morning that Watson did not have a new story, a new laugh for the President. His jokes were sometimes slightly risqué, but seldom really on the gutter level. His comments on current events were priceless examples of oversimplification or misunderstanding.

He was a professional Army officer most of his life and had a fine record. But during his White House years his knowledge of advancing military techniques bogged down badly. During the war, he accompanied the President to a nearby Army airfield for the presentation of four B-24 Liberators to the Yugoslavian government to be flown against the Nazis. Pa stood behind the President during the presentation ceremony. Standing next to the smiling aide was an Air Force general.

While the band was playing, Pa turned to his fellow general and in his rich drawl, said, "What the hell do you call those things?" Pa waved his hand toward the planes.

The Air Force man was aghast that a major general did not know as much as the average schoolboy about Army planes. He explained quietly to Watson that the ships were B-24's and were called Liberators. He also explained that they were used to drop bombs on the enemy.

Watson, with apparently naïve enthusiasm, blurted loud enough for Roosevelt to hear, "Well, well. So that's whatcha call a bomber!" Roosevelt laughed loudly, with nothing but appreciative amusement.

Watson, it must be admitted, served a purpose, but many observers—and justifiably, in my opinion—have worried that staffs may say "yes" too often to a President and "no" too infrequently. The worry is that a President will not get the best advice or service if it is continually and consciously intended to be palatable.

A President suffers when he is surrounded too much by yes men and women. His judgment can become warped if he is spoon-fed a steady diet of approval and affirmation. A staff-constructed barrier of affection can conceivably hide from the President important shifts in public opinion and in the way certain policies are being received. Actually, no President is likely to suffer too extensively from his staff's desire to please as long as he reads the newspapers and keeps track of what is said about him on Capitol Hill. But there is a tendency to turn inwards, particularly in times of widespread unpopularity.

Indeed, for Presidents as a group, it's probably a safe generalization that the longer they are in office, the more inclined they become to let history rather than the critics of the day, pass judgment on their records in the White House.

Mr. Truman probably would argue this point, but he seemed to go through a period when he regarded virtually everyone who disagreed with him as wrong. This was during a phase in which he was under heavy attack in Congress and in the newspapers, and his staff naturally sought to supply the antidote of constant assurance that his critics were soreheads who didn't know what they were talking about.

President Johnson was the same way, especially when his popularity started to fall. He seemed to need his staff as a counterbalance to the constant flow of criticism from the outside. In fact, he was fond of comparing himself to Harry Truman with regard to his critics. Unfortunately, he was not as thick-skinned as Truman when it came to ignoring criticism or dismissing, and then forgetting, individual foes. He did not have Truman's capacity for the short, cathartic profanity.

Presidential staff assistants always gain a sense of team membership. They are united against common foes; they share the aura of importance that surrounds their boss. They can get on airplanes that are ostensibly filled. Their tables at restaurants suddenly improve. They are catered to not for themselves, but for their closeness to power. They realize this, but still enjoy it.

One simple illustration of such secondary benefits involved Marvin McIntyre of Roosevelt's staff. Roosevelt gained the reputation of having as his favorite song, "Home on the Range." Actually, he despised the tune and was given to saying things like "Oh, my gawd" when he entered a ballroom and heard the band grinding out this western chestnut. McIntyre, it turned out, was the one who liked "Home on the Range" and he used to feed it to every bandleader as the Chief Executive's favorite.

The Kennedy administration had this feeling of good-humored

closeness, too, and at times the enthusiasm of some of its younger, academic types gave the somewhat unsettling impression of an attitude towards government as a "bloody good game." More than any administration I covered, there was also the attitude— even toward journalists—that if you're not for us, you're against us.

Seemingly neutral, objective observations had a way of sounding hostile if the views expressed did not support the President's policy or particular handling of a matter. Staff members were known for their congeniality, but they were also notoriously bad listeners if the conversation began to cut across the grain of Kennedy partisanship.

A President's best insurance against excessive back-slapping and judgment-warping yessism is a staff dedicated to accomplishment rather than basking in the reflected glory of the nation's highest office. True, a Chief Executive must have a completely friendly, loyal White House staff, but he also needs one or two men around him who aren't afraid to say no.

This characteristic—the talent of saying no—becomes an operational necessity in one staff position that rarely gets much publicity: the job of White House Appointments Secretary.

This person must determine to a large degree who gets in to see the President and who doesn't, how long he should devote to buying the first Girl Scout cookies and how much time he can afford to give an upset Cabinet member. He should be able to entertain a fidgety guest waiting to see the boss and to pry a talkative type away from the inner sanctum when his time is up.

Presidents tend to give this job to a man they have known and trusted long before they went to the White House. Of all the staff, the Appointments Secretary must have an intimate knowledge of the President's likes and dislikes. He must be able to sense the moods of his employer, and he must know the President's working habits as well as the President, himself.

One of the most successful men in this position was Thomas E. Stephens, a New York lawyer who held the post under President Eisenhower. One of Stephens' main attributes was a less than totally reverential attitude toward his job, other government officials, politics in general, and even the President.

He had the name-forgetting manner of Casey Stengel. He would tell about "getting behind this fellow in New York" and would be referring to Thomas E. Dewey. With close friends, he often called the President, "Eisensnipper."

Probably no man who worked for him was as devoted to Eisenhower as Stephens, or as shrewd a political mechanic, but Tom simply was devoid of the feeling of self-importance which often confuses priorities for high-ranking staff members.

For one thing, he shunned government transportation and usually walked to work. For longer trips, he would borrow a friend's ramshackle convertible. This was a significant point in a town where John Kennedy once remarked, "You can get a man for $20,000 plus a car and driver, who wouldn't come if you offered him $50,000 straight."

Stephens studiously avoided the Washington cocktail circuit to pursue a multitude of outside interests. He raised peacocks, Egyptian Salukis and Rhodesian Ridgebacks on a 40-acre farm in Southern Maryland and in a Washington apartment, grew mushrooms in his clothes closet. He was the benefactor of a ne'er-do-well gold miner in Colorado.

Stephens was regarded by some as a rather mysterious and eccentric figure, but his detachment served him, and ultimately the President, well. He had the temperament to tell Eisenhower just what he thought, particularly about nut-and-bolt political matters where Ike was something of a novice.

Once President Eisenhower was walking hurriedly through his temporary White House offices at Lowry Air Force Base in Denver and spotted an ornate sign projecting from an otherwise pristine GI cubicle. The sign proclaimed, black on gold background, "Hon. Thomas E. Stephens."

Mr. Eisenhower, quite sensitive to distinction in rank from his Army days, turned to the lean-faced, Ireland-born Stephens walking beside him and asked bluntly, "How in the world did you get to be 'honorable'?"

"Simple," came the deadpan reply, "I paid the sign painter two dollars."

The job of Press Secretary is well known to the public, but its importance is hard to overrate. A Press Secretary can make or break a modern White House administration, because a President's chief strength lies in his ability to get his ideas, programs, and principles across to the public.

Stephen T. Early was one of FDR's greatest assets as Press Secretary and counsellor. It would be unheard of today, but Early saw one of his prime duties as correcting the President when necessary.

In the 1944 campaign when Mr. Roosevelt was barnstorming for a fourth term, the train stopped at Fort Wayne, Indiana. Mr. Roosevelt planned only a brief, rear platform speech before a crowd estimated at 50,000 persons.

The President worked on his speech until a few moments before the train pulled into the station. Steve was not in the room at the time. FDR asked some of his staff, "What is the big local industry here—I ought to make some mention of it."

No one knew exactly, but finally somebody volunteered, "Farm equipment, I think. Tractors and that kind of stuff."

Whereupon the President wrote into the speech a few words of congratulations for the workers in Fort Wayne's farm implement plants, praising them for an important contribution to the war effort.

The speech draft was carried to Early for processing. One look and Steve exploded. He dashed through the train to the President's private car to inform him seconds before the speech that Fort Wayne was primarily a railroad town. Mr. Roosevelt, with a grateful nod toward Early, went out on the rear platform and lavishly praised the railroad workers of Fort Wayne for their part in vitally important war transportation.

Early in open press conferences did not hesitate to interrupt Roosevelt if Steve thought his man was getting into deep water. He would whisper in the President's ear, and then FDR would throw out his big arms in a gesture of hopelessness and say, "Well, Steve tells me I'm wrong; that it didn't happen that way. I'll have to accept Steve's version. He says . . ."

No Press Secretary since has really had this sort of role. The Truman men were experienced newspaper people: Charlie Ross, a Pulitzer Prize winner from the St. Louis *Post-Dispatch* and, later, Joe Short, a well-known reporter for the Baltimore *Sun*. But their expertise and sympathy for the problems of reporters did not substitute for the utterly confidant sort of relationship that existed between Steve Early and FDR.

Eisenhower's Press Secretary, James C. Hagerty, was the finest technical Press Secretary in my experience. Releases were letter-perfect, often helpful, and issued with an expert eye to the deadlines of various papers and news organizations. And luckily for reporters, Hagerty continually sought to open avenues for greater coverage of the White House and to keep others from closing.

Such advocacy was especially necessary in the Eisenhower administration, because the President might otherwise have sharply limited areas of coverage. Particularly in his early White House days, Eisenhower had little use for reporters and seemed to be susceptible to the negative views of Sherman Adams toward the press.

Pierre Salinger's press office was not as taut a ship as Hagerty's. Reporters often complained about minor technical mishaps, which did abound at first, and about alleged favoritism towards certain friendly reporters, which also existed to some extent. On the other hand, Salinger opened whole new channels of information to foreign correspondents and won over the hardened "regulars" at the White House with his affability and humor. He generally was effective in the role that his boss intended Pierre to fill.

Press Secretaries, however, are usually no more effective than the authority which the President gives them. President Johnson told Press Secretary, George Reedy, practically nothing about what was really going on, so reporters became hostile and Reedy was not a spectacular success in the job. On the other hand, when insider Bill Moyers took over, he could answer sensitive policy questions, tell what was on the President's mind, and, in effect, speak *for* LBJ. As a result, he was widely greeted as a big improvement. The difference really had little to do with the two men's talents—both were experienced, intelligent, and loyal—but with the President's handling of the reins.

Ron Ziegler, the current White House Press Secretary, is similarly hampered by President Nixon's firm opinions about the limited amount of responsibility his press spokesman should have. He wants Ziegler to be a mouthpiece—a conduit of carefully-prepared policy positions—and that is about all. Significantly he chose a handsome young man from the advertising business instead of someone with a news background.

It is Ziegler's cautiousness about saying anything the President could conceivably disapprove of rather than his inexperience with news, however, that occasionally gets him into hot water with reporters. Correspondents are trained to seize on subtle distinctions in phrasing as possible indications of shifts in policy. They are used to equivocation, but any waffling on substantive points is sure to bring outcries.

An example of Ziegler's cautiousness resulting in confusion occurred in early 1970. He was asked whether, in the context of the President's stated Vietnam policy, Secretary of State Rogers was wrong in saying that the Nixon plan to end the war was "irreversible." Ziegler answered:

"The point, I think, is that the plan the President is pursuing is a course of action that he is pursuing. The thing I am making absolutely clear here is that in discussing the plan and outlining the plan as he has done on various occasions, he makes reference to the three criteria (which Ziegler had explained earlier in the briefing) as they relate to withdrawal."

Later he was pressed on the same point. Was the word "irreversible" an error? He answered:

"I would not take the question in that form because we are dealing with two different discussions in two different contexts. What I'm stating to you this morning is the consistency of the President's plan, the consistency of our policy regarding Vietnam as the President has previously spelled it out and the fact that the Secretary of State was referring to the Vietnam situation as the President has stated it, referring to the plan and the course of action which the President is pursuing and has referred to, which contain the three criteria as they relate to withdrawal."

Actually, Ziegler, a well-liked young man, was struggling valiantly against not only the exacting reporters but against sharp limits on his interpretative authority. An Early could have said, "Yes, the word is inaccurate out of context." A Moyers might have said, "No, the President stands by the assessment of the Secretary, but believes certain conditions are essential."

In addition, all new Press Secretaries go through a type of hazing from veteran correspondents. Ziegler may have received a rougher baptism than normal, but each new man that I can remember got some similar treatment. For example, when the highly regarded Moyers made a rather memorable mistake early in his tenure on the job, the press room did not let him forget it for some time.

It happened one early summer evening. About a dozen reporters were waiting on one side of the White House office lobby for the issuance of a text of a speech by President Johnson to be delivered later that night.

Across the lobby in seclusion obviously of his own choice sat a stern-looking young man with thick black hair, a chunky build and wearing a dark suit of material considerably heavier than most Washingtonians wear at that time of the year.

The new Press Secretary dashed across the lobby in a cloud of cigar smoke and stopped suddenly by the couch where the young stranger sat.

"You here to pick up the copy for Labor?" he inquired, referring to the Department of Labor.

The man grunted a reply.

"Well, come with me," Moyers said.

The two of them disappeared into a section of offices where much confidential work was done for the President; an area where reporters regularly assigned to the White House were not permitted without escort and a specific appointment.

The reporters remaining in the lobby broke into laughter. A White House policeman stationed in the lobby raced after the two men. Presently, he reappeared in the lobby along with "the man from Labor," who turned out to be a new man on the Washington staff of TAAS, the Soviet news agency. We always wondered whether he had heard Moyers correctly and had simply misconstrued the question, reasoning that any good Communist was "for labor."

The people that really allow the White House to function are the Civil Service employees who work there. They range from the Executive Clerk, who instructs Special Assistants and even the President on how to handle certain types of legislation, to the assistant electrician, who often also handles the White House kennels.

This permanent staff has included some of Washington's great characters, but also some of the most tight-lipped people in government. Many more close confidants and advisers have written "inside" books which have displeased their former employers than the butlers, maids, cooks and security personnel who probably know as much or more.

They observe the behavior of the First Family and of White House guests. During the course of any tenancy in the White House, they inescapably see and hear words and actions which, if reported to the outside world as typical, would cast the most saintly Chief Executive in a rather unfavorable light.

They have one immediate incentive for keeping quiet: they would be transferred with considerable detriment to their Civil Service ratings if they made any indiscreet disclosures. An equal factor, however, seems to be a sense of privilege they feel at having been selected for White House duty, symbol of the best in government service.

One such figure was a vivacious New Yorker, Louise Hachmeister, who made history when she became the first woman telephone operator at the White House in 1933. "Hackie," as she was known to her friends and hundreds of big figures in national and international politics, served as Chief Operator all through the Roosevelt regime and was retained in the same post by Mr. Truman.

Hackie, as the first woman operator ever employed by the White House, found herself on a terrific spot. The men she succeeded were so distrustful of women that they would not give her the hundreds of departmental and official numbers they had been carrying around in their heads for years. So, she had to start from scratch, learning numbers that had to be called frequently and rapidly; most difficult of all was keeping abreast of the new agencies of the government which Roosevelt was creating at a fast pace.

Her catalogue of special numbers became the most exclusive telephone book in America. It was the product of many years of research and retentiveness. Hackie played her big switchboard like a church organ, never missing a note and rarely referring to the music. Her memory was astonishing. Not only did she recognize hundreds of voices on the telephone, but she kept as many numbers in her head.

Another nearly legendary figure among the veterans of the permanent White House staff was gardener William Reeves, who died in 1946 after tending the flowers, shrubbery and trees for Presidents for forty-two years.

It was Reeves who gained fame by becoming a shepherd during the Wilson administration, and he had his own ideas how it came about. Reeves thought Mrs. Wilson was responsible, that she felt the addition of sheep to the lawns would add to the scenic quality of the White House grounds.

The matter of the sheep was so important that the *Christian Science Monitor* reported that Wilson gave Reeves these orders: "Stop cutting the grass with the mower. The sheep are coming."

The sheep stayed, too. The flock increased from an original eighteen to forty-eight. I talked with Reeves during the Roosevelt administration about his sheep-raising days and he said, as a practical experiment in grass-cutting, the Wilson sheep operation was a flop. It seemed the sheep ate the shrubbery and flowers but not the grass, and Reeves had to mow the lawn anyway.

It is probably a good thing that, for the most part, the employees on this level are restrained by Civil Service regulations, prudence, and conscience from becoming inside dopesters. For one thing, the book market already gets glutted with the memoirs and intimate chronicles of each passing administration, authored by staff members not subject to such restraints.

Presidents are used to invasions of privacy. When the Kennedys went to Palm Beach in 1960, they ordered daily milk deliveries from a local dairy and, since there was a new baby in the family, they contacted a local diaper service. To the family's great surprise, they discovered within a matter of days full-scale newspaper interviews, complete with pictures, with their milkman and didee-wash specialist.

But Presidents usually expect more loyalty from key aides in positions of real trust, and they often are disappointed. One of the more constant inconsistencies of White House life under any administration is the manner in which members of a Presidential staff vow, promise and pledge never to disclose the little, inside details of First Family life. Then, at some mysterious point of release or disaffection for various reasons, they go to a publisher with manuscript in hand.

John Kennedy had an interesting premonition about the books that would be written about his own family and administration. Early in his term of office, a book appeared dealing with the inner workings of the Eisenhower administration.

The author, a White House staff member briefly, included in his work numerous pages of what purported to be actual dialogue of Cabinet meetings and conferences in the President's office. Kennedy, who had some professional journalistic experience in his younger days, was intrigued and somewhat appalled. He told a friend:

"If the dialogue in this book is anywhere nearly accurate, this man must have been attending the Eisenhower Cabinet meetings with a notebook on his knee under the table."

Furthermore, Kennedy said the book caused him to wonder how many members of his own administration were up to the same thing. If only the late Chief Executive could see what some of his trusted associates, employees and friends have written about him, his prophetic fears would be more than realized.

A classic example is *Jackie Kennedy* by Mrs. Kennedy's former personal secretary, Mary Gallagher. When Mrs. Gallagher was at the White House, working for Jackie, she regarded intimate questions about the First Lady as little less than challenging Scripture. Later, however, Mrs. Gallagher was more than willing, and for a substantial sum, to rip into her former boss and confirm what the White House had stoutly denied at the time—that Jackie Kennedy was sometimes a difficult First Lady who, on occasion, preferred to stay in bed reading instead of participating in White House functions.

Another type of person—besides staff and friends—with whom the President spends a significant amount of time is the foreign VIP. While it is arguable whether this class of "people around the President" represents much of a departure from the pattern of Presidential isolation, it does seem that such overseas visitors often bring out the best in American hospitality and give the President a chance to size up some of his opposite numbers in the flesh.

I remember the time the Kennedys opened up George Washington's historic home at Mount Vernon to give a dazzling party for President Ayub Khan of Pakistan. There was dancing on the boats cruising down the Potomac. It was authentic Americana and when Ayub Khan was asked by bandleader Lester Lanin if he would like to hear some specially-rehearsed Eastern music, he answered, "Oh, no, let's have U.S. jazz and rock and roll."

There was a day when White House entertaining for foreign Heads of State was self-consciously continental, from the choice of wines to the entertainment. Each state dinner seemed to be an imitation of Versailles. Eleanor Roosevelt started a trend in the opposite direction when she served hot dogs to the King and Queen of England on a picnic at Hyde Park.

President Johnson had a similar preference for informal entertaining of foreign dignitaries. He started a trend in his administration when he decided to treat one of his first important foreign visitors, German Prime Minister Ludwig Erhard, to a western barbecue on the LBJ ranch. Spareribs were served, ten gallon hats were passed around, and the result was one of Johnson's most successful diplomatic parties.

And he followed the Erhard formula with other favored heads of state. It was at a similar ranch-style party for British Prime Minister Harold Wilson that Johnson gave a characteristically graphic description of how he handled such visitors.

He had stopped by one of the dinner tables where several reporters and their wives were seated. One correspondent asked Johnson what his *modus operandi* was at such high level meetings with leaders of other countries.

"Well, I'll tell you, it's sort of like with a woman. First, you have to warm her up," said Johnson, as he rubbed the thigh of one of the wives for emphasis.

"And then," he said, with a playful pinch of the same astonished woman, "you get down to business."

FDR once told us about his slightly different system. During the war, there was a succession of visiting dignitaries at the White House. Most of them were Presidents of Latin American countries. Their visits became so frequent that between the President and the State Department Protocol Division a set formula was worked out for their entertainment.

The visiting President arrived, say at four o'clock in the afternoon. He would be met by the Secretary of State at the railroad station or airport and escorted to the White House where the President waited for him in the windowless little diplomatic reception room in the basement or ground floor. Soldiers, sailors, and marines drawn up on the South Grounds would present formal military honors, and the visitor would be escorted into the reception room where the President met him.

Mr. Roosevelt was a splendid performer at affairs like this. Maybe he had never met the person before, or at the most once. He would roll his massive, looming head and with a broad smile roar, "Well, well, well. My old friend, ——, how are you?" Mr. Roosevelt knew how to say "my old friend" in a dozen different languages. He then would present his visitor to the Cabinet and various other government officials rounded up for the occasion.

Once while visiting in the President's private car in the course of a long train trip, I asked him what he found to talk about with all these people. He laughed heartily.

"I have a system. After the visiting President has met the Cabinet, we go upstairs together and I give him a chance to go to his room and freshen up before dinner. Then before dinner, he and I meet for a drink, I give him two or three Martinis, made four parts gin to one part vermouth. Then we go into the state dinner and there are the usual toasts and starchy conversation.

"After dinner, he and I go to my study, and I have a Scotch nightcap for him. By this time he is pretty sleepy. We talk until midnight or so and then part. Next morning, I arrange to see him in my study at about ten o'clock. After we have been talking for about five minutes, Pa Watson sticks his head in the door and says my first engagement of the day already is running late. So, I say to my visitor. 'Oh, I'm awfully sorry. I had hoped to spend the morning talking with you, but they just won't let me alone!' "

Not all of the wartime visitors were so pliable, of course. One of the more difficult was the Russian Foreign Minister, V. M. Molotov, who visited FDR in 1942. Molotov was extremely security-conscious. For instance, not a single White House servant was permitted on the same floor as Molotov's room when the Russian was in his quarters. The maids were thus unable to make the President's bed when Molotov was in his own room. And only when he had gone into the comparative safety of Mr. Roosevelt's presence on some other floor could the maids enter Molotov's room to tidy up.

Madame Chiang Kai-shek also had a strange requirement. At the time of her visit, she was not in strong health and rested several times a day. And after each period of relaxation she expected her bed to be remade with completely fresh linen.

Among the most consistently eccentric and interesting visitors to the White House was Winston Churchill. Here was an example of a world leader whom Presidents really had to get to know personally in order to deal with effectively.

We got to know him over three administrations: the Roosevelt, Truman, and Eisenhower years. The first time Churchill visited Washington as Prime Minister was in December 1941. Just after Pearl Harbor he flew in to confer for about two weeks with President Roosevelt on how to stand up against Germany and Japan.

After about a week, we had a press conference with Churchill and the President. Churchill obviously knew he was up against another good showman in FDR, so to the delight of the photographers, Churchill hopped up onto his chair beside the President and stood towering above the room, waving his long black cigar with one hand and flashing his famous "V" sign with the other.

The press conference itself was a journalistic nightmare. Mr. Roosevelt quickly finished his own scant news announcements and turned things over to Mr. Churchill, who was known for a rather unsympathetic view of newsmen. Churchill rose as Mr. Roosevelt introduced him to "my wolves—my beloved pack of wolves." He took his familiar stance, one foot just a little ahead of the other, and glared at the reporters.

It was, by any standard, a tense moment. The safety of England hung by the very thin thread of bulldogged British perseverance. The United States was in mortal danger in the Pacific. The first question came from a British correspondent.

"Mr. Prime Minister," he said in a high, nasal inquiry, "are you of good cheer?"

The room exploded in laughter, with the President nearly choking on his cigarette holder.

The following summer I helped play host to Churchill at a luncheon given for him in Washington by all of the reporters' organizations. As one of the hosts, I was on the committee which welcomed Churchill to a suite at the Statler Hotel before lunch in the main ballroom.

We had drinks of every kind awaiting the Prime Minister when he lumbered in with his aides. After the introductions, Churchill stared around the living room, spied a comfortable couch and sat down. The waiter brought up a tray loaded with a variety of cocktails and straight drinks. Churchill shook his head and looked up at his hosts.

"You Americans have a savage habit, this drinking before your meals."

Having heard for years that Churchill was a handy man with a bottle, we were aghast.

"I much prefer drinking with my meals," he said. "It would be quite nice to have a whisky with lunch."

The waiter was nervous and started to back away. As he took his first step, Churchill's pudgy arm shot out toward the tray like a well-thrown dart.

"But?" he said with a grin, "perhaps . . . second thought." And he picked up a Martini.

It went down almost at a gulp and he soon had a second. His aide, a starchy young naval officer resplendent in his crisp, high-necked white uniform, sat near Churchill, just across a coffee table.

The Prime Minister picked up a canapé—caviar on toast. I was fascinated to watch his system. He hooked the piece of toast on his bottom teeth and scraped off all the caviar.

Then he looked around for a place to discard his toast. His aide had just put down his own Martini on the table and was chatting with someone. Churchill saw the glass and plopped the toast into the half-finished drink.

A second later, the aide turned from his talk to pick up his glass. A puzzled look spread over his face and he motioned to the waiter.

"I say," said the officer, "there seems to be a bit of bread in my glass. Could I have another?"

Churchill was busy talking to several people standing by his couch and paid no attention. The waiter handed the aide another Martini. And the aide took a sip, then resumed his chat. Churchill selected another canapé, this time a mammoth ripe olive.

The Prime Minister nibbled industriously at the olive for a moment, decided he didn't like it and looked around for a place to unload. And again he spotted the aide's half-finished cocktail. Plop went the olive.

I have never seen such a look of confused annoyance as on the face of the aide when he picked up his drink again to find a half-eaten oversized olive bobbing around in his glass.

We saw Churchill less frequently after the war years. It had been some time since I had seen him last when he came to Bermuda to meet with President Eisenhower and (this was 1953) the French Premier of the month, Joseph Laniel.

It was refreshing to learn from one of the Mid-Ocean Club attendants, where he was scheduled to stay, that Churchill had not changed much. Sir Winston had not yet arrived, but the club attendant said that Churchill had insisted on twin beds, although no one was to sleep in the room with him. He explained that often, after the covers of the first bed had become rumpled during the night, Churchill became irritated and liked to switch to a second, fresh bed.

Churchill arrived shortly after midday. The colonial constabulary of Bermuda and the Fusiliers, complete with a gold-horned goat, were on hand to greet Sir Winston and to herd the reporters and photographers into a rope enclosure so they would not bother the Prime Minister unduly.

(Churchill, although he was a "journalist" of some note before he entered politics, seemed to like reporters best at a distance. I once heard him instruct men of the Canadian Royal Mounted Police at a Quebec press conference, "Now don't you let those fellows stand too close to me. I don't like it at all.")

When Sir Winston's plane landed and he finally appeared, I was amazed at the physical change. He walked slowly and with apparent effort. He seemed to have a great fear of stumbling and came down the ramp from the plane a slow step at a time, peering intently at his feet every inch of the way.

His head hung lower than ever, giving him a pronounced stoop. Flesh hung in slack folds beneath his bulldog jaw. The imperishable trademark was the cigar held high and proudly. His voice seemed to have lost resonance and carrying power, but not its distinctive quality.

I was standing by Jinx Falkenberg and Ray Scherer of NBC as Winnie passed in slow review along the line of Fusiliers. Once Sir Winston spotted the goat, that was the end of the review as far as he was concerned. He waddled toward the impeccably groomed animal, wagged his head by first one horn, then the other and chortled with delight at the goat's gold trappings.

A young officer was giving the goat's biography to the PM when Churchill turned and summoned the Foreign Secretary,

Sir Anthony Eden, to his side. Eden rushed over to Churchill, apparently expecting some word of import. Instead, the Prime Minister duly introduced his ranking Cabinet officer to the ranking goat of Bermuda.

CHAPTER FIVE

First Ladies

*Certainly as much as staff assistants or visiting royalty,
First Ladies were an important factor in White House life
and the presidential administrations Smith covered. Their
personalities and activities often took on political importance. Their styles and views influenced the country, and the
public was often as interested in news of a First Lady as in
news of her husband.*

I WAS ONCE INVITED to speak to a state ladies' club convention in a southern city. The hostess-in-chief had
asked that I be sure to say something about First Ladies, and
especially to include something about one particular Presidential
wife who apparently was a figure of some notoriety among women
of the state.

It had long ceased to surprise me to find that wives of Presidents have constituencies, critics, and images of their own. They
have their own press secretaries and staffs, their own demanding
schedules and responsibilities, and, in effect, their own press corps.
But I was a little put off by the requested topic.

At any rate, after some opening pleasantries, I began the talk.

"I want to tell you a story about the wife of the President of the United States who spent so much money on high fashion clothes that she was afraid to tell her husband how badly she was in debt to New York designers and couturiers.

"We'll skip this lady's name for now," I said. "After all, the memory of her husband still is quite alive in this sentimental country of ours. But the fact remains that this First Lady—wife of the President, mother of charming children, a model for many Americans when she lived in the White House, a woman noted for her beautiful clothes—the lady was a secret eccentric in the White House, who threw away money she did not have, although at the time most Americans thought she was pretty well fixed."

There were some murmurs of objection from two or three of the younger women sitting together on one side of the room. An older woman, who looked to be an official, loudly shushed the dissenters. "Quiet, honey. The rest of us want to hear this!"

"The President was serving his first term," I continued. "He had made no decision yet about seeking re-election. However, behind the scenes, his wife was telling her closest confidantes that she lived in constant fear that he might not run again, and that if he *did* stand for re-election, he might be defeated.

"A friend asked the President's wife why she was so upset and she replied, 'I have contracted large debts of which he knows nothing and which he will be unable to pay if he is defeated.' Furthermore, the President's wife said she owed one New York store about twenty-seven thousand dollars. We know this, of course, from an account recently published by a close personal assistant to the First Lady.

"One of the great American tragedies was the assassination of this woman's husband. At the time he was murdered by the gunfire of a lone assassin, the President's wife had unpaid store bills amounting to something like seventy thousand dollars. If there was anything merciful about this tragedy, it was that the President went to his death without knowing how compulsive his wife was when it came to throwing away money."

"And I can tell you, ladies," I continued, "that Robert would have done anything to suppress this story."

There were now some looks of mistrust and confusion in the audience.

"Yes, Robert Todd Lincoln would be outraged to read this account of the conduct of Mrs. Abraham Lincoln. The First Lady's servant, Elizabeth Keckley, betrayed her position of trust in writing a revealing book, just unearthed by *American Heritage* magazine."

There were gasps of protest and audible expressions of disappointment. The women had been poised for the real dirt about Jacqueline Kennedy Onassis, now that she had fallen from her pedestal and was fair game. In fact, a few of the complaints were so vehement that I began to fear for my lecture fee, and so, I quickly started an impromptu treatise on the modern First Lady.

The incident illustrated what a point of departure Jacqueline Kennedy was in a succession of relatively non-controversial First Ladies. Not since Eleanor Roosevelt did a President's wife inspire such adulation or such contempt.

Certainly, she was new and different. For one thing, she was only thirty-two when she entered the White House, twenty years younger than most First Ladies. She was a truly beautiful woman —with an elegant figure, large, widely set eyes, delicate features, and a nearly perpetual tan. She moved with the rare grace of a woman athlete who has kept her femininity.

She was well-read, intelligent, proud and, most of all, exceptionally competent. She did many things well, and, far from her reputation as a shrinking violet, she attempted many types of activities which other First Ladies have not—and would not. For instance, one cannot readily imagine Mamie Eisenhower giving a speech before a large foreign audience in Spanish or French or Eleanor Roosevelt water-skiing on a single ski.

Her efforts at restoring some of the White House treasures and promoting American cultural interests actually represented a throwback, though, to the days of Mrs. Roosevelt. For in Eleanor Roosevelt's time, it was accepted that the First Lady had causes, programs, and, in effect, a platform, just like her husband. And after Mrs. Kennedy, there was clearly left a standard to match.

Lady Bird Johnson sensed the importance of a single distinctive contribution as First Lady. She accomplished this with her far-flung and energetic work for national beautification. It gained for her a reputation as one of the "great" First Ladies and it helped her husband politically, which was her foremost concern.

The trend toward an activist Presidential wife has changed the public's conception of her function. Just remaining pleasantly in the background like Bess Truman, for instance, would today be likened to a President without a program, a man who was just content to execute the laws of the land. Mrs. Nixon looked to be making volunteer service promotion her special project, but has gradually retreated back into the Executive Mansion and so will have to face the possible wrath of future historians.

In fact, this standard is somewhat unfair, since the minimum, behind-the-scenes chores of a First Lady, for which she receives no extra credit or praise, are the equivalent of a demanding, full-time job. She is an administrator and executive in her own right, for while her husband must run the country, she has to run the White House.

She is responsible for a system which handles mountains of mail—in a normal period 2,000 pieces a week, as many as 20,000 at Christmas time. It is she, for instance, who must insist that gift-senders receive a detailed acknowledgement, if she wants this to occur.

Despite the amount of staff, very little at the White House happens automatically. Especially on matters concerning the family section of the Mansion, the First Lady's instructions are expected and awaited. So almost every morning she confers with the Chief Usher, manager of the Presidential household, with the maître d'hôtel and the housekeeper, often with the gardener, or with the carpenter.

A White House rug needs to go to the cleaners. A curtain in the East Room shows wear. What is she going to do with a gift of fine crocheting, nine by four feet? A dozen such questions a morning are taken up on the second floor of the White House.

She must follow the food-purchasing closely. She doesn't have to stand in line at the supermarket; the shopping is done for her. But she must maintain general supervision of the menus and the spending because, outside of official entertainment, the White House food bills come out of the President's pockets and not from an entertainment allowance. And there are other culinary concerns. *Newsweek* once revealed that Lady Bird posted signs around the White House kitchen: "Please do not offer the President second helpings unless he asks for them."

Then come the public appearances, which are covered by news dispatches. These range from christening destroyers to garden parties for the disadvantaged to fashion luncheons with the wives of big political contributors. Each demands a different tone, a fresh set of "remarks," and if *Women's Wear Daily* had its way, a brand new outfit of the latest design.

With her Social Secretary, the First Lady must plan the White House social season months in advance. Conflicting dates and last-minute changes must be coordinated with the President's executive offices, and this can be as complicated as writing a new airline timetable. As the day of a state dinner approaches, most First Ladies go over invitation lists, menus and schedules in painstaking detail. She is consulted down to the arrangement of the last vase of flowers and the placement of the potted palms just before a big White House party.

Her looks, health, and style—as much as the President's—are news, and her personal appearance gets even more comment than his. A President can show up puffy-eyed for a morning engagement and the ladies in the delegation waiting in his office will coo to each other, "Doesn't he look cute, like a sleepy-eyed little boy?"

But let a President's wife appear in front of the Ladies Aid Society looking anything but beauty-parlor-fresh and the women mutter in the back rows, "My doesn't she look dreadful—and getting big around the hips, too."

In fact, this business of being a President's wife once prompted Mrs. James K. Polk to lament, "I would rather be a doorkeeper in the House of the Lord than mistress of the White House."

The focus of public attention on the appearance and womanly duties of First Ladies, however, often obscures the political influence that the wives of Presidents can possess. On most career decisions, the President's wife is usually the single closest adviser a Chief Executive has. It was Bess Truman, a person long written off in the capital as a woman of much political influence on her husband or the country, who persuaded her husband not to run again in 1952.

Lady Bird Johnson affected not only her husband's decision not to seek another term, but also his views on Head Start, health care, and other social legislation. Like Eleanor Roosevelt, she was a second conscience for her husband, particularly on welfare and distinctively humanistic issues.

Like their husbands, First Ladies have often been the victims of one-dimensional portrayal, which has obscured over the years some remarkable personalities. Lady Bird Johnson, for instance, was a perceptive political professional and an astute business-woman. Behind her praline accent and behind some less-catching moments which included appearances traipsing around the ranch in tight denim pants and a sweat shirt with a large Queen of Hearts emblazoned all over the front, Mrs. Johnson was a highly intelligent and attractive woman.

For a woman who was in her early fifties when she was in the White House, she had the trim figure of a much younger person. She had beautiful eyes and luxuriant dark hair. But most of the time she photographed very poorly because of an acquiline nose and a habit developed in girlhood of turning down one corner of her mouth when pronouncing certain words.

She worked hard at being Lyndon Johnson's wife. She learned over the years how to get her way a good percentage of the time through subtle suggestion and flattery—never a frontal clash with her husband's will. She finessed a medium-sized family inheritance into a genuine, diversified fortune, and, whatever her husband's influence, it was her accomplishment more than anyone's.

She conducted a separate whistle-stop campaign through eight key southern states in 1964, delivering forty-seven speeches in four days. This was completely unprecedented. No other First Lady had ever made a full-scale campaign trip apart from her husband.

Jackie Kennedy, for instance, dreaded campaigning. She disliked most politicians as a class, and, as she sometimes put it, "the tedious *Kaffeeklatsches* with the size-20 women." Once she began at such gatherings, she was very effective person-to-person, but she was nearly always very hesitant about getting involved.

On one occasion, I remember her initially refusing her husband's suggestion that she wade into a crowd of Democratic women with him to shake hands on the White House lawn. A minute or so after she had demurred modestly and her husband had gone ahead without her, Lyndon Johnson, then Vice President, grabbed her by the arm and propelled her into the adoring ladies, saying to Jackie, "Young lady, c'mon now, they're waiting to see you as much as the President." She ended up enjoying the event and later thanked Johnson for getting her started.

She was always less harsh on Lyndon Johnson, in fact, than many of the people around President Kennedy, before and after Dallas. And LBJ returned the feeling. While he could call the others "touch footballers" and "the little Harvards" and worse, he never had anything but affection and warm praise for Jackie.

In fact, I once heard LBJ say of Mrs. Kennedy, "There, by God, is a real woman for you, a real lady—a pretty face but a lot of brains and a lot of steel behind it. . . . You never heard her looking down her nose at me or anybody around me."

Mrs. Kennedy's capacity for personal kindness often went unreported. When the President's father, Joseph P. Kennedy, suffered a stroke in Florida in December 1961, she visited him every morning at St. Mary's Hospital in Palm Beach. He couldn't speak, but she would tell him the latest family news and make him laugh.

She had a deep friendship with her father-in-law. There were some of the Kennedys to whom she had some trouble adjusting. She wasn't the cheerleader type; nor did she accept every suggestion of Rose, the President's mother, as infallible. But she did share an independent streak and her sense of humor with the elder Kennedy.

When he died in 1969, I wrote a short story about his life for UPI. I pointed out that he had been a more progressive man than was generally thought: he had a visceral antipathy to discrimination, he had prodded his sons for many years on the importance of a Medicare plan, improving the Social Security system, ending unemployment. The piece also talked some about his personality: driving and sometimes harshly ambitious, yet humorous and warm. He was often a soft touch.

Soon after, I got a note from an unfamiliar Fifth Avenue address. It was from Jackie, who was now Mrs. Onassis and it included a reference to my story:

> . . . Thank you for what you wrote about my father-in-law. I loved him so much. You and I were lucky to have understood him —and I feel sorry for those who didn't. . . .

Jacqueline Kennedy had a mind of her own, and it was this characteristic that resulted in her reputation for being difficult. Her husband rarely objected; it was others who did.

President Kennedy, for instance, was a rapid walker and he would often quickly outdistance his wife when they were walking together. She would maintain an even gait as he forged ahead. He would eventually notice, stop, look around sheepishly and smile. And he would wait for her to catch up.

She would also move at her own pace when it was time to dress or prepare for one of their major joint appearances. This would often cause the President to pace around nervously and send someone to check on her progress, but all was forgiven when she finally showed up looking radiant and beautiful.

The breathless madonna image came largely from some of her appearances on television when she affected a little girl voice. Actually, her natural voice had a much lower tone, and she could be ribald and even profane in the company of old friends.

She had a devilish sense of humor and sometimes quite effectively hoodwinked the President. Mary Todd Lincoln notwithstanding, Mrs. Kennedy, herself, was indeed given to spending sprees for which she would often be admonished by her husband. Soon after one such semi-serious heart-to-heart discussion, Jackie rushed up to President Kennedy in a state of bright-eyed excitement.

She held out a beautifully framed painting—an abstract work consisting largely of boldly executed swirls with shadings from strong to delicate.

"Look what I got for eight hundred dollars!" she exclaimed.

The President reacted with a pithy, pained evaluation of those in the art world who influenced Mrs. Kennedy's purchase. He was beginning a general critique of her shopping habits when his wife burst into laughter. It was only then that she revealed the work to be a finger painting of Caroline's.

Another independent sort was Eleanor Roosevelt. She was the absolute antithesis of the standard political wife, whose only opinion on anything is that her husband is kind, handsome, wise and sincere and whose only contact with the rest of humanity is at her husband's side, usually cringing in the background with a fixed smile.

Mrs. Roosevelt was known as one of the original crusading women. She traveled all over the country on behalf, and actually in search of, good causes to promote and boost. If Mrs. Kennedy was Junior League, and Mrs. Eisenhower DAR, then she was League of Women Voters and Planned Parenthood.

She was an early "progressive parent." Mrs. Roosevelt did not let her children, or grandchildren for that matter, play with war toys or lead soldiers. This, she said, taught a preoccupation with killing and violence. But she saw no contradiction in putting a shooting gallery for .22 caliber guns in the basement of the east wing of the White House. Furthermore, she announced her intention to practice on the White House police's revolver range because she considered shooting a skill.

And no one but Mrs. Roosevelt would have adjusted her slip before the whole Cabinet. One afternoon in June 1942, Mrs. Roosevelt was on the front lawn with the President, the Cabinet, a group of Congressional leaders and Chief Justice Harlan F. Stone awaiting the arrival of King George II of Greece. Mrs. Roosevelt wore a white cotton lace dress. As she walked over to greet the Chief Justice, her slip was trailing at least two inches below the hem of her dress.

While standing chatting with the Cabinet members as the King's cortege entered the White House grounds, Secretary of Labor Frances Perkins, the only other woman in the gathering, whispered something in Mrs. Roosevelt's ear. Without batting an eyelash or halting her conversation with Attorney General Biddle, Mrs. Roosevelt gracefully reached inside her dress and hauled the offending slip up to proper level.

She strongly objected to having Secret Service agents accompany her everywhere she went. Amazingly—from today's perspective, at least—they often deferred to her wishes and left her unprotected. Today, a ten-man detail is responsible for the safety of Mrs. Nixon. But Mrs. Roosevelt, at least in her movements around Washington, either walked alone or with her secretary, or rode without a police escort in a White House car.

It was also Mrs. Roosevelt who made the decision to serve hot dogs to the King and Queen of England. This was not, in context, at all rude or ungracious, although it was very unusual. It was much more indicative of a charming talent for making people feel themselves and at home. It was her feeling that when royalty visited the White House or the Roosevelt home at Hyde Park, they became part of the Roosevelt household—the household did not become a temporary palace.

Mamie Eisenhower also had a no-nonsense side, far more characteristic than her image of the nice little lady with bangs and her own recipe for fudge. She was a deliberate and hard-working taskmistress around the family quarters. If a burned-out light bulb was not replaced promptly, she could display quite a temper.

Mrs. Eisenhower was extremely frugal. She instructed the kitchen to save cookies from one reception to the next, and went around turning off lights long before Lyndon Johnson thought of the idea.

Once, she and Ike went on a shopping trip in Gettysburg. The President displayed his newness at such things by simply picking up some items for his grandson and saying, "I'll take these." He didn't look at the price tags.

Mamie wandered up and down the aisles, taking much more time, and frequently commenting on prices. At one point, she admired some scarves piled up on the counter, and inquired about the cost.

When she found out, she answered, "They're lovely, but I think I'll wait until you have a sale and these are reduced. They're a little high."

First Ladies seem really to be that sort of historical figure whose effect on events can never truly be known. Certainly, at the minimum, a nagging shrew would distract a leader to some extent from his concentration on national problems. By the same token, a trouble-free, warmly supportive home life must have some positive effect on a President's confidence and equanimity.

By this point in my talk, the Amalgamated Ladies Clubs Convention was back on my side. I cinched the triumph—not to mention payment—by observing that although a woman would undoubtedly *herself* be President in this century, the current role of the First Lady was perhaps best summed up by Mrs. Johnson's words, "to bolster and sustain." The ladies thought this was fine.

CHAPTER SIX

The Lighter Side

Merriman Smith was a leading chronicler of the "lighter side" of White House life. He did not consider Presidents to be "especially funny people" or the White House a particularly frivolous locale, but he did delight at recalling some of the episodes and stories which illustrated even a chief executive's susceptibility to human foibles and problems.

PRESIDENTS, as a class, are not especially funny people. Their jokes are in the telling. You or I can tell an audience, "I apologize for the weather. It seems to have coincided with my arrival," and we will be met by blank stares. If a President says the same thing, watch the belly laughs and appreciative nudges.

It is not a case of natural comedic talent nor of real humor, but more a result of surprise. Presidents are supposed to be grave, serious and dignified. So, even a mildly bantering tone seems to strike many audiences as howlingly funny.

The same principle often pertains to the lighter moments around the White House and Washington. It is the serious backdrop of the Presidency and related institutions which allow capital story-tellers to function.

For example, the stuffed-shirt decorum of much of diplomatic life has been a foil for many slapstick scenes of the past. There was the memorable disaster of the late Senator Connally of Texas at a dinner given by the Mexican Embassy in Washington in 1947. The occasion was the state visit of Miguel Aleman, the President of Mexico, who had already been entertained at the White House and was giving a return dinner for President Truman.

I was present as a pool reporter and along with the other hundred or so guests sat in one of the freshly gilded chairs around the lavishly decorated U-shaped dinner table. When the time for the toasts came, Mr. Truman stood and proposed a toast to his host. The ladies in their delicate evening dresses, and the men in their dinner jackets, started to rise.

A harsh, ripping sound filled the room. The braver men self-consciously looked to the seat of their trousers. White-faced women stared mostly at each other. Embassy attachés turned with horror to Senator Connally, who was standing rather awkwardly because his chair had risen with him and was firmly attached to his ample posterior.

It took only a few seconds to realize what had happened. The caterer evidently had done a last minute job of gilding the chairs. The night was hot and humid. The two factors combined to make the chairs extremely sticky and adhesive.

The scene reminded one of the Marx Brothers as guests examined the large, irregular gold markings on their dinner partners' derrières, while hand-wringing Embassy personnel paced on the sidelines.

One other Embassy scene sticks in my mind from the Truman years. It was on the Brazilian trip in the same year. I had been deposited at the heavily guarded entrance of Itamarati Palace in Rio de Janeiro by my driver. Inside the palace was President Truman, poking at a plate of pheasant and truffles as the guest of President Dutra. It was my professional duty to get inside the palace and find out what was going on, but I lacked one little thing: an invitation.

But I was in my best suit of tails and, with a suntan and no haircut, I looked sufficiently Latin to get by the first wave of palace guards who seemed to be young men completely devoid of humor. Walking through their thick hedge of bayoneted rifles, I tried to hum the Brazilian national anthem to indicate that I belonged.*

I made it to the top of some red carpeted stairs before I was nailed. A guard nudged me politely toward a young man coming after me in leaps and bounds up the red rug. The young man was in evening clothes, but definitely someone in authority. He let me have a volley of Portuguese, and for some reason I remember noticing how his white tie bobbed up and down as he spoke and waved his hands.

I smiled weakly and fished in my tailcoat for a phrasebook. Thumbing frantically, I mumbled one of the first things I saw, *"Onde a quarto des homens?"* The next morning, reviewing my strategy, I discovered I had asked for the men's room.

The young man sensed something and, in English, told me, "This is most embarrassing but, sir, your invitation?"

I said in a tone intended to convey shock and hurt surprise, *"I* am Merriman Smith!"

I'll never know whether it was the way I bayed at the man or my inquiry for the men's room. But he bowed deeply and bade me enter.

But the best example for me of the frailty of high-level diplomacy will always be a little-known international incident of the Kennedy administration. Actually, it was on New Year's eve in 1960, when JFK was President-elect, that Nikita Khrushchev decided to send him a New Year's message in Palm Beach.

The President-elect, himself, was at a private party. The Russian Embassy then tried the Palm Beach Towers Hotel where the

* A White House staff member in the Eisenhower administration commented, "Smitty could look Spanish, English, Russian, French—anything. He once got into Elysée Palace by flashing a Gettysburg (Pa.) Volunteer Fire Department lapel pin."

majority of the Kennedy party was ensconced. The message was timed to be delivered at the stroke of twelve, but understandably most of the Kennedy aides were also out of their rooms.

In Pierre Salinger's suite, however, two young boys—Pierre's son Mark (age 12) and my son Tim (also 12)—were glued to the television set, waiting for the ball to drop on the Allied Chemical Building.

As soon as the big event happened, Tim went back down the hall to the Smith family room. Soon afterwards the phone rang. A heavily-accented voice asked for "President Kennedy or Merriman Smith." The call apparently had come to young Salinger who, unused at this point to a distinction between press and staff, referred the messenger to "Merriman Smith's room." At any rate, Tim, intrigued by the option of the President or his father, put on a bath robe and raced down to the hotel bar.

I had the call transferred to the bar and took down the message on the back of a menu. It was a general expression of good wishes and congratulations and, if not of earth-shattering implications, still a good news story. When I reached Salinger, I proposed a deal: he would give me an exclusive on the story, and I would not say how the message was transmitted. For one thing, it might have resulted in a trip to Siberia for the man who dictated the message to a reporter in a hotel bar.

The next day at an outdoor press conference, Salinger was asked about the message: how and when had Kennedy received it? Salinger hesitated, then looked in my direction. "Let's say," he said, "it didn't come through the normal diplomatic channels."

FDR loved all forms of repartee and give-and-take, especially with the press. Reporters, within limits, could return his barbs and kid him. When his press office handed out a "Beef Chart of Wholesale and Retail Cuts" released by the Department of Agriculture, reporters sent a query to the President.

"Mr. President: We've looked and looked and can't find the tenderloin. Respectively, The Press Room."

Roosevelt immediately returned the numbered picture of a side of beef with a notation in the margin: "Look inside!"

On another occasion we had heard that Mr. Roosevelt was

126

thinking about a long trip—it turned out to be Mexico—with a stop in Warm Springs. So we wrote a poem, decorated with crude pictures of a railroad engine and entitled, "Ode to the Spring," and showed it to Marvin McIntyre, FDR's secretary. It read:

> As we wish for sectors vernal
> Warm (like hope) Springs eternal.
> There we'd bask in liquid pleasure
> While piling up a modest treasure.
> The problem's simple, answer same—
> Let's jump to Georgia, once again.

McIntyre took our verse into the President's office. It was late in the day and Mr. Roosevelt was finishing his mail with Grace Tully, his personal secretary.

FDR studied the poem for a minute and then asked Grace for a scratch pad. Without saying anything more, he scribbled on the pad for a few minutes. He ripped off the sheet and handed it to McIntyre.

"Here, Mac," he said. "Give them this."

Mr. Roosevelt had filled the entire sheet. McIntyre called me into his office and handed the reply to me. It said:

> Your touching deep desire
> Arouses in me fire
> To send a hasty wire
> To Warm Springs in the mire
> To scrape the roads,
> Break out the corn.
> The gals is waiting
> Sho's yo born

> TO THE 3 PRESS ASSOCIATIONS ONLY
> NONE OTHER NEED APPLY

Reporters liked to remind the President about some of his far-flung business schemes. He once bankrolled a friend's idea of attempting to fence in a bay in Maine to raise lobsters more economically. The project failed when they realized that lobsters have to go to sea to spawn.

And FDR came back at them with well-aimed needling. I had been in bed one time for several days with food poisoning, but the President mistook my pallor for a bad hangover and proceeded to rib me by describing in nauseating detail how Italian vermouth, a necessary ingredient for a favorite gin drink, was made from vegetables which had rotted in Italian markets.

On another occasion, he nearly turned a group of White House correspondents into teetotalers by such tactics. They had taken on a heavy load of gin the night before and at a shipboard press conference in the Bay of Fundy the next day, he told them they probably had unknowingly gotten gin made from disintegrating fish heads salvaged from seafood wholesalers in the area.

Around the office, he would joke with the staff in the same way. His resounding laugh could be heard out in the lobby, as he would peer over the shoulder of a typist working on a response to an Odd Fellows Lodge.

"Write 'em just like they were Knights of Columbus!"

He had a talent for deflating pomposity. Sometimes he employed one of his elaborate stories for this purpose. For example, on the President's Pacific trip in 1944, the newsmen had difficulties with the President's Naval Aide, Rear Admiral Brown, who was a stickler for secrecy on the President's whereabouts. Brown was Mister Navy of the old school and he seemed to hate civilians with a passion. Here was a perfect chance for one of Mr. Roosevelt's fables.

To explain the weeks of bad weather which followed the President's party on the last stages of the journey, Mr. Roosevelt dictated his version of "Mary Had a Little Lamb" or "Admiral Brown Had a Low and Everywhere the Admiral Went the Lamb Was Sure to Go."

"Shortly after leaving Honolulu, clear blue sky, calm sea, no wind," the President related, "there appeared over the horizon a cloud as small as a man's hand. It saw us and approached slowly.

"It turned out to be one of those rare animals known as a 'low.' The party was on deck and as soon as the 'low' saw us it recognized Rear Admiral Wilson Brown, USN, and headed straight for us.

"By unanimous cursing, we persuaded it to go away while we

caught some more fish and the sun actually came out. But having transferred to a destroyer, Admiral Brown seemed to be somewhat worried and sure enough his little 'low' appeared again that evening. He was so glad to see it that it never left us. We think he fed it surreptitiously under the table. . . ."

President Kennedy had a similar sense of humor. Like FDR, he was a great needler—only a little subtler. JFK's best lines were examples of superbly spare drollery. He began a speech to the Youth Fitness Conference in 1962:

"I want to express my great appreciation at the opportunity to be here with you, and to express my thanks to all of you for having attended this conference. I asked those members of the Cabinet who felt they were physically fit to come here today, and I am delighted that Mr. Udall and Mr. Robert Kennedy and Governor Ribicoff responded to the challenge."

Like Roosevelt, Kennedy's irony was usually directed by some type of human frailty or inflexibility. He told a convention of the National Association of Manufacturers:

"I understand that President McKinley and I are the only two Presidents of the United States to ever address such an occasion. I suppose that President McKinley and I are the only two that are regarded as fiscally sound enough to be qualified for admission."

President Eisenhower seldom used humor in his speeches, saving his large stores of jokes—mostly anecdotes from Army life —for private moments. President Kennedy, however, had the timing and polished delivery of a Bob Hope. One of his best performances was at the annual Al Smith Dinner in New York City in 1960. After a string of one-liners, Kennedy appeared to be getting serious:

"Cardinal Spellman is the only man so widely respected in American politics that he could bring together, amicably, at the same banquet table, for the first time in this campaign, two political leaders who are increasingly apprehensive about the November election, who have long eyed each other suspiciously, and who have disagreed so strongly, both publicly and privately, Vice President Nixon and Governor Rockefeller."

For most of President Nixon's political life, his speeches were

given largely to serious explanation and stern rhetoric. Even off-
stage, he was a very serious person early in his career.

When he returned, for instance, from the famous trip to Latin
America in 1958 where an angry mob attacked his car and threw
stones, a friend asked with mock nonchalance, "Been away,
Dick?"

Nixon answered, "Haven't you been reading the papers?! I'll
say I've been away—we nearly got killed down there."

He had missed the joke, or possibly did not see the humor in
making light of a serious incident. But Mr. Nixon is a consum-
mate political professional, and saw from the Kennedy example
that he needed to lighten his speaking style.

So, during the 1968 campaign, he hired Bob Howard, who had
writing assignments with Bob Hope and Merv Griffin to his
credit. Howard was joined by another professional comedy writer,
Paul Keyes, of Jack Paar and "Laugh-In" background. Together
they helped a "new Nixon" emerge.

One thing that hasn't changed, though, is President Nixon's
basic reluctance to joke about anything that "hits home"—religion, money, race, and so forth. Like President Eisenhower did,
he also feels that the Presidency should not be lessened by a lack
of dignity or respect.

President Kennedy took a different, though not necessarily conflicting view. One of the uses Kennedy found for humor was to
lessen the tension or bitterness around emotion-laden political
issues. When campaigning, for example, he was often successful
at joking away—or at least, cooling down—the question of his
youth and inexperience, the issue of his Catholicism, the fears
of a family "dynasty." The late Robert F. Kennedy shared this
skill.

"There goes my farm program," the city-born New York Senator would say when a single sheet of paper blew off the rostrum
in Indiana or South Dakota.

The campaign crowds loved it. In fact, self-deprecating humor
has become a new way of joining the audience at a common level
without appearing insincere or overly immodest. Vice President
Agnew and Mayor John Lindsay are now probably the most pol-

ished political after-dinner speakers around, owing largely to a knack for this sort of approach.

President Johnson was not much for self-deprecation in any form, but he did have a well-developed story-telling sense. When LBJ told one of his favorite stories about a befuddled lobbyist at the Texas Legislature many years ago, he did it with lavish gestures, he mimicked several voices and accents, and his facial expressions ranged from glee to grave pathos.

The story took about ten minutes to tell, which is one reason why Johnson's humor has never translated very well in print. It does not travel well for it misses the setting and mood of the moment, and his yarns depended greatly on his vocal expressions and mimicry. He could conjure up the ghost of the departed Sam Rayburn with voice and facial expressions which were remarkable.

Most of Johnson's humor around reporters was Roosevelt-like teasing with a Texas twist. Once, after he walked a group of newsmen around the south grounds of the White House for nine laps in humid 98-degree weather, he said with deadpan concern, "I'd invite you all to lunch, but I don't know if we have enough hot soup."

Another time, he demonstrated this puckish trait by phoning the wife of Defense Secretary Robert S. McNamara. It was early evening and Mrs. McNamara took the call to hear the President inquiring about the possibilities of dropping by, admittedly and cheerfully inviting himself to dinner.

Mrs. McNamara was about ready to have dinner served, so she asked when she and her husband might expect the Chief Executive.

"Pretty soon now," Johnson said.

No sooner had Mrs. McNamara hung up the telephone than Johnson was at the front door. He had been talking to her by radio-telephone from his White House car—in front of the McNamara house.

In many ways, the Johnson humor resembled that of his friend, Harry Truman. Both men delighted in stories with the earthy origin of the farm or ranch. The Johnson and Truman brand of humor frequently dealt with the plight of a cowboy, a farm hand or a small town figure in his battle with the much larger outside world.

Despite his deserved reputation for salty language, Truman was deeply devout and held women in something approaching reverence. I never heard him tell a really dirty joke, certainly never in the presence of females. He told jokes in small male groups. They were usually of the Missouri barnyard variety—one mule in trouble with another, a farmer whose outhouse collapsed.

LBJ, on the other hand, sometimes shocked the ladies with his sexual similes, but this would have probably surprised him, possibly hurt him if he had known. He seemed to assume that any listener was sufficiently worldly to understand that he intended no offense or personal application. His taste in jokes was much like that of Truman, essentially barnyard and anecdotal.

Truman got many of his laughs simply by his forthright style of blurting out his true feelings about someone or something.

President Johnson amused many people just by doing some of the seemingly outlandish things that came naturally to him. In fact, political satirists used to complain privately during the Johnson administration that they were stuck in a fallow period.

Comedian Mort Sahl once explained that LBJ often hampered him by doing things that were funnier in actuality than anything a comedy writer could devise. "You start using an invented exaggeration about life on the LBJ ranch and then discover that he actually *does* herd cattle in a white Continental."

Actually, much of the "lighter side" of White House life comes with hindsight, looking back on what—at the time—were rather frightening events. A personal example involved an encounter with an over-zealous General in Rumania on President Nixon's European trip in 1969.

The Rumanians were plainly nervous to begin with on this trip. The Russians were mad at them for inviting Nixon; top Rumanian officials were scared something was going to happen to the American President. The latter fear prompted one of the country's top army generals to stay at Nixon's side literally everywhere.

More or less on the spur of the moment, the President decided he wanted to tour a big market area that caught his fancy. President Nixon understands the media and knew the value of his visit would be enhanced if he could be captured talking one-to-one with some ordinary citizens of a Communist country.

So he asked the Secret Service to bring some of the reporters right next to him. An agent later told me the President added, "Keep Smitty right on my back. I want him to stay with me at this stop."

An agent brought me up close as the President went into the market. I was dictating to U.P.I. editor Dick Growald who received my running report in a hotel room and relayed it over an open telephone line.

All this time, the Rumanian General was eyeing me. He seemed disturbed by the walkie-talkie and when he finally noticed the "PRESS" badge he became positively agitated. He rushed up and wedged between the President and me. He couldn't speak much English but pointed at my badge and said, "Press!" With that he pushed me a heavy shove back towards two Secret Service agents.

The agents, however, had been given pointed and specific orders to keep me at his back. So they shoved me back towards the President and motioned to the general to step aside. This rough handling by the American security men confirmed the general's suspicions, so he grabbed me around the shoulders and pushed back again. The Secret Service are a determined lot so, of course, they started to throw me back toward the President.

By this time, I had lost contact with Dick Growald on the walkie-talkie, had lost track of what the President was doing, and was feeling like a human ping-pong ball. I started to shove back at the general, when an agent intervened, stepped in front of the general, and allowed me to fall in again behind the President. The general started yelling about "Press" and apparently about his orders, when the Secret Service man decided to try sign language. Nodding his head knowingly, he raised a single finger to his lips in the international signal for silence and gently said, "Sh-h-h." This the general understood and he whispered for the rest of the visit.

Another example of hindsight humor involved the experience President Truman had while kissing babies during a campaign. It seems funny in retrospect, mostly because it happened to a President of the United States, but Truman was quite flustered at the time.

It was during the 1948 campaign when he was lashing the "do nothing" Republican Congress from the rear platform of his train. It was at night in a small town in Nebraska and the crowd clustered around the end of his car.

A man handed up a baby and gingerly Truman held the infant in his arms long enough for the father—and news photographers, too—to snap a picture. At this moment, the train began to pull slowly out of town with Truman still standing on the rear of his car, complete with baby.

"Stop this damned train," Truman said as genuine panic spread across his face. "I've got somebody's baby."

Out there in the Nebraska darkness, the mother's wail cut like a knife. Some of the people were roaring with laughter. The father was running beside the train, yelling, "My baby, my baby."

CHAPTER SEVEN

Presidential Campaigns: Getting to the White House

Smith wrote in his journal in the autumn of 1954:

Beside my typewriter is a small cigaret lighter which sums up those months (the 1952 campaign) in highly abbreviated statistics. The bottom of the lighter bears the signature of Dwight D. Eisenhower. Above it is a map of the United States and this inscription, "The route of Dwight D. Eisenhower, Republican Presidential candidate."

The map is criss-crossed with dotted lines, solid lines, wavy lines showing virtually every foot of the campaign: air miles, 30,505; rail, 20,871; total, 51,376 miles. Every time I look at those figures I get tired. I smell train smoke, the ink of mimeograph machines, the exhaust of warming plane engines, the vacuum cleaner scent of hotel corridors.

I hear the impersonal clatter of telegraph keys, the incessant telephones, shouting policemen, the tired voice of the candidate trying to be funny in his 20th speech of the day, the popping of motorcycle mufflers, the voice of Fred Waring rising over the roar of the crowd as he leads the chant of "I like Ike," the unwelcome voice of the telephone operator in the dark of the morning when she says, "It's five o'clock, sir, and the temperature outside is 54 degrees."

I see local politicians swarming aboard the train yipping "where's the bar," tired speech writers curled in plane seats with their exhausted arms hung loosely around the text of tomorrow's oration. I see the candidate reeling in the back seat of a convertible in Los Angeles, temporarily woozy from the impact of an unopened clump of confetti that hurtled down on his head from the window of a skyscraper.

More than anything, I suppose the little lighter brings back memories of press rooms, work cars on trains, crowded charter planes where your lap is your desk, and at least one voice crying out in anguish, "If I have to write this goddamed speech one more time . . ."

The flashback was of a single, specific candidacy, but it could have applied to presidential campaigns in general. Merriman Smith covered seven presidential campaigns and found that each prompted a certain sense of déjà vu: *the physical grind, the convention hoopla, the posturing of the political amateurs, and the systematic deception practiced by the political pros. He noticed some of the more subtle advantages of incumbency, the importance of campaign logistics on press coverage, and the absurdity of some time-honored campaign rituals. For Smith, a presidential campaign was an ordeal, a professional test, and a fascination.*

THE FIRST principle of watching political campaigns— and particularly Presidential races—is that most of what appears to be happening and most of what seems to be said is sham. Politics tends to generate a fair amount of mis-, half-, and un-truths anyway. And campaigns magnify this natural tendency.

The Presidential sweepstakes, for example, uniformly begin with the major contenders disavowing their candidacy. This is a bit of traditional showmanship which bears little relation to fact. As *Punch*, the British satirical magazine, observed in early 1968: "The Presidential candidates have so far had to face only one test of their honesty (about whether they were going to run) and all but one have lied. And the man we can trust, then? Good God, it's Richard Nixon."

Once a contender admits his candidacy, he then usually feigns ignorance of anyone else in the race. President Johnson, for instance, said in 1964 that he had no opinion as to who might win the Republican nomination. (This was at a time when Senator Barry Goldwater was the acknowledged front-runner among the Republicans.) If Mr. Johnson had said he had no forecast to make about his GOP opponent, that might have been one thing. But to say he was without any opinion whatever was another matter. This was not actual political dishonesty, but a long-revered custom by which politicians fence, weave and bob until they make their announcements at times and places of their own choosing.

When the campaign actually starts, subtle changes seem to occur in the political dialogue. Politicians start calling other politicians "politicians" again, for example. Candidates start accusing opponents of making a political issue out of questions of public policy on which opinion is divided and which, in short, are political issues. Consider the number of times in 1968 that one candidate or another was heard to say that he did not intend to trifle with national interests by making the war in Vietnam a political issue. Then, for the next fifteen minutes he usually talked about Vietnam and the unrealistic, immoral, or misguided positions of the other candidates.

A curious doctrine of "flexible sin" emerges in campaigns. In one election year, we hear pointed observations that if the Republican President would only stay in Washington instead of traipsing off to Gettysburg, we might not be in such a mess with Castro. The Republicans dutifuly scream "dirty politics."

Two years later, Republicans imply that if the Democratic President would only stay in Washington instead of frittering away time on Cape Cod, we would not be in such a fix in Cuba.

Democrats know the proper response, too, and cry "dirty politics."

Rhetoric in political campaigns, in fact, is usually so consistently self-justifying and disingenuous that when candor makes a rare appearance, the effect can be shocking. Rose Kennedy made a brief statement in 1968 that was really just a series of truisms, but her mere statement of the obvious was big news in the campaign season because she had been frank enough to make it.

Asked about the family's financial backing of Senator Robert Kennedy in 1968, his mother said: "It is our money and we are free to spend it any way we please. It's part of this campaign business—if you have money, you spend it to win. And the more you can afford, the more you'll spend. The Rockefellers are like us—we both have lots of money to spend on our campaigns."

The problem was that, unknowingly, Mrs. Kennedy had tampered with some well-entrenched campaign mystique—stress your underdog status, finesse any questions about money or personal wealth, dramatize, or at least affect, humble beginnings.

The log-cabin image may seem a little outmoded in a day and age when the U.S. economy is around the one trillion mark, but its attraction has always been strong. Even Adlai Stevenson, a millionaire, was known for the hole in his shoe and Nelson Rockefeller's frayed collars have been objects of interest and analysis.

At the national conventions, campaign pettifoggery shifts into high gear. For instance, regardless of the predetermined outcome of any convention, there must be demonstrations. These are fascinating folk dramas. They really have no counterparts elsewhere in the world and, in fact, often mystify foreign scholars who come from abroad to observe how America elects a President.

For the most part, these convention demonstrations are bought and paid for by state delegations to herald the sterling qualities of a native son who in truth does not have a chance of being nominated for anything outside his home precincts. But signs and banners are printed, imitation straw hats equipped with brilliant borders, musicians hired more for their ability to bull through a crowd than play, and plastic enlargements of state products manufactured.

At the 1960 Republican convention in Chicago, one group of strolling minstrels was spotted demonstrating powerfully for five favorite sons from five different states. The horn blowers apparently had only minutes in which to duck into the nether regions of the convention hall, change hat-bands and emblazoned shirts, pick up music for the next state song and swirl back onto the floor.

When a nominee is picked and the campaign goes on the road, the pattern of little white lying shifts, but continues. One of its first post-convention symptoms is the inflated crowd figure.

Invariably, most of the reporters traveling with a Presidential candidate estimate the crowd at a political rally on their own and find that it is far under that of the ranking police official present. It is old journalistic custom, however, to quote an authority for a political crowd estimate. Thus, the public is treated to some rather interesting figures.

When Senator John F. Kennedy spoke in Detroit on Labor Day, 1960, the police estimated his crowd in Cadillac Square at about 50,000 to 55,000 persons. The *Detroit News* then did a rather unfair thing; unfair to the campaign year estimator. The paper took a large photographic blow-up of the crowd, marked it off into equal sections and counted every single person who was visible. The total, police count notwithstanding, was under 27,000.

And the story is told of a leading Republican campaign strategist who went to a Notre Dame football game. A friend asked him to estimate the crowd.

"I suppose there are about 50,000 here today," he said, "but if a candidate were speaking, it would be somewhere near 200,000."

And that tells the story of most campaign crowd figures.

Celebrities are solicited, sometimes hired, to add glitter to campaign platforms. Candidates start claiming that they have discovered some Irish, Jewish, or Italian ancestry in their family trees, depending on the audience. (When FDR told an Al Smith dinner audience in New York that he thought he was part Irish, Fiorello H. LaGuardia was said to have remarked, "If Frank Roosevelt is Irish, I'm a Chinaman with a haircut.")

Spontaneous demonstrations begin to be laboriously organized. The famous "Bring Us Together" sign that President Nixon spotted in a crowd and made the subject of his post-election victory speech was not just a little girl's homemade plea. It was spray-painted the night before Mr. Nixon noticed it in a Deshler, Ohio, gymnasium under the guidance of a Republican advance team.

As the press starts to report some of these relatively minor, but illusion-shattering aspects of a campaign, relations between candidate and reporters often become somewhat strained. And other unavoidable factors can compound the friction.

For example, a candidate out of sheer necessity and in the interests of consistency, uses the same phrases and sentences over and over again. He polishes anecdotes on crowd after crowd until they work perfectly—if a crowd hears them for the first time. The press party traveling with the candidate, after hearing the same speeches repeatedly, tends to jump on minor variations. What may seem to the traveling press as a shift in policy may be nothing more than a matter of rewording old material. But the press is charged with saying things never intended by the candidate.

Each candidate, when he parades through a city, is followed by cars and busloads of traveling journalists and broadcasters who, intent on their work, look out at the crowds with less than happy faces. They are working, trying to size up the crowd and besides, they see this sort of thing day after day—and several times a day, at that. Their facial expressions tend to remind some spectators of adult delinquents being shipped off to rehabilitation centers. Local party leaders see this lack of fiesta spirit and seize upon it as vivid proof of press prejudice.

(Former President Dwight D. Eisenhower, new to the ways of campaigning in 1952, asked his people plaintively, "Isn't there anything you can do about all those sour-faced fellows riding behind me?")

At some point in a Presidential campaign, every reporter asks himself the obvious question—what does all the carnival, show business atmosphere have to do with the Presidency, particularly in times of nearly perpetual crisis. The answer has to do with the old whipping boy, the American electorate. The sad truth is that millions of Americans still do not care tremendously about looking over the men for whom they vote and it takes a little showmanship to get the public away from other forms of entertainment and to come to a rally to see what the candidate is like in person.

But this has always been true. Revelations like Joe McGinnis' *The Selling of a President* are insightful, but really only recount the latest version of a recurring phenomenon.

For instance, cynics and so-called liberals frequently took the Eisenhower campaign staff to task for the stagey qualities of their techniques. These critics hooted at the audience warm-up with entertainment personalities, the advance squads of confetti and placard distributors indicative of an approaching Eisenhower visit. But nothing undertaken by the Eisenhower camp ever quite approached Adlai Stevenson's 1952 campaign visit to his birthplace at Los Angeles.

Democratic officials got together the best planning talent Hollywood had to offer for Stevenson's visit. Shortly before the Democratic candidate was to visit the humble house where he was born, helpful campaign workers distributed among the press many handouts on the program of the day, including one seemingly inoffensive and uninformative document labeled "Routine —Stevenson visit to birthplace."

The reporters, most of them at any rate, gave the accumulation a quick glance. Some of the more alert—or bored—newsmen suddenly leaped into action. The "routine" sheet was anything but that and it virtually destroyed Stevenson's visit "home."

The first item on the sheet read like a movie shooting script.

"11:00–11:05. Stevenson dismounts from car in front of walk leading to porch. Crowd and party are held back in order to allow Governor to walk alone up the steps and to the front door. This should be done with reasonable reverence, in such a manner as to give camera men a dramatic shot of an historical figure returning to the place of his birth.

"Stevenson is met at the door by Miss Bertha Mott, current oc-

141

cupant of the house who says, 'Since I was a little girl, it has been my ambition to fetch a glass of water for a President. May I have that honor now?' (All this in a light, friendly vein.)

"Stevenson accepts and enters the house. When he enters, those outside shout: 'We want Adlai!' At the same time, those actively participating in the ceremony take their positions on the front porch and, as Adlai comes out (and waves to the crowd) they usher him to his seat on the porch."

The concluding scene of the Democratic homecoming for Stevenson was equally impressive. He walked around the interior of the house for a few minutes, then returned to the porch. Incidentally, he never got his glass of water because Stevenson's press agents found out about the script and changed the plans so that poor Miss Mott had virtually no chance to get off her "since I was a little girl" line.

Stevenson received two surprise gifts—his birth certificate and a "Native Son's Bear Flag." The script then continued:

"11:20–11:21. Stevenson standing with Native Son's Bear Flag in one hand and Birth Certificate in the other, holds them aloft and concludes with a remark to the effect that any man who has all this and the State too can't help but win!

"(APPLAUSE)

"11:25. Cavalcade departs."

In fairness, this sort of appearance did not really typify Stevenson's campaigns. For one thing, such orchestration is considered fine by most candidates, but they tend to want to do the orchestrating themselves. They want to write the script, not have it written for them.

This is true of incumbent Presidents in particular, for they have more leverage and greater opportunity to manage events than do challengers. A moonshot, a summit conference, a dramatic government appointment—an incumbent President can time any of these according to his own domestic political needs if he chooses to do so.*

* One of the worst positions, though, it seems to me, is that of the incumbent Vice President running for President. Just as John Kennedy saddled then Vice President Nixon in 1960 with every defect of the Eisenhower administration, so Richard Nixon, himself, was able to blame Hubert Humphrey in 1968 for every shortcoming of the Johnson administration.

Smith as a young reporter in Georgia in the 1930s. He later grew a mustache to make himself look older when he came to Washington in 1940. By 1941, at the age of twenty-seven, he was White House correspondent for United Press.

Smith takes notes at left as President Roosevelt and Winston Churchill answer questions at the White House in 1942.

As President Roosevelt toured the country's military installations by train in 1943, a constant companion was his dog, Fala. The little terrier was once "almost denuded," Smith wrote, when some sailors at Pearl Harbor started clipping off locks of Fala's coat for souvenirs.

Long after President Truman had left the White House, he and Smith had maintained contact by correspondence and occasional banquets like this one. Once, when President Johnson visited Independence, Missouri, to see Truman, Smith warmly greeted the former president and inquired after his health, family, and so on. LBJ, who witnessed the scene, remarked laconically to an aide, "I guess the only way for a president to get any affection from Smitty is to leave office."

Three wire service reporters (Smith in the middle) phone in competing stories after one of Truman's presidential press conferences.

Candidate Eisenhower calls to Smith at a campaign stop in Brooklyn in 1952. Smith was typing on the ground since no press tables were available.

United Press International Photo

This picture—taken as Smith was asking President Eisenhower about the defense of Formosa in 1955—was the first photograph permitted to be taken at a presidential news conference.

Two of Smith's children meet President Eisenhower and Secretary of State Christian Herter at Gettysburg as a Secret Service agent looks on. After the introduction, Smith reported to Ike, "Marvin Arrowsmith (the AP man) wants equal time next weekend. And *he's* got nine kids."

Smith covered Winston Churchill's White House visits during three ad-.
ministrations: Roosevelt's, Truman's, and Eisenhower's. Here, Churchill
poses with the Eisenhowers on the North Portico.

Merriman Smith once played the Augusta National Golf Course's four-teenth hole to find out why President Eisenhower was always complaining about it.

White House, Abbie Rowe

Shortly before a White House Correspondents' banquet, a news story appeared about President Kennedy cutting his finger while slicing some bread in the White House kitchen. Smith decided an appropriate gift for the president should be something practical—so here he gives him an automatic bread slicer.

Merriman Smith was an avid amateur photographer and often took shots of presidents and their families as he traveled with them. This was taken as Mrs. Kennedy was leaving Mass in Middleburg, Virginia.

President Kennedy introduces Merriman Smith to an old friend.

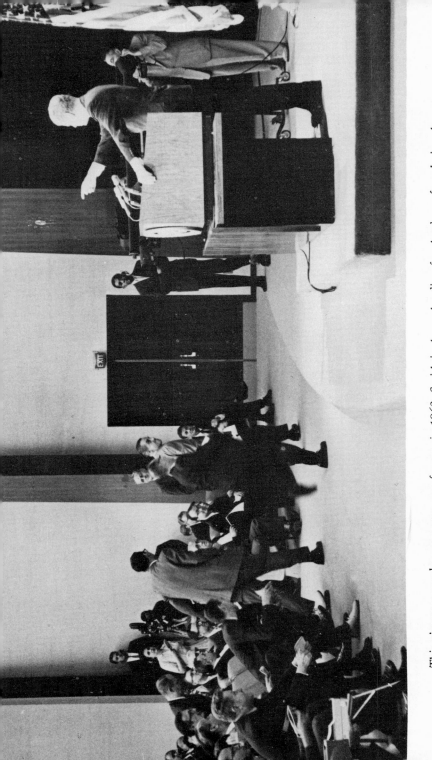

This picture was taken at a press conference in 1962. Smith is shown heading for the door after closing the conference with the traditional "Thank you, Mr. President." President Kennedy, however, decided to take one extra question. When the question turned out to be about a "serious disagreement" between JFK and Mayor Wagner of New York, the president laughed and commented, "Mr. Smith was right, as usual."

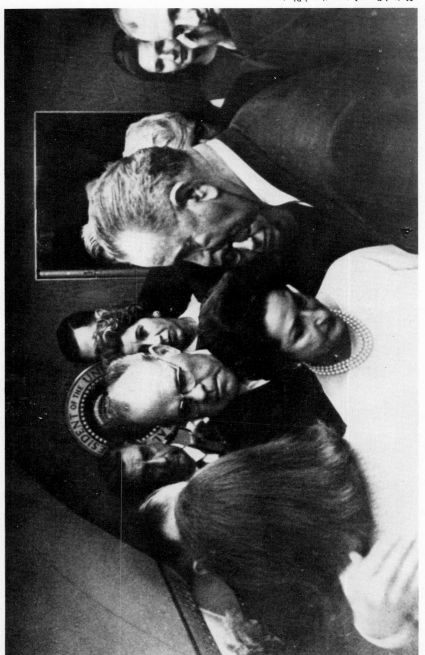

Merriman Smith (on the left, by the presidential seal) in the cabin of Air Force One in Dallas, November 22, 1963.

Smith posed for this UPI publicity shot after winning the Pulitzer Prize of 1964 for his coverage of the Kennedy assassination in Dallas. His private reaction: "I've been writing for 25 years. Why couldn't I have won it for something else?"

One of the hazards of a White House reporter's profession. Here, President Johnson had taken reporters on a walk around the South Grounds, even though it was raining.

Merriman Smith, President Johnson, and AP colleague Doug Cornell at a working lunch. The LBJ inscription: "To Smitty—a professional. Lyndon B. Johnson."

President Johnson shares a plane seat with Smith as he talks to reporters. This was taken during the 1964 campaign.

Smith took this shot of President Nixon after the president had finished a round of golf in San Clemente. "... a rare shot of Nixon at ease" was Smith's notation in his photo file.

A classic pose for any reporter. Fresh paper and carbons in the typewriter. Then it's time to think up a fresh lead for the story. This was taken in a San Clemente press room in 1969.

Another plus for an incumbent is a built-in recognition factor for himself and his family. I remember one of Harry Truman's favorite ploys, which he used for appearances at the rear end of his private railroad car which had been equipped with a blue velvet curtain.

He could finish his talk and say with a sort of bashful boy smile, "How would you like to meet my family?"

The crowd always went for that, loud and long. Then the President would say with an acquiescent shrug of the shoulders, "Well, all right."

"First, Mrs. Truman—the boss."

The crowds gave her a good hand as she stepped between the opening of the velvet curtains. She rarely said a word, but waved. Then came the climax of the show.

"And my daughter, Margaret."

This invariably brought a blast of applause louder than any of the President's "hang the Republicans" lines did. Margaret swept through the curtain with a gracious smile and a wave to the crowd.

And about that time the loud speakers on the end of the car reverberated with a series of rising and falling wails, signaling the departure of the train. In fact, this routine became so standard that wags aboard the train began to refer to the First Family in vaudevillian terms as "The Three Traveling Trumans." But the appearance made a lot of political sense. Crowds wanted to see pretty Margaret of the concert stage as much as they wanted to see the Chief Executive. Poor Governor Dewey had a perfectly nice family, but no one knew them, and hence they didn't possess the same drawing power.

(The technique of ending an appearance by having the train pull away from the crowd while the candidate is still speaking was also a favorite of Lyndon Johnson's when he was barnstorming on the Kennedy ticket in 1960. When he wanted to leave, he would nudge aide Bobby Baker who crouched next to him with a walkie-talkie. Baker would give the command and LBJ—still talking—would shout, "They're taking me away from you, folks. I want to stay with you, but they're taking me away! . . . Vote Democratic! Bye!")

Incumbents also like to strike various Presidential poses to stress their statesmanlike qualities and experience at the helm. A classic example was President Johnson's posture in the 1964 campaign against Senator Barry Goldwater. LBJ would dramatically recreate the Cuban missile crisis for his audiences—when "Khrushchev and John Kennedy stood eyeball to eyeball with their knives pokin' each other in the ribs . . . until Khrushchev sent those missiles back to Russia."

And he had another great line to sum up the peace issue: "Just remember this when you go to the ballot box on Tuesday—who do you want to be sittin' beside that hot line when the telephone goes ting-a-ling and the voice on the other end says, 'Moscow calling.'"

The most vivid example of a President devising and carrying out his own election strategy was, for me, FDR's fourth term campaign in 1944. Many political experts to the contrary, Mr. Roosevelt, at the outset, did not want to run again. Age was beginning to tell on him. He had lost much of his vitality. The spectre of illness was increasingly visible.

But it was a thing he had to do. He was like a fire horse refusing to go to pasture. His love of political warfare, his vanity and his firm belief that the country needed him got the best of his judgment.

His attitude toward Governor Thomas E. Dewey, the 1944 Republican candidate, was one of unvarnished contempt. He shuddered at the thought of Dewey in the White House. But he felt, too, that if he did not run, the Democrats had little chance of winning against Dewey with any nominee they might select.

This was the situation as of July 11 when he ordered the doors of his office locked and then read to more than two hundred sweating Washington correspondents the text of his letter to Democratic Chairman Robert E. Hannegan, agreeing to accept the nomination.

"You have written me," Mr. Roosevelt wrote Hannegan, "that . . . a majority of the delegates have been directed to vote for my renomination. . . ."

Reporters snickered. Who knew better than the President how the delegates were lined up?

Furthermore, the President said he would not run "in the usual partisan, political sense." His dramatic voice boomed into the domelike ceiling of his office.

"But if the people command me to continue in this office and in this war, I have as little right to withdraw as the soldier has to leave his post in the line."

The President finished reading and grinned up at the reporters.

"Now," he said. "You've got your news—go on and get out!"

Shortly afterwards, the President left to "visit the troops" on the West Coast. When he returned to Washington, he continued to maneuver. He faced the problem of just how to campaign. Throughout the war, his public appearances were virtually discontinued. Security governed everything. And everything was secret. But the President realized that a candidate cannot run off the record.

He decided to make four major campaign appearances outside the capital—in New York, Philadelphia, Chicago and Boston. And he opened his campaign in Washington in late September with an address to the Teamsters Union dinner at the Statler Hotel.

He set out deliberately to pick a dock-walloping brawl with the Republicans, knowing that a political battle of such proportions would turn out a heavy vote. Also, he wanted to make Dewey lose his temper, knowing that an opponent moved by anger is more easily tripped than one who is campaigning coolly.

The President accused the Republicans of being liars, cheats and swindlers. And the teamsters went wild.

One excited teamster-Democrat behind me showed his approval of Roosevelt's nastily sharp lines by beating a silver bread tray with a soup ladle. The noise was terrific. Two tables away, another loyal teamster applauded by smashing glasses with a wine bottle, taking a full swing for each of the President's punch lines and sending a shower of glass to the floor.

The President reveled in the thunderous ovation, bread trays and all. And he was never in better form. His sarcasm reached an all-time Roosevelt high when in a mocking voice he protested Republican attacks against "my little dog, Fala."

Shortly before he died, I asked the President if he had set out deliberately to get Dewey mad. He laughed, taunting me with a remark that he thought the results made the answer obvious. Dewey, it must be remembered, blasted back at him two nights after the Teamsters speech in an address which the Democrats used during the rest of the campaign to accuse the Republican candidate of twisting the truth. Thus, Dewey seemed to have taken the bait just as Mr. Roosevelt had hoped and expected he would.

Next came the horrible New York City trip. The President was determined to show the people of New York that he was not a dying man as the campaign whisperers were picturing him. And in so proving, he nearly killed off his staff and the reporters with him.

It was a cold, rainy day in late October. And in this terrible weather, the President toured the boroughs of New York for nearly five hours. He had a special heater under his legs in the rear seat of the car, a flannel undersuit, a fur robe around most of his body and his heavy navy cape. And he stopped once during the trip to go to the bathroom and change his upper garments which were soaked by water oozing down his neck.

I rode in an open Secret Service car just behind the President, sans heater, fur robe, flannel undersuit or a change of clothes. All I had was a raincoat and hat. I was drenched to the waist by the time the procession reached upper Broadway to begin the slow journey down to Times Square.

After speaking that night at the Waldorf, the President went to Hyde Park for a week end. He was loudly gleeful the next morning when the doctor couldn't find a trace of a sniffle in him, but reported that several of the brawny young Secret Service men had picked up bad colds.

If anything, Presidential campaigns have become more grueling over the years. Air travel and television both were hailed as means of making campaigning less hectic, but neither has had that effect. In fact, the airplane just enabled candidates to do more "whistle-stopping" per day than they used to do by train. Less time is taken for travel between stops, but this also means that less time is available for things like sleep, food, laundry, and the like.

And television has never supplanted the personal appearance as once anticipated for the simple reason that the most effective type of television appearance is that of a candidate meeting crowds on the stump. Although TV has become an overwhelmingly powerful campaign medium, no candidate yet has been able to run out of a studio. So rallies, parades and clambakes continue, if only to provide raw material for Walter Cronkite.

Campaigns thus become tests of stamina as well as tests of philosophies and personalities. A candidate's staying power becomes a political variable along with his looks, background, and voting record, and accordingly his personal physician often takes a key position in the traveling entourage. The campaign doctor arranges for rubdowns at the end of the day, mends hand cuts inflicted by handshakes, and concocts special potions for throat disorders which threaten his man's speaking voice. He dispenses bandages, medicine and advice to other members of the party—staff and press—who also have to stagger through the campaign's closing push to Election Day.

A campaign doctor often faces some rather unusual medical calamities. More than one campaign worker has been turned into a human pin cushion by lapel buttons falling off an overhead rack. And there was the case of the unlucky policeman in one of FDR's campaigns.

It seems a woman leaned out of an apartment window along the parade route to yell "Yea Frank!" She gave the "Frank" so much emphasis that her upper plate popped out of her mouth and dropped toward the crowded street. A split-second later a stalwart, dignified uniformed policeman let out a yelp of pain. The teeth had made a solid hit on his head, then splattered over the street.

My personal campaign disaster happened during the 1948 race. It resulted, however, in a minor journalistic coup. As so often is the case, luck figured prominently in the scoop.

As the Truman campaign train was pulling into Berkeley, California, I leaned far over the rail to get an early glimpse of the size of the crowd, reception arrangements, and so on, for I already had a text of the President's remarks and wanted to file a story immediately. As it turned out, I leaned too far, because I lost my balance and toppled off the train, landing on a steel guy wire.

The committee waiting to welcome President Truman evidently thought I was dead. To get me out of the way they stuffed me into a telephone booth at the station. It turned out to be the only telephone within miles and we got a ten-minute beat on the story.

Down the stretch, caring for the creature comforts of the press can reap political benefits. The 1968 Nixon campaign probably neutralized the natural sympathies of many of the traveling reporters for Hubert Humphrey by making everyday life with their candidate considerably more livable than with HHH. Lose a newsman's luggage, bring him into a small town after all restaurants are closed and no food or drink is available, forget to arrange for telephones at an airport stop—do any or all of the above and watch the most objective reporter grow a little querulous.

The Republicans generally have more money to combat logistical problems of high-speed campaigning. The Nixon campaign, for instance, went to some effort and expense to provide midnight buffets for reporters coming in off the road, telephones in the middle of nowhere, overnight laundry service, and so on—not to mention accurate schedules for the next day's events and readable advance texts. But sometimes it is simply a matter of heads-up planning. For instance, James L. Hicks, a Negro reporter traveling with Stevenson in 1952 was refused accommodations at a campaign stop in New Orleans. Hicks and the other white reporters, too, were vocally indignant. A lot of bad feeling and bad publicity resulted. The Eisenhower campaign, on the other hand, avoided the problem by juggling schedules so that the candidate and his entourage never ended up in a segregated Southern city at night.

Besides physical and logistical pressures, a candidate has the added burden of maintaining an image of all-American charm and equanimity during a campaign. The famous example of a candidate losing his cool with negative political results was Dewey's trouble with the railroad engineers in 1948.

He was addressing a track-side rally when the train began to move backward into the crowd and hundreds scattered in squealing alarm. Dewey reacted by roaring that his engineer "must be a lunatic." And everywhere Dewey traveled after that night, he saw written in the dust of hundreds of boxcars, "lunatics for Truman."

The road to the White House is strewn with many such pressures and potential obstacles. Consider some of the other essentials for a Presidential candidate. Food: A potential President may be utterly allergic to shellfish and break out in zebra stripes when confronted by lobster, but he'd better not say anything about it in New England. A President who lets it leak that he dislikes fried chicken would be President without the votes of countless Southerners.

And family problems! During a political campaign, a would-be President who spanked one of his children would be regarded as an arch-fiend. The opposition could start intimating that he also has been known to get a little rough with his wife. And a candidate must love animals. Two or three lovable mutts in his family can produce more votes than an M.I.T. degree. Try to think of a successful Presidential candidate who ran without a dog. As for religion, a man may go a lifetime with little or no attendance at church, but we forgive the past if he starts showing up at any church with regularity while he's running for office.

Opposition political professionals pick up most deviations from these norms and can dispassionately exploit them, charging all varieties of character weakness and moral turpitude. In fact, this becomes so routine that political pros can often remain relatively easy rivals—certainly much more so than amateurs whose candidate has been unfairly attacked or wronged in some way. The latter are really the ones who stir up most of the heat in campaign feuds.

Volunteers are essential to any campaign, but sometimes the political veterans of both parties despair of the enthusiastic semi-pro, be he on the left or right. For one thing, the more fire he breathes, the more he (or she) requires a good deal of channeling and effort. Their well-meant money-raising efforts, for instance, sometimes actually cost the party money. An inexperienced fund raiser may let a potentially large contributor off the hook by selling him a $100 dinner ticket when a more experienced political money man would have tapped the contributor for several thousand dollars and forgotten the dinner ticket.

Volunteer workers who get to be around the candidate are generally recognizable by the number of buttons they wear. Their reasoning seems to be that the more they wear in the way of identification the greater their sense of authenticity—and the greater their sense of belonging. The latter factor is highly important to a candidate who benefits when his volunteers feel they are part of his "in" group. But the multitude of buttons always just seems to confuse the policemen and the reporters whom they're designed to help.

A Nixon staff member in 1968, for instance, typically wore a small gold "N" in his lapel, then a multi-colored, small bar saying "Nixon-Agnew," plus another button or two in red, white and blue proclaiming that the wearer was "Staff."

And the Kennedy people in 1960 had another interesting button problem. It involved a Hollywood actress who otherwise was quite an effective and diligent campaign worker. She was a bosomy young woman, disconcerting to many males under normal circumstances. But when she put two teacup-size Kennedy buttons on her upper front, it had the effect of spotlighting her physical endowments.

This delighted the news photographers, but one of the campaign graybeards, a man in his early thirties, had to be given the delicate task of convincing her that one relatively small button was in better keeping with the sought-after image of national leadership.

It is a strange bond that grows among the people on an extended campaign trip. Violent competitors in my business will put aside their typewriters and work together diligently to help a luckless colleague who is caught in a crowd and having trouble getting back to the group, or one who is suffering from near pneumonia and needs help getting out a story.

Many of the natural barriers between candidate and reporter tend also to break down. There are few personal secrets of substance among people who live together in a campaign for weeks at a time. Birthdays, songs, and stories are shared in idle traveling hours. An almost family-like closeness grows, which is one reason good news organizations in the interest of objectivity rotate reporters from candidate to candidate.

On the campaign trains of the 40's and 50's, the inhabitants usually lived in individual rooms, but there was much over-the-back-fence conversation in the hallways with bathrobe and slippers as accepted attire. Some even bought small potted plants for the windows. Portable radios blared day and night in awkward dithyramb with the never-silent mimeograph machines.

Even today, somewhere on a campaign plane, every hour of the twenty-four a typewriter taps a staccato accompaniment to the drone of the engines. Individual rallies, speeches, and cities blur and leave behind the memories of the campaign constants of travel and fatigue, and so these bits of sound and motion are the images of a Presidential campaign that a reporter retains. Anyone who actively participates in them thinks of them first of all as ordeals. But they *can* be valuable—for the people and reporters—as a means of learning about potential leaders.

The skillful obfuscation and campaign trickery are always there, but there are just too many opportunities for revealing moments in a Presidential race for a simply plastic or insincere candidate to remain undiscovered.

As Theodore H. White, author of "The Making of the President" books, once noted: "The best time to listen to a politician is when he's on a stump on a street corner in the rain late at night when he's exhausted. Then he doesn't lie."

CHAPTER EIGHT

On the Road:
White House Travel Yarns

Perhaps no facet of the presidency changed so dramatically during Merriman Smith's tenure at the White House as the character and pace of presidential travel.

It took Franklin Roosevelt as long to go across the country in 1944 as it took Lyndon Johnson to make a round-the-world tour in 1967. Aboard Air Force One with President Nixon, Smith could phone in a story from the air, while on President Truman's whistle-stop train tours, it was often a major problem to find a Western Union outlet along the way.

Whatever the conditions, it was part of Smith's job to follow presidents on all major trips. He went with FDR on his off-the-record wartime trips and accompanied President Truman to Potsdam and Wake Island. He was with Truman board the U.S.S. Augusta when the news of the A-Bomb explosion at Hiroshima arrived.

He traveled with then President-elect Eisenhower when the latter fulfilled his campaign pledge to "go to Korea"

*and was with him in Paris in 1960 when the "Big Four"
summit conference blew up over the U-2 incident.*

*He went with Kennedy to Ireland, with Johnson to
Southeast Asia, with Nixon to Rumania, and wrote articles,
books, and diaries of every major presidential trip since
1940. The following chapter contains a distillation of Smith's
observations about presidential travel—its changing nature,
the insights it can provide, the color and anecdotes behind
official communiqués.*

FACTS AND FIGURES describing Presidential travel rarely
startle people anymore. We accept that a modern Chief
Executive can leave the White House in the morning to dedicate
a midwest dam or building project and be back in Washington
for a White House dinner.

The newspaper statistics—"President Johnson's globe-circling
Christmas journey covered 27,000 miles in sixty flying hours over
five days" or "More than 50,000 police will guard President Nixon
during his five-nation European tour"—impress but do not astound in the age of the moonwalk.

The more incredible thought in the 1970's is that it was not
until the Eisenhower administration that air transportation—
planes and helicopters—finally gained true ascendancy over train
travel. And that as late as 1947, the President of the United States
had to check with the Justice Department to see if documents
signed outside the United States would have constitutional va-
lidity.

It seems strange to recall that on this same 1947 trip—with
President Truman to a major inter-American conference in Brazil
—the traveling party totalled only twenty-five, while over 150
reporters accompanied President Nixon to Europe in 1969.

Today, scores of specialists precede any traveling President to
provide instantaneous communications facilities for his entire
entourage. Office supplies, special foods and water, medical equipment, and limousines are shipped ahead for the Presidential
party. Security and protocol arrangements are checked and re-
checked. Permits are procured for walkie-talkie radios, firearms,
and motorcades.

Visits are scheduled—again by expert specialists—down to the minute. Even such items as "recreation opportunity for press" are noted on some of the Nixon administration travel schedules. It was certainly not always this way.

Presidential trips, particularly in the Roosevelt and Truman administrations, used to reflect to a far greater degree than they do now a President's own personality and idiosyncracies. One simple reason is time. Trips took longer in those days, and reporters and Presidents, living at relatively close quarters, got to know each other better. On the other hand, today's trips are more efficient, in many ways more informal, and probably accomplish more.

Travel with FDR was, even in the context of the 1940's, amazingly leisurely. Mr. Roosevelt delighted in a slow speed train. He knew the various roadbeds of the country better than some railroad men. And he knew that reducing the rate of speed meant an easier ride. He also wanted the opportunity to sit by the window of his private car and study the passing countryside.

He loved to astound his guests with amazingly detailed knowledge of the geography of the country through which he was passing. He kept before him a small, neatly folded road map on which he followed the progress of the train. Passing through some ordinary milkstop, the President would roar out to the person nearest him:

"This is the town where General Blank did so-and-so."

Or moving through a wooded part of the Northwest, he would boom:

"Look at those trees—need cutting, but the Park Service won't let anybody in there."

When we went from Washington to San Diego with Mr. Roosevelt in 1944, the trip took more than five days. The speed of the train rarely went above thirty-five miles an hour. This was so slow that the batteries on the sleeping cars would not recharge themselves sufficiently and the train had to stop every two nights to pump power into the batteries from the big Diesels in the radio car.

In fact, the trip—off-record at the time—was so slow and boring that I rode through most of Oklahoma atop the engine cab, waving to astonished trackwalkers who never before saw a man riding on top of an engine.

But the President was happy. Nobody could reach him on the telephone. He followed his beloved hobby of geography. And he was able to bone up on the war situation before talking with Nimitz and MacArthur in Hawaii.

Traveling with Mr. Truman was like being on the road with a high school basketball team and a coach who let the players have their fun. Mr. Roosevelt loved the splendid. Mr. Truman liked little towns and small talk in the lobby of a small hotel which, if not cleared out by Secret Service agents, would be populated by shoe salesmen and hardware drummers.

When President Truman used to move through the nation by train, every stop was a new story, all this in addition to the major speeches he made at the more important stops. The big, set speeches were not too hard to handle because an advanced text was furnished and the story written long before the actual performance.

On most train trips with Mr. Truman, the correspondent had to stay in a state of perpetual alert because the President was relatively unpredictable. A few minutes after the train left Washington, he usually walked through each car, shouting greetings to everyone.

On one trip—to Fulton, Missouri, with Winston Churchill— he went on up to the engine and drove it, donning gloves and cap to do the job in regulation style. And reporters never knew at what stop Truman was going to make an impromptu speech from the rear platform of his car.

The unscheduled platform appearances drove the reporters nearly daffy, and made for many hours of nervous worry. They never knew when the President was going to say something newsworthy. Thus, at each stop, the reporters would bail out of their cars and race for the rear end of the train. The President would come out on the platform of his car, wave and acknowledge the cheers of the station crowd.

And then he might speak. And the stop might last no more than three or four minutes. During that period, the newspapermen—the wire service reporters, at least—had to record the President's words, dash back to their rooms, bat out a few paragraphs and hand them to a Western Union representative before the train pulled out.

The most elegantly written prose is, of course, of no use in a situation like this if the reporter cannot "unload" to get it to his office and on the wires, in print, or on the air. When the story becomes hot enough, rather extreme measures are sometimes taken to file a dispatch. Once we were up in the boondocks of northern California during the Truman campaign, the train was not due to stop for some time and Mr. Truman had been saying some highly printable things about Stalin—"I like old Joe, but he is a prisoner of the Politburo . . . had a case of Atlee-itis . . ." We had a big story and no way to file it.

One of the United Press regional men was on the trip with me and I told him that we had to get this story filed and the only way was for him to jump off at the next town. He didn't much like the idea but he finally agreed that if the train would slow down at the next town he would jump off.

Then I got the White House transportation man to have the train slowed down and the man jumped. He caught up with me about two days later. He said he didn't know how fast the train had been going when he jumped but that he had run for about a hundred yards before he could start rolling. United Press got about a 45-minute beat on that story.

(Press room folklore eventually had it that I had wrapped the man in pillows and personally shoved him out the door, but this is exaggeration. Actually, we were simply operating on an old principle—the theory of the expendable reporter.)

The really newsworthy Presidential trips in these years were the big wartime conferences. A Presidential trip to a foreign country is always big news, but these events, we knew, would make history. It is actually stretching things a bit to say we "covered" the meetings at Yalta and Potsdam since we never were permitted within miles of where the conferences took place, but we (the three wire-service men) did usually manage to tag along, after a fashion.

We traveled back from Yalta with FDR and waited in Berlin

for Truman, but in each case the American President deferred to the wishes of Messrs. Churchill and Stalin that American press not be allowed to cover the meetings. And, in each case, the Americans were repeatedly scooped by the British press. Churchill, and even Stalin, would leak a personal version of the proceedings of the foreign press while the Americans had to rely on hopelessly bland official statements.

(This seems to be a recurring pattern in coverage of international meetings between Heads of State which has persisted to this day. Naïve U.S. press officials and the Presidents whom they advise get led down one garden path after another by shrewd foreign public information specialists.)

We did, however, accompany FDR on the sea voyage back from Yalta. He seemed a little guilty about our absence from the conference and spent each morning on deck trying to give us plenty of news.

Here was an example of how the slower pace of shipboard travel and freer access to the President, himself, gave reporters greater chance to test the Chief Executive's thinking and measure his mood at historic junctures than modern, jet-speed trips provide. This is not to say that longer exposure leads to more dramatic disclosures, but only that signs of things like worry or exhilaration or fatigue are more easily seen and reported.

For instance, in light of some of the recent theories of how Stalin "fooled" or "tricked" Roosevelt at Yalta, I've tried to recall any signs of doubt about the conference in FDR's mind on the trip home. And I can't. The President occasionally referred to Stalin's general stubbornness, but always in affectionate "Uncle Joe" terms. He appeared genuinely to like the Russian leader. And as with any man with whom he had to do business or bargain, Roosevelt was totally confident he would come out on top.

On the other hand, it is much more difficult to say, for instance, whether President Kennedy appeared "shaken" or "scared," as some have claimed he did, by the belligerancy of Nikita Khrushchev at their first meeting in Vienna. Even the Pool reporters riding with Kennedy on Air Force One only saw him for a few minutes in the period after the meeting. They could hardly get a sensitive reading of his reaction in such a short time. Kennedy may have felt surprise at Khrushchev's tone as much as anything else, but it was simply very hard to tell.

If the Yalta trip did fail to produce much hard news on Allied strategy decisions or developments in the war, it did include what may have been the most amazing meeting ever held between an American President and a foreign Head of State. The event was not really part of the Crimean conference, but happened as a side trip to the Middle East.

President Roosevelt had wanted to visit with an Arabian leader and had invited King Ibn Saud of Saudi Arabia to meet him on board ship in the Suez Canal. The King accepted and the American Navy dispatched a destroyer, the USS *Murphy,* into the Red Sea to pick him up.

Three days later, in mid-morning, the crew of the President's cruiser manned the port rail to watch the approach of the destroyer bearing the royal party. Old Navy hands blanched and shook their heads in disbelief at what they saw.

The *Murphy's* deck space was covered with colorful rugs. Beautifully striped desert tents were rigged above them. On the fantail, a small herd of sheep milled about. Standing vigilantly poised were ten fierce-looking guards. They were resplendent in brilliantly colored robes and the sun gleamed off their lavishly jewelled belts, daggers and huge Arabian scimitars.

The King himself sat in the bow of the destroyer on a large, gilded thronelike chair. At his feet were many rich carpets. He was an impressive, large man despite being quite old. It was his first trip outside the country.

We learned that the tents were up because the King had wanted to sleep out of doors, having turned down the captain's cabin. The destroyer had had to travel at reduced speed lest the wind blast the Arabian tents from her decks. The sheep were brought along for both religious and eating purposes. Cooking was done on deck over small charcoal braziers. In addition to the key members of his government, the King brought along the royal astrologer and fortune teller, the royal food taster, and the chief server of the ceremonial coffee.

The ship's navigator kept the party posted on the location of Mecca and a direct radio circuit was set up from the *Murphy* to the Prime Minister waiting there. Each half hour the radio operator, who was the Saudi Arabian Director of Communications, would call Mecca and would ask, "O.K.?" Mecca would reply, "O.K." and sign off.

This was the sort of thing that Roosevelt really enjoyed. He grandly greeted the King and invited him to lunch in the flag captain's cabin. In deference to the Mohammedan abstinence from alcoholic drinks and tobacco in any form, FDR ordered the "smoking lamp" out on both ships.

After a long meeting at which they explored many problems of the Middle East, the King gave the President four colorful sets of Arabian attire, complete with multi-colored burnooses and gold head bands.

The President, in return, gave one of his own wheel chairs which Ibn Saud had admired. Mr. Roosevelt proudly told us that the King, wounded nine times in his long and courageous career as an Arab warrior, said it would save him many steps around his palace.

Roosevelt loved these meetings, loved the pomp and royalty and calling world leaders "Winston" and "Joe." When he died, however, the new President was left to deal with men he didn't know, in diplomatic situations with which he was unfamiliar. Thus, watching Harry Truman go to Potsdam to meet Churchill and Stalin was very different from studying Roosevelt at Yalta.

What one saw in the case of Truman was the determined, if slightly self-conscious entry of the new President into big-time, big-stakes world politics. I think he realized better than anyone his lack of experience at this level of international discussion, but he did not appear awed in the slightest.

Crossing the Atlantic, we were able to get an interesting insight into Mr. Truman's approach to his first big conference with other Heads of State. The wire service men stood with him one afternoon, watching a shuffleboard game on the forward deck of the cruiser. The brisk wind rippling over the bow fluttered his tweed cap.

The President said quite seriously that he would rather have done anything else in the world at that time than leave the country. The only reason he consented to make the trip, he said, was to shorten the war. To emphasize the all-business nature of the trip, he cancelled ceremonious stops in Oslo, Copenhagen, and London.

Germany had collapsed and Japan was growing weaker. The President hammered home repeatedly at the same theme—he was on his way to Europe for one primary reason—to save American lives. He wanted to avoid an invasion of the Japanese home islands if possible. The atomic bomb had yet to be tested, so the shortest route to a quick victory over Japan seemed to be Russian participation in the Pacific War.

The President said he was determined that Russia's entrance in the Pacific War would have to be guaranteed at the start of the Potsdam Conference. He reasoned that American aid was indispensable to the rebuilding of Europe, but that not one American dime would go into the project until we were assured of more help in defeating the Japanese.

Stalin did not arrive on what was supposed to be the first day of the conference, July 16 (1945), so the President took advantage of the free time to go for a brief tour of central Berlin. We got a chance to talk with him a few minutes underneath Hitler's famous balcony of the then-shattered Chancellery. Mr. Truman seemed somber and moved by the utter destruction of downtown Berlin. He looked at the balcony where Hitler had stood and motioned toward the ruins.

"It just shows," he said, "what can happen when a man overreaches himself."

He looked around at the other buildings, once proud symbols of Nazism and now only burned out shells.

"I never saw such destruction. I don't know whether they learned anything from it or not."

As the President drove back to Babelsberg over the *autobahn,* his car passed long and weary processions of old men, women and children laboring under heavy bundles of their few remaining belongings. These were people in constant search for food and shelter, and seldom did they seem to find anything.

There was an awful stench that covered Berlin shortly after

VE-Day. It was the smell of death, rotting bodies and the charred remains of buildings. A rubble dust hung in the air most of the day. The people were dirty. Few smiled. Almost every block had its queue of silent, forlorn people waiting to buy a few slices of bread.

Stalin showed up the next day and the conference got underway. The press party headed for its quarters in a Berlin suburb. We didn't see Truman again for nearly ten days, when we finally joined him at a military headquarters in Frankfurt. It was there, in what had once been the library of a handsome German home, that I think I first really appreciated President Truman's candor and his way of handling pressure.

"How are things going?" I asked him.

He shook his head and said vehemently "they"—obviously Stalin and Churchill—were giving him a run for his money. He said they were "trying to push the new man around a little."

Most seasoned observers had predicted as much, and Mr. Truman's analysis was hardly detailed or profound. What struck me then, however, was that FDR would never have considered making such an admission nor telling a reporter anything so revealing. Truman's response to the "pushing" was also characteristic.

When one of the polished diplomats spoke of an *aide memoire*, Truman spoke of a memorandum. When someone referred to the complexities of an issue, the President would talk about basic principles.

When Stalin went to call on Churchill, hordes of NKVD agents and more than fifty expert Russian riflemen covered the one-mile route of his bulletproof sedan. Going to Churchill's quarters the same evening, the President, James F. Byrnes (then, the Secretary of State) and William Leahy (Admiral Leahy, Truman's military advisor) walked down the road from their house to the British headquarters, accompanied by two Secret Service agents.

As had happened before, the big news on the Potsdam trip came when we least expected it. On what apparently was the anticlimax cruise home, the President called us in to the green, felt-covered table in the flag cabin, normally used for poker, and calmly told us about the successful explosion of the first atomic bomb.

Two days later at lunch, the captain interrupted the President's meal to hand him a small sheet of white paper. Hiroshima had been bombed under perfect weather conditions and with no opposition. The next day Russia went to war with Japan.

The next administration began with more wartime travel, but ended with a new concept of Presidential globe-trotting. Dwight D. Eisenhower initially made his mark as a Presidential traveler when, as President-elect, he visited the front lines in Korea. Ironically, though, despite the Korean trip and his military background, one of the most distinctive innovations in Eisenhower's presidency was his unprecedented peacetime use of personal diplomacy.

He visited 34 countries during his term of office, still a Presidential record, and was the first U.S. President to visit Asia while in office. He actually changed foreign travel for a President from a political liability—Teddy Roosevelt had been roundly denounced for merely visiting the Panama Canal Zone—to a political advantage.

Now, no administration is considered complete without at least one major good-will tour abroad. Besides diplomatic business, foreign trips are taken to mold public opinion—as some of President Johnson's trips to Southeast Asia—or to solidify credentials with ethnic voting blocks—as President Nixon's tour of Ireland —or for any one of a variety of domestic political reasons.

Actually, in one sense, even Eisenhower's second term trips to Europe, Asia, the Middle East, and South America were political innovations of a sort. They were a solution to the problem of finding something constructive for a "lame-duck" President to do in his last twelve to eighteen months in office.

Particularly in the case of the small nations, a visit by a U.S. President had symbolic connotations. It indicated, by the actual presence of the most important man in the United States in, say, Morocco, a level of American concern which might not otherwise have been assumed.

This philosophy was not without critics. The effects of good-will tours, some argued, are highly perishable. Cheering crowds do not change basic diplomatic interests. Presidential visits can misleadingly raise expectations: of the American people who may expect some noticeable increment in peace or security to come from the trip or of the host country who may assume that increased aid or assistance will result.

Presidential visits can stir up dormant political tensions in foreign countries and can expose a Chief Executive to physical danger and the U.S. to damaged prestige. Finally, such trips expend large amounts of time and money and manpower.

Eisenhower was aware of these costs and acknowledged the risks, but he had a rather sophisticated view of the external or incidental benefits which could accrue from Presidential tours.

First, there was the opportunity of fostering good will between two other nations. When he was in India in 1959, for example, Nehru told him Iran could solve many of her problems by going ahead with badly needed land reforms. On the way home Eisenhower relayed this opinion to the Shah in Teheran, and later the President sent a note to Nehru about the conversation. Eisenhower was able to report that the Shah would do everything possible to push pending land reform legislation through his Parliament—and he did.

The President realized the touchy situation between India and Afghanistan, but it was not too delicate for him to tell both Nehru and King Zahir that he hoped, and the free world hoped, there would be no trouble on their border.

Eisenhower believed that much of the pay-off from Presidential trips abroad is of such undramatic quality that most of us tend to overlook it. He was speaking particularly of the results of foreign explorations in personal diplomacy on the people at home.

He was reasonably certain that because of his own travels millions of Americans through their newspapers, magazines, radio and television had learned more of the nations than they would have absorbed ordinarily. He thought his trip to Asia and the Middle East was particularly important in this respect as millions of Americans truly for the first time in their lives were exposed to stories and pictures of places known to most of them only as strange lands located vaguely somewhere out there. Afghanistan was a good example. He was there only a few hours, but there was probably more in the newspapers about Afghanistan that day than appears in most secondary school texts.

There was another, sometimes subtle effect of Presidential travel which Mr. Eisenhower never mentioned—at least to me— but which I think exists. Perhaps the most important benefit is to give the most powerful man in the world a chance to see and feel and even smell other peoples and cultures of the world. These are the people, after all, whom the superpowers by definition affect. Presidents are often so isolated anyway that it is necessary for them to see other lands and ways of living, if only fleetingly and superficially, in order to maintain some perspective.

In Afghanistan, for instance, President Eisenhower saw scenes rarely witnessed by a Westerner. In the countryside, the crowds were made up predominantly of men and children; tribesmen wrapped in heavy woolen robes of brown and dirty white, many of them covering the lower part of their faces in a protective reflex born of mountain cold, desert dust and the presence of strangers.

What women there were in the rural areas watched from afar, standing in shrouded, veiled groups beside dun-colored village walls far back from the highway. Many of them quickly averted their eyes to the ground as the procession passed.

Some of the Afghan men, after initial reticence, became so excited that they began rolling themselves in human balls and hurtling from the hillsides towards Ike's open Daimler. As the motorcade entered the capital city of Kabul, dozens of smiling men literally tried to climb in with him.

It was this Asian trip that I think was the biggest eye-opener for Mr. Eisenhower. He was exposed for the first time to the vast continent—the human masses, the somewhat mystic quality of Indian society, the relationship of the people to certain charismatic leaders. And I know he saw a side of Nehru that he had not previously appreciated.

It happened in the pungent Indian dusk on Kitchener Road leading twelve miles from the Palam Airport into the center of New Delhi.

The President was clutching the shoulders of a husky Secret

165

Service agent, James J. Rowley (now Chief of the U.S. Secret Service), seated before him in an open Cadillac convertible. Eisenhower held his right arm over his forehead to shield his eyes and mouth as he tried to stay on his feet in a vortex of screaming, wildly gesticulating Indians and their smothering floral offerings.

Behind the shield of his arm, Eisenhower looked out at a scene never before witnessed by an American Chief Executive, the mass adulation of India that quite literally came close to killing with its kindness. Men, women and children, crushing against the cars of the President's motorcade in what approached mass-hysteria, had poured into New Delhi by train and truck, in rough lorries and overloaded busses, by camel cart and thousands simply by foot.

They jammed Kitchener Road in numbers never seen before by a world leader under similar circumstances. True, Eisenhower was the first American President to visit Asia. True, the Indian government had encouraged and even facilitated the turnout. But also true, the people of India turned out in masses that no one foresaw.

The crowd was estimated—conservatively—at one million, which really only meant that it was more people than anyone had ever seen before. Later evaluations figured the crowd at more than two million.

Beside Eisenhower in the beseiged automobile that moved only inches at a time sat a man with a rosebud on his shoulder, a man whose face throughout the world symbolized peace and gentleness, a modest white cotton cap over his deep brown eyes, India's Prime Minister Jawaharlal Nehru.

Nehru was worried. He nibbled at his upper lip and stroked his chin, hunched down in the wild melee of flower blossoms and warily eyeing the intense young men in turbans and shirtsleeves leaning into the car to roar the Urdu welcome, *"Hind Eisenhower ki jai!"* (Hail Eisenhower). The Prime Minister looked up apprehensively at the standing Eisenhower as the visitor reeled and ducked under the impact of the heavier bouquets and garlands.

Lean, hard Indian police, turbans askew and their starched khaki shirts and shorts beginning to wilt with sweat, shouted and swung at the crowd with *lathis,* a slender wooden stick much like

166

the old swagger stick of the American Marines but longer and partly covered with leather. Much of the time, the only light on the turbulent scene came from the ceremonial lantern bearers from small villages whose ancient beacons wobbled and sometimes disappeared in the rolling waves of humanity.

The long procession was bound for Rashtrapati Bhavan, home of India's elderly President Rajendra Prasad and once the regal palace of British viceroys.

Indians crushed to the front of the crowd used what English they knew in calling out to Eisenhower. Dusk had turned to night, but some of the Indians proudly shouted "Good morning, Ike," and with all the smiling dignity possible under trying circumstances, Eisenhower replied, "And good morning to you, sir."

The President bent down toward Nehru to say, "I've never seen anything like this in my life," when a heavy bouquet arched over the car dropped in a sticky clump on the back of the visitor's neck. Ike straightened up and smiled nervously.

The procession inched into Connaught Circus, a famous, central area of shops and restaurants and a large, circular park. A massive electric display sign glowed atop one of the higher buildings, but some of the gleaming, hot letters were obscured by Indians clinging precariously to the iron structure of the sign that rocked slowly under its load of humanity.

Motorcycle police ahead of Nehru's car tried vainly to bore a hole in the crowd, but the people spilled over the motorbikes and between the legs of the club-swinging police, who were forced back to a protective line up against the Cadillac. A police jeep lost in the mob beamed a loudspeaker into the jam while an officer pleaded with the crowd to avoid injury.

Fever-eyed men, their jet-black hair gleaming in sweeping movie floodlights at Connaught Circus, thrust their grinning faces as close to Eisenhower as possible to scream, "Zindabad, zindabad."

Two cars away from the President, a veteran Indian journalist said, "They're wishing him long life. Some of them are saying, 'Long live the king of America.' "

As far as the eye could see, in front and behind, to either side of the President's car stretched an undulating crash of human bodies buckling under pressures from the rear of the crowd. One thought of newsreel pictures of asphalt pavements in an earthquake.

Five young Hindus in turbans of green and orange and yellow locked arms and burrowed beneath the police to come up beside the President's car, yelling, "Gude day Aye-zen-huer, New Yawk, New Yawk." The President bowed and shouted back, "New York.

Ten minutes, then fifteen minutes passed with no noticeable progress around the circular park. The crowd was becoming more volcanic and Nehru decided to act. He leaped to his feet beside Eisenhower and began to tongue-lash his people in Hindi. His voice was all but lost in the storm.

I was watching from about fifty feet away, literally imprisoned inside an ancient American-made car. It was stifling hot, but it was necessary to keep the windows closed to avoid torrents of marigolds. With the windows down, by now nearly hysterical Indians were reaching for jacket buttons, scraps of note paper, half-smoked cigarettes, anything for a souvenir.

An Indian friend explained, "This is a religious experience in a way. One word for it is *drashan*. I cannot translate it exactly, but it means generally spiritual betterment for having been in the presence of a great man."

"If I didn't know better," I said uneasily, "I'd say these people were drunk."

"One can become quite intoxicated just from the excitement of contact with other humans," he said. "That is what is happening now."

Nehru suddenly disappeared from our vision. A security car blocked a clear view from our car and I tried leaning out the window, but had to retreat from the clutching, snatching people in the street. It was not until later that I learned why Nehru vanished. He had leaped from the car down into the crowd and sailed into the police for not doing their utmost.

One particular policeman seemed to have displeased him. Nehru tore the officer's *lathi* stick from his sweaty hands and shoved him angrily toward the jerking, pushing spectators.

Shouting shame and disapproval at the crowd, he took a few swings with the stick himself before tossing it back to the startled policeman, then plowed like a zealous halfback toward the police jeep with the loudspeaker, pulled himself up into the open vehicle and stormed at the crowd—they were behaving frightfully in front of visitors and they'd better fall back or get hurt.

The cars began to creep out of the circle and when I could see the President's convertible again, Nehru was back in the car and troops on horseback were rearing and prancing into the crowd to open a narrow traffic lane.

It took only a few minutes more to reach the red stone corridors leading into Rashtrapati Bhavan and the cars swept through the heavily guarded gates into a peaceful cobblestone courtyard. It had taken us two hours and ten minutes to come twelve miles from the airport. I ran over to the side of the President's car and he and Nehru alighted. The floor of the open convertible was more than a foot deep in orange-yellow blossoms.

"What did you think of that welcome, Mr. President?" I asked.

He turned, brushing flower petals from his dark jacket, and looked fleetingly at Nehru, who seemed much more weary than Eisenhower.

"You saw it." Eisenhower smiled. "You write it."

If the reception in India was the peak of Eisenhower's travels, the low point was clearly the failure of the Paris Summit in 1960. It illustrated for Ike and future Presidents the back-fire potential of face-to-face talks, particularly between Cold War adversaries. Once more, the interesting news was not to be found in the official communiqués, but behind the scenes.

The details of the May 16 meeting have been amply recorded: Khrushchev's demand that Eisenhower apologize publicly for the U-2 flights, punish all those responsible, promise not to do it again and, above all, for Ike not to come to Russia (as had been planned).

Eisenhower, noted in the past for a sulphurous temper, knew this was not the time to cut loose with invective. Sitting across the table from the Russian in a classical decorated conference room on the second floor of the Elysée Palace, Eisenhower with studied, determined restraint told Khrushchev that the flights had been halted and would not be resumed, that they were conducted only because of Russia's refusal to join the free world in exposing armaments to full view and that for the sake of keeping the summit going he would be willing to negotiate separately on the question of the flights.

Khrushchev would have none of it and when the meeting ended in the early afternoon, the principals left de Gaulle's heavily guarded courtyard one at a time. Khrushchev smiled in the cocky manner of a man who had just drubbed an offensive neighbor. Macmillan seemed wan and droopy. Eisenhower smiled thinly on the palace steps as he said goodbye to de Gaulle.

While the meeting was in progress, the Russian attitude toward the West manifested itself in the courtyard of the palace as we watched through the curtains of the tiny office of M. Perlou, personal press attaché to de Gaulle.

Automobiles of the principals were drawn up on the shady side of the courtyard. The Russian security men and drivers remained entirely to themselves, refusing to have anything to do with the American, British and French security men who gossiped with each other during the long meeting.

Khrushchev's chauffeur looked like the classic villain in an American wrestling show except for his bright green felt hat. On the day before the meeting when Khrushchev visited the Elysée Palace to call on de Gaulle, the driver was tieless and wore a light gray shirt open at the throat.

A French reporter gave his office a colorful description of the driver, but an editor misunderstood and put together a story about how Khrushchev himself arrived at the palace for a formal call on the French President with no tie, but wearing a bright green hat.

The story spread through Paris quickly and the Russian Embassy must have taken note, because when the man drove Khrushchev to the palace for the Monday meeting, he had on the same gray shirt and green hat, but this time a tie.

The Russians were so jittery during the Monday meeting that the Soviet security agents brushed aside the fact that they were within the jurisdiction of the French President and forcibly prevented French cameramen from photographing Khrushchev's empty automobile.

The one and only full session of the Summit was an hour behind schedule in beginning, the delay requested by the Russians without explanation. Ike was informed and came late. The Soviet, British and French delegations were seated when he arrived.

The French Chief of Protocol showed the President to his seat. Before he took his chair, Eisenhower greeted his fellow conferees individually. When he came to Khrushchev, the President bobbed his head in a quick bow and said, "Good morning, Mister Chairman."

Khrushchev glared back, grunted and turned to look at the Soviet advisers beside him.

Later, we found out that Khrushchev on Sunday told de Gaulle virtually everything about the planned denunciation of Eisenhower except one major item. He neglected to tell de Gaulle in advance that he planned to withdraw his invitation for Eisenhower to visit Russia.

When the President drove back to the Embassy Residence and his big black Cadillac bumped softly into the walled entrance yard, his jaw was sternly set. There were patches of red above his cheekbones. He seemed to be clamping down on himself until he could get inside and blow up, which, incidentally, he never did.

One of the Americans who sat behind Ike during the meeting said it was a most curious session, obviously charged with drama and excitement without the participants seeming to be excited themselves.

"They looked like heavy-stake poker players late at night," this man said. "It was the coldest gathering of human beings I believe I've ever seen. They were almost antiseptic in their dealings. Not once during the three hours was there a smile or even a colloquial aside to relieve the tension."

Initially at least, it was the view of President Kennedy and certainly of his Secretary of State, Dean Rusk, that Presidential foreign tours were not of deep diplomatic importance; that diplomacy was more effective on the ambassadorial level and moving to the ministerial level only when major agreements were to be locked up and final language agreed upon. This may have been in part a reaction to some of the mixed reviews for Ike's country hopping. At any rate, early in his administration, Mr. Kennedy and his advisers thought Presidential participation in diplomacy on foreign shores should be kept to a minimum.

Once Kennedy did start traveling overseas, however, he began to change his views. He found that attitudes of a host government could be influenced significantly by such non-institutional factors as crowd demonstrations, particularly if the turnout went far beyond expectations of the host.

Kennedy became quite sensitive to his receptions overseas. This was in keeping with his administration's emphasis on international understanding, the Peace Corps, journalistic exchanges, and the like, but preoccupation with the "turnout factor" became most apparent in Kennedy's tour of Italy.

His reception in Rome, coming at the post-luncheon nap hour, would have embarrassed the spectators at any self-respecting supermarket opening. Yet the Italian trip was salvaged in Kennedy's eyes by a massive and wildly enthusiastic crowd in Naples, helped along by the feverish efforts of the United States Information Service and his ace advance man, Jerry Bruno.

Certainly Kennedy's most enjoyable trip as President was to Ireland, his ancestral home. It is doubtful whether this trip made great strides toward world peace or will end up in an important place in history, but it was the most charming Presidential trip I can remember.

Within hours after the President reached Ireland, much of the population seemed to forget that he was born in America. At every stop, buildings were decorated with banners proclaiming, "Welcome Home, Mr. President." One placard held high in the airport crowd said, "Johnnie, I hardly know ye." And the Irish newspapers were beside themselves. One of the more subdued headlines in the Dublin *Evening Press* read: "A FANTASTIC TRIUMPH!"

The weather lived up to Irish tradition as the President began his sentimental journey to the tiny towns from which his family sprung. As Kennedy boarded his helicopter on the lawn of Ambassador Matthew McCloskey's residence, the weather was wet and cold. The Irish called it a mist. In the United States, it would have been regarded as a light rain.

The flight from Dublin to Cork had to be made at relatively low altitudes varying from 800 to 1,000 feet in order to stay beneath the leaden gray cover of rainclouds and swirling mist.

When the President arrived at the Collins Barracks in Cork, other members of his party were bundled up in trenchcoats and hats, but Kennedy alighted from the plane hatless and minus an outer coat.

The motorcade through the streets started through a barracks gate so narrow that the big White House touring car with its top down had difficulty negotiating a tight turn. The President rode standing up in the rear seat, waving constantly to the handkerchief and flag-waving crowds that jammed the sidewalks and slipped over the curbings.

The county folk who proudly identify themselves as "rebel Cork" hung from house windows, over field-stone walls and from stout wooden police barricades to call their greetings to the President. Bagpipe bands along the route saluted Kennedy with shrill Gaelic tunes.

After Mayor Sean Casey formally accorded Kennedy the high honor of becoming a free man of Cork, Kennedy delighted the Town Council and dignitaries crowded into the Council Chamber with a homespun, informal presentaton of the Irish members of his staff.

The scene was the high vaulted room in which the Council meets to govern the city of Cork. Trumpeters with golden horns heralded the President's entrance with a melodious fanfare. Kennedy was escorted down the center aisle by the Mayor in his brilliant robe of scarlet and precious furs. Then followed the Council Members in their scarlet robes.

Kennedy took great delight in introducing his personal assistant and chief greeter at the White House, Dave Powers, who on the steps of the hall had met seven first cousins whom he'd never seen before. Kennedy asked Powers and all seven cousins to stand up for a bow. Powers, a native of Charlestown, Massachusetts, is an Irishman as avid as de Valera himself.

Then Kennedy presented his pastor in Palm Beach, Florida,

Monsignor Jeremiah P. O'Mahoney, who was visiting Ireland. Kennedy got a heavy laugh from Americans in the audience by describing the Monsignor's "poor, humble flock" at St. Edward's Church in Palm Beach.

Next the President introduced his chief legislative liaison officer on the White House staff, Lawrence F. O'Brien, and Representative Edward Boland, D-Mass., whom Kennedy said represented the 85 Members of Congress who were of Irish descent.

"I don't want to give the impression that every member of this administration is Irish," the President said. "It just seems that way."

He spotted standing back in a doorway another proud Irish-American, James J. Rowley. Kennedy called Rowley to the front of the Chamber for a bow.

"Those members of the Secret Service who are not Irish are very embarrassed about it," the President said with a broad smile.

At another stop in New Ross, the President introduced members of his family—his sisters, Eunice Shriver and Jean Smith, AFL-CIO President George Meany whose parents came from Ireland, and Ambassador McCloskey.

"And I want you to meet," Kennedy shouted, "the only man here who does not have a drop of Irish blood, but who's dying to——"

He then presented Angier Biddle Duke, the dapper U.S. Chief of Protocol. There was a loud cheer.

Kennedy turned to Duke and said, "See, Angie, how nice it is?"

After the New Ross ceremony, the President set out by motorcade over a winding, narrow road to Dunganstown and a visit with some of his distant relatives. It was in Dunganstown that a hearty and somewhat elderly doctor who had been delivering the babies of the community for more than forty years presented the Chief Executive with a lambskin rug.

Then for the benefit of a fairly large audience and television cameras, the doctor boomed out that the rug was to be put beside Mrs. Kennedy's bed when she had the twins in August. And within a very few minutes, the entire community of Dunganstown accepted as gospel fact that the Kennedys were expecting twins.

President Johnson's international travels—particularly to the Pacific and Southeast Asia—resembled, I always thought, nothing so much as grand political campaign tours. There is something about being out of the country that often brings out the best in Presidential performance before crowds, and Johnson, in any country, was at his most comfortable "on the stump" telling Texas stories and pumping the flesh.

Despite the serious diplomatic purposes of his trips to Asia, my most vivid memories of Johnson were with the street crowds in Australia. He loved being with these demonstrative people—in many ways like Texans—who would whoop and yell at LBJ's anecdotes and fist-thumping homilies, old stuff to audiences back home.

He told one Sydney crowd that the accomplishments of his administration could be summed up in one word which he spelled out, "F-R-I-E-N-D," and then translated:

"F—Food production not only for Americans, but the entire world.

R—Recreation (plus beautification and conservation).

I—Income reflected in jobs and good wages for 77 million Americans.

E—Education, with 18 education bills recommended by the administration having passed Congress.

N—Nursing homes for the elderly, along with Medicare.

D—Defense."

At another stop, using a hand microphone and the public address system built into the White House bubbletop limousine, Johnson told one nighttime street crowd, "After we stop the aggression in Vietnam, we're all coming back here and have a big barbecue!"

It was this same built-in microphone that provided a rather graphic example of the cross-cultural exchanges of experience that can occur when a Presidential entourage swirls into another society.

In Bangkok, men and women still bow and curtsey in the presence of their King and Queen and Their Majesties usually are rigid examples of formal behavior when they are on public view.

So, the people of Thailand could hardly believe it when Johnson's limousine passed by and a voice from within boomed —over the hidden public address system built into the car— "Thanks for coming out to see us."

Late one night in the Philippines, there were some startled people at street intersections when the big American car zipped by and out of nowhere thundered LBJ's voice, calling out, "Mahbuhay," the Philippino version of welcome.

At one point, the loudspeaker boomed right into the face of a rather bedraggled looking man standing at curbside in a run-down section of Manila and he waited to hear no more. He took off down the nearest alley, running as fast as he could.

That President Johnson could have made informal, campaign-style trips was really traceable to President Eisenhower's innovations. There was a time when it was regarded as required that when Heads of Government met, it had to be for a minimum of three days. This gave the principals time to exchange banquets and luncheons, visit local monuments and conduct their formal business as time permitted.

Eisenhower was actually the first to break this pattern. He proved in his trip to India that an American President could visit countries along the way for no more than a few hours, providing a clearly understandable explanation was made to the host country.

The new view may have brought needed informality to Presidential travel, but it also brought a grueling pace matched only by the last days of a national campaign. The wear on clothes, health, tempers and nerves has become a factor to be reckoned with by White House schedulers.

Furthermore, from the standpoint of personal vanity, the press is starting to get bad notices from these endurance tests. A columnist in Guam wrote in 1967 of the appearance of the LBJ press party as it straggled off an airplane after 20 hours in flight:

"Did you ever see a scroungier bunch in your life? They were the oldest, wildest battle suit clothes, bagged and sagged. They generally have long hair and red eyes, and are just a case of how professional people shouldn't look out in public. But they do their job well, and maybe are too high up in the intellectual ladder to worry about looks and appearances."

The Nixon approach to foreign travel seems to indicate—so far, at least—an understanding of the symbolic nature of Presidential visits. When President Nixon traveled early in his administration to carry the message of a "lowered U.S. profile" around the world, he geared the nature of his appearances accordingly. There was not a lot of ceremony, nor were there strenuous efforts made to turn out the huge, flag-waving crowds.

The President pointedly took a modest, conservative stance in private discussions with foreign leaders, mostly asking for their opinions and assessments of common problems. Another reason for the stripped-down style of visits was that Nixon advisers knew that the President could not match the European receptions of war-hero Eisenhower or the photogenic Kennedy. So, they simply decided not to try to compete on that level and risk unfavorable comparisons.

The future of Presidential travel will, I think, remain intertwined with domestic politics. It is a sure-fire way to attract massive news coverage to a President and *away* from another, potentially unpleasant domestic news, as President Johnson sensed at the time of the Fulbright hearings into the Vietnam war. Also, it seems invariably true that a President's ratings in the popularity polls rise during and after a major foreign trip.

A danger which may arise with future travel may come from just those qualities of the American Presidency which make such trips possible: modern technology, organization, size, wealth. If the purpose of Presidential visits is mostly symbolic, then the appearance of giant Uncle Sam swooping down on particularly a third-world country could have negative effects.

Nevertheless, it seems inevitable and desirable that an American President will go to Black Africa in this decade and to Mainland China.* The omission of especially the newly independent African states from Presidential itineraries in the past has become something of a disgrace.

* Smith's prediction was made in early 1970, some eighteen months before President Nixon's announcement that he planned to go to China.

CHAPTER NINE

Presidential Retreats: Custodial Coverage

Not all presidential travel was as glamorous to cover as trips to European capitals, the Orient, or historic summit conferences. Often, in fact, the job of shadowing a president meant hours of just sitting and waiting in hotel lobbies, airports, or small town diners.

This surveillance reporting often became quite important, though. Smith was one of three reporters along on a routine trip to Warm Springs, Georgia, when President Roosevelt died. It was on a vacation trip that President Eisenhower had a serious heart attack.

Besides the possibility of unexpected news breaks, being with a president in the off-stage setting of a Gettysburg or a Johnson City or a Hyannis Port often revealed a human side to chief executives not so apparent in Washington.

THE DICTIONARY defines a ghoul as a "demon who robs graves and feeds on corpses."

That, according to President Roosevelt was the proper description for the role played during the war by two colleagues and me. He used the term affectionately—sometimes. And then again, when he felt a trifle miffed about our presence, he added the label, "vultures."

"You wire service men," the President said to us one night early in the war, "are just sitting around like vultures waiting for something to happen to me. Isn't that right?"

We told him:

"Not exactly, sir. We're here *in case* something happens." *

Thousands of miles were traveled. Mr. Roosevelt's ghouls were with him, just like the little boy's shadow. And it was on one of his "ghoul's" trips that he died, and we were there to report it, fulfilling plans that had been made and changed a hundred times.

Before there was any suggestion that Mr. Roosevelt was not in tiptop health, White House correspondents rehearsed in their minds, over and over again, what they would do when "it" happened.

"It" was death or serious injury, from natural causes, accident or assassination.

"It" has to be thought about by men who cover a President because when bodily harm or pain comes to a Chief Executive, it is the hottest news an American reporter can possibly handle.

"It" is one big reason correspondents accompany Presidents on such inconsequential trips as to church in Washington, or to a boring banquet in the evening not three blocks away from the White House.

Suppose a drunk driver smashed into the President's car? Suppose a run-down jalopy careened into the side of his motorcade? If White House reporters were not on the spot to inform the world immediately, they would be severely criticized by their editors. The public would be bitter because it did not know exactly what happened.

---

* This was during the period when all of President Roosevelt's trips were off-the-record, but on which the wire services (then, UP, AP, and INS) sent reporters for delayed coverage purposes or in case of personal tragedy involving the President.

It is possible to go on supposing for pages. Heart attack? Food poisoning? An injurious fall?

All these things happen every hour to hundreds of Americans and there is no particular reason to believe that a President of the country is immune. And when "it" happens to him, the welfare of the nation is affected. The effect goes into every household, every family. And for that reason, the public has a right to know at all times what the President is doing and where he is.

During the war, this public right was abrogated by military security; i.e., the fear that an enemy agent would assassinate Mr. Roosevelt. Actually, the secrecy was mostly transparent. Reporters knew when he left town, and each time, for example, that he arrived in Hyde Park for a weekend, his procession of automobiles drove through the heart of Poughkeepsie in full view of the public.

Some out-of-town columnists would occasionally print "exclusives" about FDR's movements, as if they had managed great scoops, but, in fact, the information was common knowledge to most of the Washington press corps who were voluntarily complying with a self-censorship request.

All reporters were quite welcome aboard Mr. Roosevelt's train during the fourth-term campaign. Virtually every restriction on reporting his movements was lifted for the campaign. But the minute he was elected, slam went the lid again, and again I was a ghoul, riding thousands of unreported miles on the Presidential train between Washington and Hyde Park and rarely writing a line because of the military security which disappeared so amazingly when there were voters to be wooed, but reappeared when the ceremony was over.

The challenge to the reporters in those days was to survive the crushing boredom of custodial coverage. Newsmen took up poker, bridge, stamp-collecting—practically anything to make the long hours of train travel pass more quickly. All sorts of minor feuds and contests developed between the correspondents during the lengthy trips with President Roosevelt, who was rarely aware of what was going on in the cars ahead of his private quarters.

One of the most memorable contests was waged between Fred

Pasley, then a reporter for the New York *Daily News,* and any-body who came within shouting distance.

On a quiet day in Poughkeepsie, N.Y., where the press berthed when Mr. Roosevelt was in Hyde Park, Pasley went for a long walk and came back to the hotel with a live, red rooster.

The hotel clerk, just after a night when someone had put a dozen live lobsters in the bed of another reporter, was a little testy and offered to escort Pasley to the street if the chicken was not abandoned immediately.

"You, sir," Pasley said in his foghorn voice, which could fill whole rooms without effort, "are speaking of the rooster I love."

The press party was leaving that night anyway so the room clerk's threats were meaningless.

Pasley took the rooster aboard the Presidential train at de-parture time and proceeded to the dining car where he ordered two Martinis—one to be served in a saucer.

Somehow, Pasley got the rooster to drink the Martini, and then betting began. As the poor, besotted chicken flopped over on the table, Pasley called for odds on when his pet would be able to stand.

The diner steward was apoplectic, not knowing from one moment to the next when Mrs. Roosevelt or someone of equal rank would walk through the car and witness the contest.

Pasley eventually collected all the bets, then retired to his com-partment, after renting the upper berth for the chicken.

All this changed, of course, when the trips were put back on the record and reporters had stories to write again, but Presidents continued, and still do, to resist coverage of non-official travel.

There was a time when President Eisenhower found it hard to believe that reporters had to go everywhere he went, in and out of the capital. Sometimes he even expressed dismay that they were along on purely recreational trips.

But if he continued to harbor any such ideas, they were not evident after his 1955 heart attack on a vacation trip to Colorado. He said after this, "I know they have to be there, but I'm afraid I won't make much news."

And he did not make much news, until something happened

—to him, or elsewhere in the world—and then he made lots of news. Presidents eventually come to understand the feast-or-famine pattern to a White House reporter's professional routine. It always seems to take a while, though. I once incurred President Truman's unmistakable wrath for objecting to an unaccompanied trip he made early in his White House term. It involved his mother, whom he revered.

She was ninety-three years old in November, 1945, and we asked if Mr. Truman would fly out to see her. Inquiries of Press Secretary Charlie Ross brought no answer, however. Other White House officials insisted Mr. Truman had no such plans.

On the morning of her birthday, however, the President got up early and took a look at the weather. It was just after dawn on a Sunday and the weather was excellent. So, the President ordered his plane. And with no public announcement, he flew to his mother's little cream-colored frame cottage at Grandview, Missouri.

Many newspapers, and particularly Washington newspapermen, first heard about the flight from radio broadcasts. While Mr. Truman was at his mother's home, he telephoned Roy Roberts, then editor of the Kansas City *Star,* and announced his presence. Roberts in turn notified other news offices.

I shared the view of a number of reporters that the President, being head of the country, is pretty much public property and should not make long plane flights without public knowledge.

Mr. Truman began his return flight in midafternoon, landing in Washington shortly after eight o'clock. I was at the airport to meet him, along with other reporters and photographers. When he stepped from the plane, we began questioning him.

I said to the President during the course of questioning:

"Mr. President, some of our customers (papers and radio stations, in those days) were a little worried about your making a long plane flight without any advance knowledge. Is there any explanation?"

Mr. Truman's almost ever-present smile disappeared. I could see the sharp expression on his face in the light of the flaring flashbulbs of the news cameras.

"No, there isn't any explanation. And I don't intend to make any. I don't have to."

Another reporter tried to put a question, but the President continued to talk.

"I just wanted to go out and see my mother without any fuss and fanfare. I just took a notion to go see her and I did."

"But, Mr. President," I asked, "have we in any way ever caused any fuss or fanfare, or caused any interference with a visit to your mother? We were concerned mainly with the plane flight."

"No, you have not caused any fuss," the President said slowly and firmly with a pointed glare in my direction, "but I just took a notion to go see my mother and I did."

The example I've been giving in recent years to press secretaries and others who complain about the omnipresence of reporters is the time when John Kennedy learned he had become the father of a boy. It was after one in the morning and he was 13,000 feet over the Florida coast. This was one "routine" trip we were glad to have made.

He was then President-elect and had spent a tranquil 1960 Thanksgiving Day at his Georgetown home with Jackie and Caroline. The following Sunday was going to be Caroline's birthday. She had opened some of her presents in advance, and shortly after 8 p.m., the President-elect kissed the ladies good-bye and headed for the Washington airport.

He was bound for ten days in Palm Beach where he could rest and work on plans for his new administration without the pressures and interruptions of Washington. Mrs. Kennedy, who had suffered two previous miscarriages, was near the end of an apparently satisfactory pregnancy.

In consultation with her obstetrician, Dr. John W. Walsh, the Kennedys had planned on her entering Georgetown Hospital on December 12 to have the baby by Caesarean section, and President Kennedy had planned to return from Florida by December 5 in plenty of time. Then, after the baby was born, they were going back to Florida for Christmas at his family home in Palm Beach.

That was the plan. But all of this changed abruptly as the

184

President's private plane, the *Caroline,* neared Palm Beach. A few minutes before the *Caroline* was scheduled to land, Kennedy's pilot, Howard Baird, sent word via the stewardess, Janet Derosiers, that an important telephone call awaited him on the ground.

When the landing ramp of the Kennedy Convair was lowered, the President-elect emerged smiling to the cheers of 100 or so spectators out to greet him. It was 12:25 a.m. An airline passenger agent handed him a slip of yellow paper. It said Mrs. Kennedy had been taken to the hospital.

He headed quickly for the small terminal at the Palm Beach airport. His press secretary, Pierre Salinger, who arrived on the earlier press plane, had opened a telephone line to the hospital. His brow furrowed with concern, Kennedy picked up the instrument.

A voice at the other end said she was the nurse in charge of the floor and she had no information beyond the fact that Dr. Walsh had taken Mrs. Kennedy into surgery and the nurse assumed the Caesarean operation was then in progress.

Kennedy put down the phone and headed for his own plane. He gave a few soft-voiced instructions to his own pilot, explaining that he was returning to the capital immediately and would travel aboard the American Airlines charter, a DC6B which could make the flight faster than the Convair.

There was a wild scramble on the ground—baggage had to be unloaded from ground vehicles and rushed to the DC6B. Ground crews raced up with a fuel truck. With his ship refueled, the pilot took off for Washington at 12:50 a.m.

Shortly after 1 a.m., Kennedy clamped on a set of earphones in the pilot's cabin. A slow smile spread over his face as he listened.

It was the National Airlines office back in Palm Beach reporting that he'd just become the father of a boy and mother and child were both doing well. Salinger announced the news over the plane's loudspeaker system and the newsmen and Secret Service agents applauded. The time was 1:15 a.m.

Kennedy's smile was a trifle pale, but he was obviously relieved. Actually, he was more pleased than he indicated. Several times during the 1960 campaign, he predicted flatly that Jackie would produce a boy.

After he arrived at the Washington airport, a white sedan sped him—sometimes at over 60 miles an hour—to the hospital some six miles away. Without a topcoat in the freezing winter weather, he raced quickly up the steps to the main entrance of the hospital and plunged through a crowd of reporters, photographers and well-wishers, including the nurses and nuns who ran the hospital.

It was 4:15 a.m. as he reached the bedside of his wife and then peered into the softly lighted interior of an incubator where snoozed their son, John F. Kennedy, Jr.

Later, standing outside his red-brick home not far from the hospital, Kennedy seemed much more the excited young father than the next President of the United States.

He thought everybody was "fine"—Jackie, John, Jr., the doctor, the nurses, everybody. And he was particularly pleased when asked the name of his son.

"Why, it's John F. Kennedy, Jr. . . . I think she decided—it has been decided—yes—John F. Kennedy, Jr."

The location of any new President's "retreat" is always of special interest to the men and women who will have to, as part of their jobs, follow him there: White House reporters, Secret Service agents, Signal Corps communications men, members of the permanent White House logistical staffs. Thus, there were cheers when President Nixon acquired his home at San Clemente, when Kennedy offered Cape Cod and Palm Beach. And groans as the regular travelers contemplated the lobby of the Hotel Gettysburg or the barrenness of Johnson City.

These communities, in turn, reacted in differing ways to the invasion of Presidential parties. The upper-crust hunt country town of Middleburg, Virginia, plainly did not rejoice when the Kennedys—"new people" themselves—brought in a crowd of working reporters and photographers in their wake. The battlefield museums and roadside cafés near the Eisenhower farm at Gettysburg, however, built new wings and planned for prosperity.

186

Hyde Park, New York, was always notable for the way it reacted with unreconstructed nonchalance to the Roosevelt presence. It had known the Roosevelts, after all, for generations, and
saw no reason to get excited just because another one of them
had become President. (It is also interesting that FDR never
carried Hyde Park or surrounding Dutchess County in any political race—for Governor or President.) [Smith was correct with
one exception: FDR carried Dutchess County in the guber-
natorial race of 1930.]

I recall especially one election when President Roosevelt went
to Hyde Park's old, white-frame town hall to vote in the 1942
Congressional elections. The President attracted little attention
when he appeared. A few villagers waved to him and he nodded
greetings in return.

To Moe Smith, one of Mr. Roosevelt's tenant farmers, went
special honors for the day. Mike Reilly, supervising agent of
the White House Secret Service detail, appointed Moe special
agent. When the big Secret Service car rolled up to the town hall,
Moe went to Reilly and said:

"Sir, I want to report there are no strangers on the block."

Secret Service men carried FDR up the creaking wooden steps
of the hall and then he stood up on his braces. He walked in
slowly and stopped at the table presided over by J. W. Finch,
Chairman of the District Three Election Board.

Finch looked up over his spectacles at the President and asked
gravely:

"Name please?"

"Franklin D. Roosevelt."

"Occupation?"

"Farmer," Mr. Roosevelt replied. "I think that's what I said
the last time."

Every Presidential vacation home must be toured at least once
by the press. This has become an unwritten rule. The color of
drapes, thickness of carpets, and organization of the kitchen are
duly recorded and then printed in the Sunday supplements and
on the women's pages of hundreds of newspapers.

One of the more candid such visits happened unexpectedly on

Christmas Day, 1963, not long after Lyndon Johnson became President. I always considered the tour—one part Southern hospitality, one part impulsiveness, one part lack of consideration —an illustration of the unfathomability of LBJ.

The President had just finished chatting with a group of 30 to 35 reporters on the front lawn of his ranch home. Inside the house, more than 20 relatives awaited the start of Christmas dinner. Without so much as an instant of warning, the President suddenly said to the assembled news and photographic corps:

"I think a number of you have not seen the inside of my house. How would you like a tour?"

Truthfully, most of the reporters were not wildly enthusiastic about the idea because the President had given them several good news stories, it was getting into early afternoon and high time for them to race back to Austin to file their dispatches. But they could not gracefully turn down such a Presidential invitation. There also was the fact that this was the first opportunity for many of them to get a close-up view of the interior of Johnson's home.

There was much head-bobbing and voices of approval and appreciation. The First Lady, however, walked to her husband's side and said, "We're having a party here for them (the press) in just a couple of days and don't you think we could do it then?"

LBJ gave her a broad grin and said gently, "No, I think we'll do it now."

"But, sweetheart, dinner is ready and that dressing isn't getting any better the longer we wait," Mrs. Johnson said with a smile that was a trifle brittle at the edges.

The President cast a glance at her, then turned to the reporters, calling "Come on, follow me—we'll start through this door here."

In we trooped, dirty shoes and all. Scattered around a front living room was a group of adults, male and female, looking as people who might have been waiting for a behind-schedule bus.

This vista of forlorn faces did nothing to deter the proud President who merely explained their presence to reporters with an aside, "Those are some of my kinfolks."

188

We went first into his comfortable, thoroughly western study, then into the dining room with a picture window overlooking his private air strip and on into one living room, then another. In this room, the Chief Executive tried a side door but found it locked.

He rapped on the door and called, "Lady Bird, let me in."

A brief pause. Johnson turned, not sheepishly but in calm, matter-of-fact statement, to the reporters, "You know what—she's locked me out."

He knocked again and this time it was opened—there was Lady Bird smiling ever so bravely. This, we learned, was the gateway to the actual living quarters—the bath and bedchamber of the President and his wife. He pointed first to the left, saying, "That's my bathroom," and indeed, it was. It resembled the holiday or Sunday morning clutter of any family bathroom with bottles of vitamins, hair curlers, toothbrushes, dentifrice tubes without their caps and a few used towels.

"We'll go through here," he said, motioning to another door, "because I want you to see our bedroom, and also, the door on the other side of the room is the easiest way out of the house from here."

We could see at once why the First Lady had delayed the tour momentarily. The bed was made, but barely. She apparently had time only to fling the covers over the pillows. Night clothes still were scattered around, but the valiant lady had done her best to present some semblance of order.

For a reporter, the most valuable part of making these non-business trips with a President is to get a view of the man in a different setting, away from the pressure-cooker atmosphere of the oval office. A good example was our experience with President Eisenhower, whom we got to know better from a few guard-down encounters in Colorado than in months of official Washington appearances.

One simple but revealing incident happened when we accompanied him on a fishing trip to Pine, Colorado. We had watched the President angle for trout during the morning and then had gone into town to file our stories and grab a large lunch of several cheeseburgers. We were in no particular hurry to get back, figuring that the President would come in from the stream and eat his box lunch, prepared that morning by his valet, under the nearest tree.

When we got back to streamside, however, the President was on the porch of an adjacent ranch building, pulling off his heavy waders. He called, "Come on everybody let's go down the stream a bit and I'll cook you some of the best fish you ever ate." As I mentioned in an earlier chapter, Eisenhower had relatively few personal dealings with reporters so the invitation came as a distinct surprise.

He drove through freshly cut hayfields and over narrow cattle trails to a towering tree beside the South Platte River. Apparently the fish-fry was a spur-of-the-moment idea. The sight of the morning trout caught by members of the party, the fish glistening in the protective wet grass, was too much for the cook in the President, so he and Aksel Nielsen, a friend from Denver, started planning.

First, they had to borrow two big skillets from the wife of a nearby farmer. Then they borrowed a pound of butter, some bacon, salt and pepper and a box of yellow cornmeal. The President apparently had cooked here during a visit in 1952. He knew exactly where he wanted to go and guided the procession of cars to a boulder a few feet from the stream.

He went at the task of organizing his outdoor kitchen with energetic dispatch. He bustled around like an active camp leader, gathering firewood himself and telling others what was needed. Some of us were instructed to bring rocks from the stream to build the fireplace, others cleaned the fish and the firewood detail fanned out through the woods.

One Secret Service man was sent on a mission of high importance—placing a watermelon in a hillside spring. A citified camper came struggling back with an armload of wood big enough to stoke a furnace.

"That's a little big," the President said. "We need it small and dry so we can get a quick bed of coals."

The fireplace formed quickly and the President's cook fire flared up, sending a slow spume of smoke into the shafts of sunlight that broke through the massive tree overhanging the boulder. It was a warm, lazy day and even the grasshoppers seemed to be taking it easy during the noon hour.

The President pushed his blue fishing hat to the back of his head and squatted by the campfire. He peeled the wrapper from the pound of bacon and broke up the slices with his pocketknife. Soon he had bacon sizzling in one of the skillets. Into the other skillet went about half a pound of butter, which he melted carefully, seeing that it didn't scorch before he was ready to use it with the fish.

He discarded the bacon to drain on a brown paper bag, then began to blend the bacon drippings and butter, pouring back and forth from skillet to skillet. I had had no idea Ike was such a chef.

"Now we can get down to business," he said, picking up a plastic sack into which he poured cornmeal, salt and pepper. He dumped several trout into the bag and shook it vigorously.

"Stand back," he said as a general announcement, "I'm getting ready to work.'

The two pans were popping and sizzling over the hot coals as the President with tender care eased several trout into each skillet. He kept the pans moving so the trout did not stick. The iron skillet handles got hot, but Ike merely took out a handkerchief and wrapped his hand to prevent a burn.

It seemed only a very few minutes before the President speared one of the fish with a borrowed fork and held it up proudly.

"Who wants the first fish?"

Several persons suggested he should have it.

"Heck no," he said, "I've got a lot of cooking to do."

The three reporters edged into the background, mindful of their recent cheeseburgers. We were not entirely sure that we were supposed to eat or merely act as spectators.

The President spotted our retreat and halted it immediately.

"Here, you guys," he said, "come here and get some of these fish. Why do you think I'm cooking them?"

We tried to make flimsy excuses, but too flimsy. Within seconds each of us had a trout-laden paper plate.

Mr. Eisenhower refused to eat a bite himself until he saw that the three reporters were distressingly well fed, plus Nielsen, Schulz and the Secret Service agents.

One SS man seemed to catch Ike's eye. The President served him one of the first fish. I watched this man closely because I knew he was in somewhat the same fix I was in. Some of the agents had eaten bountiful box lunches of ham and chicken sandwiches before they knew they were to be guests at a Presidential fish fry.

This particular agent ate one fish and showed great gusto, probably a bit too much enthusiasm because the President returned to him only a few minutes later with another trout.

"Oh no, Mr. President," protested the agent, "I don't want to be greedy. I've had far more than my share."

The President dumped the fish in the fellow's paper plate and returned to his fire. The agent ate the fish, but it was obvious that he was under considerable gastronomic strain.

Several of us were lying in the grass, contemplating our overstuffed stomachs. The President got up from his rock stove and bore down on us with two whopping rainbows, the largest fish in the catch.

"Who's ready?" he cried with the enthusiasm that only an amateur cook can summon under such circumstances.

The President looked toward me.

"Mr. President, I don't want to be selfish," I said. "But I think you ought to know this—that agent over there wants another and I think he's afraid to tell you."

I pointed toward the stuffed SS man. The agent's eyes rolled in silent distress as the President moved toward him with a loaded frying pan. It is somewhat difficult to explain, but in such cases, one just doesn't come out and tell the President of the United States that he does not want another of the President's prize creations.

"Why didn't you say you were hungry?" the President demanded.

Dutifully, the agent held out his plate. He shot a murderous glance at me, then picked up the trout. As he bit into the fish, he had a look of gritty determination you see on the face of a ship captain in a British movie just as the destroyer goes down firing.

"Look at that boy go," said Mr. Eisenhower gleefully. "Who says he isn't hungry?"

CHAPTER TEN

Two Deaths

Two of the awesome moments in America in the middle years of the twentieth century were the sudden deaths of President Franklin D. Roosevelt at Warm Springs, Georgia, on April 12, 1945, and the assassination of President John F. Kennedy in Dallas, Texas, on November 22, 1963.

Merriman Smith was at Warm Springs with Roosevelt and eighteen years later was riding in a press car behind Kennedy in Dallas when the fatal shots were fired.

No other American was such a witness to both of these occasions. His graphic and poignant accounts of each—it was his coverage in Dallas that earned him the Pulitzer Prize—captured the high drama of those acts that moved the world so profoundly.

It was a beautiful April afternoon at Warm Springs, and Bill Hassett and I were lazing away on the front porch of his cottage talking about hush puppies and Brunswick stew. Hassett was the secretary who made most of the trips with Mr. Roosevelt.

"I'll bet," Hassett said, "the President hasn't had any Brunswick stew in years. He'd enjoy some, too."

195

"Why don't we have one of the Meriwether County barbecue experts run up a pot of stew for the old man?" I asked.

The next thing: Hassett and I were talking over barbecue plans with Ruth Stevens, the manageress of the small Warm Springs Hotel.

"We," said Ruthie, "will have us one damned good barbecue."

Ruth and the owner of the hotel, Frank Allcorn, worked like demons for several days lining up the chef, his assistants and some hillbilly musicians. Allcorn got two small hogs, a lamb and a side of beef. The Brunswick stew specialist was imported from nearby Newnan.

Finally, the magic day. Hassett came tearing down the side of Pine Mountain in his station wagon just before lunch. A smartly uniformed Marine leaped from the car in front of the hotel. He carried a glistening bugle. The Marine took up his position inside the lobby while Hassett sent for me. He gave me my instructions. I was to announce him as he entered the lobby.

Bill signaled the Marine who then proceeded to assail the eardrums of the lobby loafers with four blasts of "Attention." I strode in just as Ruth burst in from the kitchen. Hassett handed a brown envelope to the Marine who bore it across the lobby to Ruth. She turned a dull white.

Ruth's hands trembled as she opened the envelope. "The President of the United States," she read, "accepts with pleasure your kind invitation to barbecue . . ."

April 12, 1945, was the date of the barbecue, to be given at the Pine Mountain home of Allcorn, an Atlanta broker who bought the Warm Springs Hotel to satisfy his love of small-town life.

We decided to limit the party to the travel crew—the President's staff, the three wire service men and, of course, Ruth and the mayor. This was to avoid social complications on Warm Springs Foundation where an invitation to eat with the President established a person's social position for years to come.

The party was supposed to start at four o'clock. The staff was to come thirty minutes ahead of the President to permit a few head-start drinks before the Boss arrived. He was scheduled to reach the mountain cottage at four-thirty. I spent most of the morning of April 12 on the mountain, helping Ruth and Allcorn get organized. We tasted the barbecue—and the old-fashioneds—and by three in the afternoon we seemed to be squared away.

I had to go down the mountain to the Foundation for a few minutes and ran into Alice Winegar, Hassett's secretary. Alice looked a little strange as she darted across one of the Foundation's clay streets. I yelled at her.

"You folks better be getting ready," I told her. "Don't be a minute later than four o'clock."

Alice didn't say anything. She just looked terrified.

"What's the matter?" I asked her.

"Nothing, Smitty," she said. But I knew she was lying. I thought at the time something big must be brewing; that she was a little preoccupied, but it never occurred to me that anything truly earth-shaking was about to happen. I went to the hotel, changed clothes and drove on to the Allcorn cottage.

At four o'clock the first guests began to arrive. The Brunswick stew was bubbling in a huge cook pot, country fiddlers were playing "The Cat and the Chicken" and everyone was in expectancy of the chief executive's arrival. Four-ten came and Major Dewitt Greer, head of the White House Signal Corps unit, arrived. He made a quick check on the short-wave radio units which were placed in Allcorn's barn for the Secret Service.

At four-twenty I became a little irritated because the secretarial staff had not arrived. I had visions of their cars clogging traffic for the President on the narrow one-way road leading up the mountain to Allcorn's house. I excused myself from the party and walked back to the barn where Wayne Shell, a Signal Corps sergeant, was sitting by his short-wave portable, reading a Western magazine and waiting patiently for the end of his shift.

"Wayne," I asked, "how about letting me call the White House to see if the Boss is on his way?"

Waiting for the radio check, I looked out at the party. It was one of the happiest gatherings I'd ever seen. A warm spring sun bathed the valley below the small mountain and the air was an appetizing combination of odors—the crisp, crackling fat of the hogs, the warm pungency of the Brunswick stew and the added touch of civilization, the slightly barroom smell coming from a table laden with old-fashioneds.

The President, Hassett had said, will stay about an hour, then he will have to go to a minstrel show being staged for him by the children of the Foundation. We had arranged a special chair from which Mr. Roosevelt could gaze down the beautiful valley, and still hear the country fiddlers. He was to be served no barbecue, but just a bowl of the stew and a drink or two.

The sergeant mumbled into his hand microphone.

"Indiana to Pine—Indiana to Pine—come in please."

"Pine to Indiana—Pine to Indiana—go ahead."

"Is there any sign of movement?"

"No—no sign of movement."

I leaned over to Shell.

"Let me have the mike a minute, please."

"Pine—who is this please?"

"This is Anderson. Who is this?"

"This is Smitty, Andy. What is going on down there?"

"Smitty, I honestly don't know. No cars have arrived. There just isn't anything doing."

"The President is supposed to be here in a few minutes."

"Yeah, I know. But there's nothing moving as yet. Want me to give you a call?"

"No, Andy, I'll get on the phone and talk to Hackie."

Anderson was the Secret Service agent on duty at the front gate of the Little White House. Hackie was Louise Hackmeister, the chief White House telephone operator.

I trotted to the door of Allcorn's cottage and asked his pretty daughter if they had a telephone. Yes, she said, on the wall in the next room.

It was a coffee-grinder type of set and it took several minutes to reach the Foundation switchboard.

"Ring the White House board," I asked.

A few seconds and Hackie's crisp, "Yes, please" came in through the receiver.

"Hackie, this is Smitty. Why aren't you people on the way? What's holding things up?"

Hackie's voice sounded almost unreal. Usually, she was very level-headed. But this time her voice was panicky. She was shouting.

"I don't know, Smitty," she said. "But Mr. Hassett wants to see you. Get the other two boys and go to his cottage as fast as you can."

I put down the phone and ran out into the driveway. I saw Bob Nixon of I.N.S. and Harry Oliver of A.P. standing together. I went over quietly and said, "Come with me."

We walked toward Greer's big, fast Signal Corps Lincoln. He saw us and came running.

"What's up?"

"Can you take us down to Hassett's cottage right away? Something awful big is going on."

We saw Ed Clement, of the Southern Bell Telephone and Telegraph Company.

"Ed," I shouted, "get some circuits lined up to Washington, will you?"

We started down the narrow, twisting mountain road, all speculating about what the big break would be. We agreed it was the capitulation of Germany.

Greer drove the car and when we hit the paved road leading to the Foundation, the speedometer needle was tickling ninety miles an hour. In a cloud of dust, Greer pulled up in front of Hassett's cottage and we dashed inside.

I was the first one through the door. Hassett was standing near the fireplace of his living room, his face gray and mournful. I looked over to the couch and saw Grace Tully and her assistant, Dorothy Brady. Both of them were crying softly and literally wiping their eyes on each other's shoulder.

When I saw Grace Tully's tear-swollen eyes, I knew she was not crying about the end of the war. I remembered there were four telephones in Hassett's cottage. And one was only about two feet away from me—on the radiator of his living room. I honestly had no exact idea of what was happening, but I knew it was big and tragic.

Hassett cleared his throat and fiddled with two or three small

pieces of paper in his hands. He stepped away from the fireplace
into the middle of the room, and I picked up the telephone.

"Gentlemen," he said, "it is my sad duty to inform you that the
President . . ."

"Number please?" said the operator in my ear.

"Priority one—Washington—" I said softly.

Hassett continued.

"The President died at 3:35 this afternoon."

"Executive 3430," I finished to the operator. "My name is
Smith."

I heard the telephone switchboards yanked apart, and then—
it seemed hours, but it was only a few seconds—I heard the most
welcome voice I ever heard in my life—Romilda Flanagan, our
operator in Washington.

"United Press," she chirped.

"Flash!" I roared into the telephone. I could also hear Oliver
and Nixon screaming because I had grabbed the living room
telephone. Hassett quickly steered them into rooms where there
were other instruments.

Julius Frandsen, U.P.'s extremely quiet and calm news editor
in Washington, answered with a soft "yes?"

"Roosevelt died at 3:35 Warm Springs this is Smith," I jab-
bered.

"Dictate," Frandsen said and hung up his phone.

I started dictating to the typewriter girls in Washington, and
I didn't find out until some time later that Steve Early, the
President's press secretary who was in Washington, beat me by a
few minutes with the first news.

Steve had telephoned the wire service offices in Washington at
about the same time we were getting the news from Hassett.

We dictated for a few minutes, then stopped to make notes,
continuing this stop-and-go process for several hours. A tired
young man in a sweaty khaki shirt and trousers helped us. He
was Howard G. Bruenn, the Navy doctor who was with Mr.
Roosevelt when he died.

Bruenn mopped his face with a limp handkerchief and said
with a hopeless shrug, "It was just like a bolt of lightning or

getting hit by a train. One minute he was alive and laughing. The next minute—wham!"

"Howard," we asked, "did you see this thing coming?"

"This wasn't the sort of thing you could forecast. Doctors just can't say 'this man is going to have a cerebral.' It doesn't happen that way. He'd been feeling fine. He was awfully tired when we first came down here. You saw him the other day—wasn't he in fine spirits?"

Yes, the President was in fine spirits that day, but he looked unhealthy.

I had been horseback riding near the President's cottage most of the morning of April 5 when a Marine courier found me on a back road and told me to proceed to the President's quarters immediately. I didn't know what to do with the horse, so I tied him to a tree in the garden behind Bill Hassett's cottage—and found later that the horse hungrily did away with the owner's prized bed of pansies and lilies.

The three press association reporters were ushered into the small, comfortable living room of the Little White House at about two o'clock in the afternoon of April 5. The President had been in day-long conference with Sergio Osmena, then President of the Philippine Commonwealth.

Mr. Roosevelt was sitting in his favorite spot in the house— before the living room fireplace. The President was in a friendly and easy mood, but his hands seemed to tremble more than ever as he fitted a cigarette into his famous, scorched ivory holder. If we had only known it was his last press conference, we would have better noted the smallest details.

Osmena was Mr. Roosevelt's guest only for the day. They had discussed distant plans for a day they hoped would not be too distant—the day of complete Philippine independence. Little Osmena, looking frail after a recent operation in Florida, nodded and smiled agreement as the President talked.

Mr. Roosevelt coughed lightly at frequent intervals, but he smoked chain fashion. It was a beautiful, tranquil afternoon and I could not understand why the President, the great lover of the outdoors, was not out with Osmena in the small convertible.

The interview was about over. Mr. Roosevelt began to fiddle with various papers on the card table beside him. And the reporters saw that one of the greatest news wells the world has ever known was about to go dry—for the moment at least.

He kidded us about the bad golf that was being played on the Warm Springs course.

"Have a cig?" he said, shoving his pack of Camels across the card table toward me. He used that expression often and it was so out of character. "Have a cig" seemed to belong more to the flappers and sheiks in John Held, Jr., cartoons than in the vocabulary of a Roosevelt.

His hands shook so badly he could hardly get the cigarette out of the package. I leaned over to light it for him, but he said no thanks, he had some kitchen matches of his own. He seemed to gather all his strength and control into the lighting of the cigarette. It was an intense thing. I wanted not to watch.

I didn't see him again to talk with before he died. Two days before his death, however, the President was taking a quiet afternoon drive in his little open coupe and nearly ran me down. I was riding a very nasty horse which I had rented for the afternoon at the village drugstore. They had everything in that store.

As I reined in the horse to let the President and the accompanying Secret Service car pass, Mr. Roosevelt bowed majestically to me. The car was moving slowly and the President spoke. His voice was wonderful and resonant. It sounded like the Roosevelt of old. In tones that must have been audible a block away, Roosevelt hailed me with: "Heigh-O, Silver!" As far as I was concerned, those were his last words.

Actually, however, he spoke his last words on April 12, just before 1:15 p.m. (Central War Time). It was before lunch and the President was killing two birds with one stone. He was at work on official papers which had arrived from Washington that morning, and posing at the same time for Elizabeth Shumatov, one of his favorite artists.

He had been in gay spirits. He was feeling so much better than he had in previous weeks that Bruenn that morning had telephoned an enthusiastic report on his condition to Admiral McIntire, who was in Washington.

Mr. Roosevelt sat where he could see the sun-bathed valley of dogwood trees west of his little cottage. He remarked what a fine day it would be at the barbecue. The war news was good that morning. The Washington dispatches looked fine. Let's see—there were two more bills Hassett had brought for his signature. The President leafed through the papers in front of him. Suddenly, he clapped his hand to the back of his head like a man slapping a fly. His face wrinkled into a heavy frown.

The President said softly, "I have a terrific headache." Then he collapsed. The massive, heavy upper part of his body rolled over against the side of the chair. The artist leaped to her feet. The President's cousin, Laura Delano, ran from the rear of the room.

"The President!" they called. "The President has fainted!"

Into the pleasant, sunny room dashed Arthur Prettyman, the President's valet. Miss Delano grabbed a telephone and called for Bruenn who was just leaving the swimming pool a mile or so away. Prettyman ran into the kitchen and summoned a Filipino messboy. They lifted the President's sagging body from the chair and bore it into his small bedroom a few feet away.

Prettyman did what he could to see that his chief was comfortable. He loosened Mr. Roosevelt's belt and tie. The President looked very sick. His tortured breathing could be heard throughout the cottage. His tremendous chest rose and fell as though a large pump were operating it. He was in his last fight.

Within a few minutes, Bruenn rushed into the cottage with George Fox, the Navy pharmacist who gave the President nightly rubdowns and always traveled with him as a first-aid or emergency specialist. They gently removed Mr. Roosevelt's blue suit and put pajamas on his limp body.

Bruenn telephoned his chief in Washington. McIntire in turn telephoned Atlanta and asked Dr. James Paullin, famous southern internist who had consulted with McIntire before on Mr. Roosevelt's health, to hurry to Warm Springs.

While Paullin was en route, Bruenn did everything possible to keep the President alive. Fox tried gentle massage and moved the President's arms. Mr. Roosevelt's eyes were open, but they were unseeing eyes. Fox called to the President, asking him to show some sign of recognition if he could hear his voice. But the eyes just stared straight ahead.

Paullin arrived after a wild automobile ride, and his diagnosis agreed with Bruenn's—a massive cerebral hemorrhage. It was just a matter of time. And at 3:35, Warm Springs time, Mr. Roosevelt's tortured breathing stopped.

Bruenn, Fox and Paullin were the only ones in the room. The doctors bent over the bed. They looked at each other. The President was dead.

The night of April 12 was truly a nightmare. It was a horrible, discordant symphony of people shouting for telephones, automobiles racing along dusty clay roads, the clatter of telegraph instruments and typewriters.

The President was to have attended a minstrel show put on by infantile paralysis patients in wheelchairs and on crutches. It was to have been their dress rehearsal with the President and a few members of his party as the only audience. But he died two hours before the show was to start and the wheelchair brigade out of the tiny playhouse was a throat-clutching sight. Their idol, their ideal, their biggest source of hope was gone.

The three White House correspondents, having to carry almost the entire brunt of the coverage because the White House was loath to have the sorrowing Foundation overrun by strange reporters and photographers, wrote all night. I wrote until I thought another word could not come out of my typewriter. Then would come a message from Washington—"We now need a piece about . . ." And the typewriter would go on.

Mrs. Roosevelt, McIntire and Early arrived around midnight. Steve gave us the funeral train plans as they developed. I still had to pack and check out of the hotel, so I signed off my wire to Washington and went into the village. Sorrowing, miserable people sat along the high curbstones, talking in low voices. Their faces were pictures of fear

Shortly after nine o'clock the next morning, the Secret Service notified the three White House reporters to get in a car and go to the Little White House. We were to come back to the train in the funeral procession.

The cortege left the Little White House at nine-thirty. A hot southern sun bathed the green hills and valleys the President loved so well. The route was down a winding clay road to Georgia Hall, the central building of the Warm Springs Foundation, and thence about a mile to the little railroad station.

Troops from Fort Benning, most of them combat veterans, stood shoulder to shoulder at present arms along the way. An honor guard walked ahead of the hearse.

Mrs. Roosevelt had requested that the hearse stop momentarily at the entrance of Georgia Hall—just a brief stop, the kind the President had made every time he left Warm Springs in the past. The President always had waved and assured the patients of his return within a few months. This morning, they knew too well he would not be back. Just as the hearse stopped, a Negro Coast Guardsman, Chief Petty Officer Graham Jackson, stepped from behind the columns. Jackson was one of the President's favorite musicians and he had his accordian with him.

Tears were streaming down Jackson's black cheeks as he lifted his accordian and began the soft strains of Dvořák's "Going Home." Kids buried their faces in their elbows and wept loudly. Case-hardened nurses and doctors sniffled and looked at the ground. Only the very young—those too young to know—seemed to be tearless.

There was old Tom Logan on the edge of the crowd. For fourteen years he had waited on the President at Warm Springs. As the white-haired Negro stared at the hearse bearing the body of his friend, his frail frame shook with sobs and he prayed, "Lord God, take care of him now."

As the procession started to move again, Jackson edged closer to the slow-moving automobiles and began, "Nearer, My God, to Thee," the most solemn song of the Protestant faith.

Many of the soldiers along the line of march cried softly as they stood at rigid attention.

It was about fifteen minutes before the train left, so I dictated during that period to Washington. I was so choked with emotion, myself, that it was difficult to speak coherent sentences.

I saw the conductor wave his arm to the engineer, so I turned the telephone over to Fowler and sprinted for the train. It was beginning to move as I climbed aboard. I walked back to my drawing room and flopped in the seat.

IT WAS A BALMY, sunny noon as we motored through downtown Dallas behind President Kennedy. The procession cleared the center of the business district and turned into a handsome highway that wound through what appeared to be a park.

I was riding in the so-called White House press "pool" car, a telephone company vehicle equipped with a mobile radio-telephone. I was in the front seat between a driver from the telephone company and Malcolm Kilduff, acting White House press secretary for the President's Texas tour. Three other pool reporters were wedged in the back seat.

Suddenly we heard three loud, almost painfully loud cracks. The first sounded as if it might have been a large firecracker. But the second and third blasts were unmistakable. Gunfire.

The President's car, possibly as much as 150 or 200 yards ahead, seemed to falter briefly. We saw a flurry of activity in the Secret Service follow-up car behind the Chief Executive's bubble-top limousine.

Next in line was the car bearing Vice President Lyndon B. Johnson. Behind that, another follow-up car bearing agents assigned to the Vice President's protection. We were behind that car.

Our car stood still for probably only a few seconds, but it seemed like a lifetime. One sees history explode before one's eyes and for even the most trained observer, there is a limit to what one can comprehend.

I looked ahead at the President's car but could not see him or his companion, Gov. John B. Connally of Texas. Both men had been riding on the right side of the bubble-top limousine from Washington. I thought I saw a flash of pink which would have been Mrs. Jacqueline Kennedy.

Everybody in our car began shouting at the driver to pull up closer to the President's car. But at this moment, we saw the big bubble-top and a motorcycle escort roar away at high speed.

We screamed at our driver, "Get going, get going." We careened around the Johnson car and its escort and set out down the highway, barely able to keep in sight of the President's car and the accompanying Secret Service follow-up car.

They vanished around a curve. When we cleared the same curve we could see where we were heading—Parkland Hospital, a large brick structure to the left of the arterial highway. We skidded around a sharp left turn and spilled out of the pool car as it entered the hospital driveway.

I ran to the side of the bubble-top.

The President was face down on the back seat. Mrs. Kennedy made a cradle of her arms around the President's head and bent over him as if she were whispering to him.

Gov. Connally was on his back on the floor of the car, his head and shoulders resting in the arms of his wife, Nellie, who kept shaking her head and shaking with dry sobs. Blood oozed from the front of the Governor's suit. I could not see the President's wound. But I could see blood spattered around the interior of the rear seat and a dark stain spreading down the right side of the President's gray suit.

From the telephone car, I had radioed the Dallas bureau of UPI that three shots had been fired at the Kennedy motorcade. Seeing the bloody scene in the rear of the car at the hospital entrance, I knew I had to get to a telephone immediately.

Clint Hill, the Secret Service agent in charge of the detail assigned to Mrs. Kennedy, was leaning over into the rear of the car.

"How badly was he hit, Clint?" I asked.

"He's dead," Hill replied curtly.

I have no further clear memory of the scene in the driveway. I recall a babble of anxious voices, tense voices—"Where in hell are the stretchers . . . Get a doctor out here . . . He's on the way . . . Come on, easy there." And from somewhere, nervous sobbing.

I raced down a short stretch of sidewalk into a hospital corridor. The first thing I spotted was a small clerical office, more of a booth than an office. Inside, a bespectacled man stood shuffling what appeared to be hospital forms. At a wicket much like a bank teller's cage, I spotted a telephone on the shelf.

"How do you get outside?" I gasped. "The President has been hurt and this is an emergency call."

"Dial nine," he said, shoving the phone toward me.

It took two tries before I successfully dialed the Dallas UPI number. Quickly I dictated a bulletin saying the President had been seriously, perhaps fatally, injured by an assassin's bullets while driving through the streets of Dallas.

Litters bearing the President and the Governor rolled by me as I dictated, but my back was to the hallway and I didn't see them until they were at the entrance of the emergency room about 75 or 100 feet away.

I knew they had passed, however, from the horrified expression that suddenly spread over the face of the man behind the wicket.

As I stood in the drab buff hallway leading into the emergency ward trying to reconstruct the shooting for the UPI man on the other end of the telephone and still keeping track of what was happening outside the door of the emergency room, I watched a swift and confused panorama sweep before me.

Kilduff of the White House press staff raced up and down the hall. Police captains barked at each other, "Clear this area." Two priests hurried in behind a Secret Service agent, their narrow purple stoles rolled up tightly in their hands. A police lieutenant ran down the hall with a large carton of blood for transfusions. A doctor came in and said he was responding to a call for "all neurosurgeons."

The priests came out and said the President had received the last sacrament of the Roman Catholic Church. They said he was still alive, but not conscious. Members of the Kennedy staff began arriving. They had been behind us in the motorcade, but hopelessly bogged for a time in confused traffic.

Telephones were at a premium in the hospital and I clung to mine for dear life. I was afraid to stray from the wicket lest I lose contact with the outside world.

My decision was made for me, however, when Kilduff and

Wayne Hawks of the White House staff ran by me, shouting that Kilduff would make a statement shortly in the so-called nurses room a floor above and at the far end of the hospital.

I threw down the phone and sped after them. We reached the door of the conference room and there were loud cries of "Quiet!" Fighting to keep his emotions under control, Kilduff said, "President John Fitzgerald Kennedy died at approximately one o'clock."

I raced into a nearby office. The telephone switchboard at the hospital was hopelessly jammed. I spotted Virginia Payette, wife of UPI's Southwestern division manager and a veteran reporter in her own right. I told her to try getting through on pay telephones on the floor above.

Frustrated by the inability to get through the hospital switchboard, I appealed to a nurse. She led me through a maze of corridors and back stairways to another floor and a lone pay booth. I got the Dallas office. Virginia had gotten through before me.

Whereupon I ran back through the hospital to the conference room. There Jiggs Fauver of the White House transportation staff grabbed me and said Kilduff wanted a pool of three men immediately to fly back to Washington on Air Force One, the Presidential aircraft.

"He wants you downstairs, and he wants you right now," Fauver said.

Down the stairs I ran and into the driveway, only to discover Kilduff had just pulled out in our telephone car.

Charles Roberts of *Newsweek* magazine, Sid Davis of Westinghouse Broadcasting and I implored a police officer to take us to the airport in his squad car. The Secret Service had requested that no sirens be used in the vicinity of the airport, but the Dallas officer did a masterful job of getting us through some of the worst traffic I've ever seen.

As we piled out of the car on the edge of the runway about 200 yards from the Presidential aircraft, Kilduff spotted us and motioned for us to hurry. We trotted to him and he said the place could take two pool men to Washington; that Johnson was about to take the oath of office aboard the plane and would take off immediately thereafter.

I saw a bank of telephone booths beside the runway and asked if I had time to advise my news service. He said, "But for God's sake, hurry."

Then began another telephone nightmare. The Dallas office rang busy. I tried calling Washington. All circuits were busy. Then I called the New York bureau of UPI and told them about the impending installation of a new President aboard the airplane.

Kilduff came out of the plane and motioned wildly toward my booth. I slammed down the phone and jogged across the runway. A detective stopped me and said, "You dropped your pocket comb."

Aboard Air Force One on which I had made so many trips as a press association reporter covering President Kennedy, all of the shades of the larger main cabin were drawn and the interior was hot and dimly lighted.

Kilduff propelled us to the President's suite two-thirds of the way back in the plane. The room is used normally as a combination conference and sitting room and could accommodate eight to ten people seated.

I wedged inside the door and began counting. There were 27 people in this compartment. Johnson stood in the center with his wife, Lady Bird. U.S. District Judge Sarah T. Hughes, 67, a kindly faced woman stood with a small black Bible in her hands, waiting to give the oath.

The compartment became hotter and hotter. Johnson was worried that some of the Kennedy staff might not be able to get inside. He urged people to press forward, but a Signal Corps photographer, Capt. Cecil Stoughton, standing in the corner on a chair, said if Johnson moved any closer, it would be virtually impossible to make a truly historic photograph.

It developed that Johnson was waiting for Mrs. Kennedy, who was composing herself in a small bedroom in the rear of the plane. She appeared alone, dressed in the same pink wool suit she had worn in the morning when she appeared so happy shaking hands with airport crowds at the side of her husband.

She was white-faced but dry-eyed. Friendly hands stretched toward her as she stumbled slightly. Johnson took both of her hands in his and motioned her to his left side. Lady Bird stood on his right, a fixed half-smile showing the tension.

Johnson nodded to Judge Hughes, an old friend of his family and a Kennedy appointee.

"Hold up your right hand and repeat after me," the woman jurist said to Johnson.

Outside, a jet could be heard droning into a landing.

Judge Hughes held out the Bible and Johnson covered it with his large left hand. His right arm went slowly into the air and the jurist began to intone the Constitutional oath, "I do solemnly swear I will faithfully execute the office of President of the United States . . ."

The brief ceremony ended when Johnson in a deep, firm voice, repeated after the judge, ". . . and so help me God."

Johnson turned first to his wife, hugged her about the shoulders and kissed her on the cheek. Then he turned to Kennedy's widow, put his left arm around her and kissed her cheek.

As others in the group—some Texas Democratic House members, members of the Johnson and Kennedy staffs—moved toward the new President, he seemed to back away from any expression of felicitation.

The two-minute ceremony concluded at 3:38 P.M. EST and seconds later, the President said firmly, "Now, let's get airborne."

Col. James Swindal, pilot of the plane, a big gleaming silver and blue fan-jet, cut on the starboard engines immediately. Several persons, including Sid Davis of Westinghouse, left the plane at that time. The White House had room for only two pool reporters on the return flight and these posts were filled by Roberts and me, although at the moment we could find no empty seats.

At 3:47 P.M. EST, the wheels of Air Force One cleared the runway. Swindal roared the big ship up to an unusually high cruising altitude of 41,000 feet where at 625 miles an hour, ground speed, the jet hurtled toward Andrews Air Force Base outside Washington.

When the President's plane reached operating altitude, Mrs. Kennedy left her bedchamber and walked to the rear compartment of the plane. This was the so-called family living room, a private area where she and Kennedy, family and friends had spent many happy airborne hours chatting and dining together.

Kennedy's casket had been placed in this compartment, carried aboard by a group of Secret Service agents.

Mrs. Kennedy went into the rear lounge and took a chair beside the coffin. There she remained throughout the flight. Her vigil was shared at times by four staff members close to the slain chief executive—David Powers, his buddy and personal assistant; Kenneth P. O'Donnell, appointments secretary and key political adviser; Lawrence O'Brien, chief Kennedy liaison man with Congress, and Brig. Gen. Godfey McHugh, Kennedy's Air Force aide.

Kennedy's military aide, Maj. Gen. Chester V. Clifton, was busy most of the trip in the forward areas of the plane, sending messages and making arrangements for arrival ceremonies and movement of the body to Bethesda Naval Hospital.

As the flight progressed, Johnson walked back into the main compartment. My portable typewriter was lost somewhere around the hospital and I was writing on an over-sized electric typewriter which Kennedy's personal secretary, Mrs. Evelyn Lincoln, had used to type his speech texts.

Johnson came up to the table where Roberts and I were trying to record the history we had just witnessed.

"I'm going to make a short statement in a few minutes and give you copies of it," he said. "Then when I get on the ground, I'll do it over again."

It was the first public utterance of the new Chief Executive, brief and moving—

"This is a sad time for all people. We have suffered a loss that cannot be weighed. For me it is a deep personal tragedy. I know the world shares the sorrow that Mrs. Kennedy and her family bear. I will do my best. That is all I can do. I ask for your help—and God's."

When the plane was about 45 minutes from Washington, the new President got on a special radio-telephone and placed a call to Mrs. Rose Kennedy, the late President's mother.

"I wish to God there was something I could do," he told her, "I just wanted you to know that."

Then Mrs. Johnson wanted to talk to the elder Mrs. Kennedy. "We feel like the heart has been cut out of us," Mrs. Johnson said. She broke down for a moment and began to sob. Recovering in a few seconds, she added, "Our love and our prayers are with you."

Thirty minutes out of Washington, Johnson put in a call for Nellie Connally, wife of the seriously wounded Texas Governor.

The new President said to the Governor's wife:

"We are praying for you, darling, and I know that everything is going to be all right, isn't it? Give him a hug and a kiss for me."

It was dark when Air Force One began to skim over the lights of the Washington area, lining up for a landing at Andrews Air Force Base. The plane touched down at 5:59 P.M. EST.

I thanked the stewards for rigging up the typewriter for me, pulled on my raincoat and started down the forward ramp. Roberts and I stood under a wing and watched the casket being lowered from the rear of the plane and borne by a complement of armed forces body bearers into a waiting hearse. We watched Mrs. Kennedy and the President's brother, Atty. Gen. Robert F. Kennedy, climb into the hearse beside the coffin.

The new President repeated his first public statement for broadcast and newsreel microphones, shook hands with some of the government and diplomatic leaders who turned out to meet the plane, and headed for his helicopter.

Roberts and I were given seats on another 'copter bound for the White House lawn. In the compartment next to ours in one of the large chairs beside a window sat Theodore C. Sorensen, one of Kennedy's closest associates with the title of special counsel to the President. He had not gone to Texas with his chief but had come to the air base for his return.

Sorensen sat wilted in the large chair, crying softly. The dignity of his deep grief seemed to sum up all of the tragedy and sadness of the previous six hours.

As our helicopter circled in the balmy darkness for a landing on the White House south lawn, it seemed incredible that only six hours before, John Fitzgerald Kennedy had been a vibrant, smiling, waving and active man.

CHAPTER ELEVEN

Post Mortems:
The Traumas of Transition

The Roosevelt and Kennedy deaths in office had the common effect of spawning disbelief and recrimination. The flood of books about the assassination in Dallas kept alive a public unwillingness to accept the fact that one pathetic little man, acting alone, could, in effect, have removed the president of the United States. Who had allowed this to happen? Where was the Secret Service?

The Roosevelt death raised another set of questions. They involved the issue of how much the public is entitled to know about the health of a president. If the public is misled, it may be cheated out of an intelligent vote or tricked into accepting the leadership of an incapable chief executive.

Even on the president's funeral train from Washington to Hyde Park—as Smith was to write afterward—conversation was permeated with doubts about the truthfulness of past reports on Roosevelt's health.

WHEN I BOARDED the funeral train for Hyde Park that night, the porter told me that most of our party was in the diner. I went in and sat down with William C. Murphy, Jr., then covering the White House for the Philadelphia *Inquirer* and later the publicity director for the Republican National Committee.

The train was so long and heavy that the crew found it difficult to get it started. A coupling broke three times. The third time, Murphy remarked laconically, "The Republicans have always known that it would be difficult to get Roosevelt out of Washington."

A lot of judgment was passed that night on the way to Hyde Park. One school of thought said the public had been misled by not having a true and full report on Mr. Roosevelt's health long before his death, particularly during the fourth term campaign. Another group took the other side, arguing that the public had been given the whole story; that the President's death was as unexpected to his doctors as it was to the public at large.

If Dr. McIntire was at fault for not telling the nation more about the President's health, the fault was not his alone. Due largely to the frequent prevalence of untrue rumors about Mr. Roosevelt's health, members of his staff and his close friends bent over backwards to deny any suggestion of poor health.

To the best of my knowledge, Steve Early was completely honest in what he said about Mr. Roosevelt's condition. But Steve didn't say much about it, unless the President had a cold or some other minor ailment which was sufficient to keep him away from the office. When this was the case, Steve always supplied bulletins, sometimes several daily, giving temperature readings and other details. It seemed to me, however, and in retrospect, that the older Mr. Roosevelt got, the less his staff tried to say about his health.

The last public report on his health came from the President himself. On March 1, 1945, he reported to Congress on the Yalta conference. For the first time before such a large public audience, the President sat in his wheel chair and did not stand for the speech.

"I hope you will pardon me," he told a joint session of the House and Senate, "for the unusual posture of sitting down during the presentation of what I wish to say, but I know you will realize that it makes it a lot easier for me not having to carry ten pounds of steel around the bottom of my legs, and also, because of the fact that I have just completed a 14,000-mile trip.

" . . . I am returning from this trip that took me so far, refreshed and inspired. I was well the entire time. I was not ill for a second until I arrived back in Washington and here I heard all the rumors which had occurred in my absence. Yes, I returned from the trip refreshed and inspired. The Roosevelts are not, as you may suspect, averse to travel. We seem to thrive on it."

The President might have been more convincing if he had looked better. His voice that day in the crowded House chamber was thin. He sounded poor on the radio. His delivery was listless and spotty. He misread sentences. His head sagged as he read from his big, black notebook.

As we passed second and third judgment in the diner of the funeral train that night, one reporter made the point that it was a mistake not to have performed an autopsy on the President's body and with a full, public disclosure of the results.

That would have been a sure antidote for the rumors that swept the country in the days following his death. There are to-day, for example, people who believe Mr. Roosevelt was murdered. Some swear that he committed suicide. One magazine actually printed an article alleging that the cerebral hemorrhage which killed him was the third he had suffered.

Then there were reports that he died of cancer, of tuberculosis and/or poisoning. There was a rumor current in Harlem for a time that he had not died at all, but had gone stark raving mad. This rumor obviously fed on the fact that his body did not lie in state or in public view before the funeral.

Plainly these rumors are untrue. The word has the record of three distinguished medical men—McIntire, Bruenn and Paullin —for the cause of the President's death. Their reputations and their established integrity, plus the lack of any established facts to the contrary, make it necessary to accept their stated cause of death.

But the record does not seem as unquestionable on reports of his health in advance of the President's death. McIntire reported at the end of the Yalta trip that Mr. Roosevelt was in "tiptop" condition. Yet, it was during the same period that Secret Service agents were assigned to protect Vice President Truman.

Mr. Truman did not ask for the agents. McIntire did not request or recommend them. So, what was the answer? The higher-ups of the United States Secret Service obviously were worried about the President's health. To be on the safe side, they assigned a detail of agents to guard the Vice President.

If the people close to the President did not believe he was in failing health, I think they were kidding themselves. As a layman, I saw many indications, not of approaching death, but of sagging vitality. I realized, too, that we could not expect the Administration to be so politically inexpedient as to announce, for example, that "President Roosevelt is now a tired and worn out old man, and is having trouble regaining his strength and energy." But that seemed to me about the size of it.

> *Another common feature in the two transitions from fallen leader to new president was the bitterness that crept into the relations between the outgoing staff and the new assistants and secretaries. The Kennedy staff was totally loyal to JFK and understandably resentful of reminders of Texas, after Dallas. And the new Johnson people were mostly Texans. To the Roosevelt crowd, Harry Truman and his staff were pretenders. FDR had been larger than life—and now this little man.*

Roosevelt died in April and I then faced the pain and clumsiness of adjusting to a new President, this plain admixture of the farm, the haberdashery and Pendergast politics. During his first few days in the White House, I thought first that it was awful, then pitiable the way he tried to do business with the door to the great oval office wide open. He seemed dwarfed by the surroundings as he peered through his heavy glasses and smiled at V.I.P. sightseers who were paraded by the open door by various staff members and hangers-on.

It was not until sometime later that I learned Truman knew as well as anyone that he could not for long transact business on semi-public view, but he suffered through several days of the open-door policy largely to oblige his staff. He knew only too well that his assistants were being put through bitter hazing by the Roosevelt staff which found it almost impossible to accept that their great leader had fallen.

The incoming Truman staff, small as it was, lacked the urbanity and know-how of the Roosevelt staff which, after all, had been in place at the White House for more than twelve years. It seemed only natural that FDR's lieutenants and their girls friday knew the executive ropes far better than the small Truman group which came down from his Capitol Hill offices awed and a bit bewildered. But still there was considerable friction and even enmity.

Sadly, this apparently is true when there is a sudden and unexpected shift of command at the White House. The same sort of shock-spawned bitterness was to show itself again when another Vice President, Lyndon B. Johnson, succeeded the murdered Kennedy.

There were some around Kennedy who were so shaken by his death that they could not help discharging this grief in the form of anti-Johnson remarks and acts. I heard one otherwise highly responsible White House secretary refer to Johnson as "that stupid son of a bitch" simply because he was out on the south lawn frisking with his two beagles.

"His dumb dogs don't have sense enough to return a ball—and Charlie could do that," she said. Charlie, of course, was Kennedy's terrier and in the minds of some of the Kennedy staff, Johnson's introduction of beagles to White House living was nothing more than tasteless aping of the fallen hero. It did not occur to them, in the state of mind they were in, that Johnson's dogs antedated his coming to the White House.

Another well-known secretary at the White House stood up

under the advent of Johnson and his way of doing things for about two weeks, then quit cold without so much as an hour's notice of departure.

The climate in the winter of 1963–64 being what it was, it is now all the more amazing that Johnson did not order the White House staff uprooted and either fired or reassigned almost immediately. The fact that he did not showed a certain amount of forebearance, as well as appreciating the difficulty of a situation in which he needed the services of those who might have very definite reservations about his qualifications.

It must be said in behalf of the Johnson entourage that its members acted to the best of their ability not to be overbearing or demanding. They came not as supplicants, but as equals, and inquiring eagerly how certain procedural matters had been handled in the past.

What seemed to anger both the Johnson staff and the Kennedy staff who decided to stay on was that some of John Kennedy's ardent admirers, as well as employees were unable apparently to avoid saying to the newcomers, "This is how this must be done" or "This is the way we do it."

The new President and his staff were as sensitive as the workers-in-residence about their ignorance of White House routine, but it galled them to hear Kennedy employees saying, in effect, that their way was the only way.

This was not a uniform fault by any means, but it showed up often enough to make the transition a bit more painful than it was under the weight of the natural, tragic circumstances.

Smith took a relatively detached, professional view of the interstaff problems surrounding the deaths of Presidents Roosevelt and Kennedy. He was able to put such White House quarrels in perspective. This removed and philosophical stance is somewhat deceptive, however. It obscures the emotions that a reporter, like any other person, cannot help but feel. Actually, he wrote both of the foregoing analyses several years after the deaths and, in truth, it took a while for him to adjust to the new presidents, too.

A look at excerpts of an unpublished diary entry for November 22, 1964, reveals that one year after Dallas he was still preoccupied by the Kennedy assassination. And just as he had implied in print that the Kennedy staff was using resentment to vent grief, so, privately, he was doing the same thing.

Albert Camus said, "You cannot create experience. You must undergo it."

Perhaps this is why today, the first anniversary of JFK's death, left me cold as far as radio broadcasts and overdone newspaper tributes were concerned. I felt none of the choking, weepy sense of loss that I did a month after Dallas. The difference probably being that I'm sober today, I was drinking then.

In JFK's death, my sense of loss has taken the form of simply being unable to accept in my guts the coarse image and patois of LBJ. This really is no slam at LBJ. He can't help being what he is, but I've never adjusted successfully to his image for any length of time. I think he has done one hell of a fine job as President thus far and thank God he beat Goldwater so soundly. Perhaps my feelings are superficial and not really important, but I know that around JFK my frailties would have been far more accepted than by LBJ. Perhaps the Johnson attitude is better for the country.

I felt Kennedy understood me and my (professional) problems; that he never talked down to me, threatened me or attempted flattery. He was a consumate politician and God knows, Johnson is even more so, but I never got the feeling that Kennedy was lying to me—at least, in private or off-guard conversation, whereas I challenge the sincerity of LBJ's hang-dog piety, his turkey-trot dancing with women I know he detests; the oiliness with which he approaches tourists at the White House gate.*

---

* It should be noted that this description of Johnson represented only a temporary evaluation on Smith's part. He later developed a sincere respect and, indeed, affection for LBJ and even took to making some speeches defending him against "personal villification from so-called dissenters." But at the time of the above diary entry, Smith's attitude was bitter and negative.

Smith had experienced similar resentment—partly a feeling of protective interest in the dead president and partly the feeling that the new people were somehow usurpers— when the Truman transition began after the Roosevelt funeral. As Smith was to write:

I really gave little thought to the new President until after the funeral at Hyde Park, concentrating instead on covering the drama and the national shock produced by the death of a wartime commander-in-chief.

The funeral was over and I was walking with a colleague down a railroad track beside the Hudson River toward the train for Washington, stumbling over the crossties in a fog of weariness for it had been several days since I had slept.

There ahead of us was the big White House train and somewhat absently I noticed a new private car was on the rear end, not the old Roosevelt car.

My friend said, "Let's go up and say hello to the new President."

"Who?" I must have sounded more stupid than fatigued.

"Harry Truman, you idiot. You know him."

We crawled up the steps at the rear of the car and the new President came to the door. First he greeted my friend, then turned to me. He was smiling, but it was a smile of sympathy, not a happy look.

"I know you must be awfully tired and awfully sad," he said to me, "because you knew him so well—and you were there."

As the shock of Roosevelt's death and the emotional impact of the funeral began to wear off, I was fighting to keep control of myself. All I could do was mutter my thanks and turn to leave.

Truman took my arm and led me inside the car. A waiter was

A colleague of Smith's had a theory about his change in attitude toward presidents. "Smitty seemed to despise each new president. Then came the point of grudging respect, then finally a feeling of warmth, almost protectiveness. But at first, new presidents seemed incompetent and arrogant. It was a cyclical thing. I think he was just at the grudging respect stage with Nixon."

passing drinks and Truman handed me one saying, "Here, this may make you feel a little better."

I looked around the small sitting room of the private car and saw only strange faces. I learned later that some of the men were from the House and Senate and I knew them quite well, but my powers of recognition were blotted out by an inner rage—what were these *strangers* doing on *Roosevelt's* train?

CHAPTER TWELVE

Protecting Presidents

Throughout his career, Merriman Smith saw a range of possible threats and dangers to presidents and their families. Besides Dallas, he was a witness to the attempt on President Truman's life in front of Blair House in 1950. He reported a plot to kidnap Caroline Kennedy from Florida in 1961. He saw Lyndon Johnson surrounded by an angry mob in Sydney, Australia, and saw President Eisenhower tear-gassed in Uruguay.

He noticed how different presidents handled the theat of assassination and personal fear and how the White House acted as a magnet for angry, disturbed persons. Even his own correspondence files contained numerous crank letters ("Dear Mr. Smith: President Kennedy is not dead. A Jewish conspiracy arranged to have a double in Dallas and is holding the real John Kennedy captive . . .").

Smith lived so closely with Secret Service men that he came to share their views on many of the problems involved in protecting presidents, but he also saw the way they could be diverted from their primary duty.

A STRANGER SPOTTING these fellows in a group might assume they were young insurance men bound for their weekly bowling date. Viewed singly in a supermarket checkout line, one of them might resemble a manual training teacher and part-time athletic coach from the neighborhood junior high.

Actually, their backgrounds are varied. Practically all have a college degree or some advanced training in law enforcement. Some come from metropolitan police forces; others are recruited from investigative agencies or the military. An average agent on the White House Detail of the Secret Service might be in his mid-thirties, a former Villanova halfback, married—with a family, an Irish name, and ten years of experience in protective work.

Much of the time, they talk in wanted-poster prose ("my daughter is twelve years of age"), but most are gregarious, sentimental hale-fellows off the job. On the job, they are trained within inches of their patience and potential to be the most deadly competent bodyguards in the world.

All are crack shots with either hand. Their pistol marksmanship is tested on one of the toughest ranges in the country. The bull's-eye of their target is about half the size of the one ordinarily used on police and Army ranges. They must qualify with an unusually high score every thirty days, and if any one of them—or any of the White House police, which falls under Secret Service jurisdiction—falls below a certain marksmanship standard, they are transferred.

Agents must also qualify periodically firing from moving vehicles. This accounts for the requirement to shoot well with either hand. A right-handed agent might be clinging to a speeding car with that hand and have to shoot with the left.

Besides the .38 caliber revolver (which they prefer over automatics which have a tendency to jam), agents must also be proficient with high-velocity automatic rifles, 12 gauge shotguns, so-called sniper rifles, crowd-control gasses and shortwave radios. They are drilled in life saving, first aid and depending on the tastes of a First Family, horseback riding, sailboat and high-speed motorboat handling, skiing and ballroom dancing. They are judo and karate experts, and in certain administrations, authorities on infant care.

They attend periodic schools through their service, with a range of cram courses in business administration, biological warfare, advanced psychology, criminal law procedures as they change under appellate and Supreme Court decisions—and survival in event of nuclear attack. In this latter course, they study the possibility that an enemy attack on Washington could come from the ground, not the air, through a miniaturized atomic device hidden by saboteurs in a centrally-located building.

The trademark, in fact, of the Secret Service is their contingency planning and checking. This was once thought by some critics to be overdone and wasteful, but obviously not any more.

When the Chief Executive leaves the White House, even for a brief dinner meeting at a local hotel, the Secret Service spends hours checking over the rooms and corridors to be used by the President. They examine elevator housings and cables. Under their direction, firemen check the last re-fill dates on fire extinguishers. The names of cooks, waiters and busboys are checked against master government files to make sure that no one with a past record of violent crime gets near the Chief Executive.

This was started during the war when it was once found that in a hotel where Mr. Roosevelt was scheduled to visit, there worked fifty aliens, several persons with serious criminal records, and one man wanted for murder in Texas. The very proper and dignified hotel management was mortified, but it was many years before a President ever again entered this particular hotel.

Even when a President goes to church, the Secret Service makes an inch-by-inch check of the building. The pastor is asked to furnish in advance a list of the congregation members likely to attend. An agent invariably sits in the pew directly behind the President and several others are scattered through the church.

Particularly when a President goes out of the country, the Secret Service is on the alert for hidden microphones and recording devices. The agents are assisted in this type of detection by specialists from the Army Signal Corps, assigned to the White

House. If a foreign host thoughtfully provides a shelf of books for the visiting President, advance agents looking over the layout are supposed to take every book from its resting place and check it for hidden microphones. Toasters, clocks, radios, heaters and stoves are taken apart sufficiently for specially trained agents to determine whether any sort of threatening equipment is hidden inside.

Secret Service men are also constantly tested for health and endurance. An agent with a contagious disease threatens the President's health and even an agent with a cold is sent home to recover completely. The training of the White House detail is so finely coordinated that any one member below par could threaten its efficiency in emergency.

Agents visit the gym and nearby handball courts to maintain their wind for the miles of running they have to do. Jogging alongside the President's car when it is moving slowly through crowds or along parade routes, they keep a sharp lookout for people who might dash out toward the motorcade or suspicious persons lurking in upper windows.

Since these "secret" agents scarcely can avoid being seen and photographed, they strive for the most forgettable coloration possible—no distinctive hats, bright-button blazers or theatrical haircuts. They tend to conservative business suits and, in crowds, they are distinguished only by small lapel buttons worn largely for the benefit of local police.

Away from the public eye, the Secret Service keeps track of literally hundreds of threat cases. A computer aids in their "preventive protective intelligence" program, which in an average year deals with more than 20,000 cases. Senior agents inspect the bulletproofing of the family windows on the second floor of the White House; they specify armor-plating on the bottom of new Presidential limousines.

But it isn't enough and they know it. These agents live most of all with fear and frustration. Despite all the training, all the planning, every contingency precaution, the bitter irony remains that in the final analysis it may not do a bit of good.

Every effort made by the Secret Service is marginal. They can increase a President's protection by a fraction or reduce dangers by a percentage, but the truth they've been made to face is that the really large, credible threat to a President is impossible to combat—at least under our current conception of democracy. Any agent and any President knows deep down that a person willing to give up his own life can take the life of the President.

A chief executive, unless he is to be enclosed in a protective vacuum, must undergo this risk if he is to maintain any sort of personal contact with the public. And as bad as our country's record is for political assassination, no President will be the first to say the time has come for letting security take precedence over personal contact.

So, the agents continue their efforts at the margins and Presidents learn to deal with the risk and with fear in their own ways. Truman, the target of a very close attempt on his life in Blair House, became belligerent when he talked about it. Eisenhower never spoke of his personal safety, except to say that it was in the hands of specialists and not his concern.

Kennedy could be very fatalistic and even maudlin about the subject. Once, in fact, on a holiday weekend, John Kennedy acted out his own assassination in a game of charades. It seemed funny to his friends at the time. At least, they laughed. As one guest took a home movie, he slumped to the floor after being hit by an imaginary bullet, and another friend doused him with ketchup.

Kennedy, however, had the trait of plunging ahead extra strongly into something of which he was unsure or afraid. This was his own way of overcoming fear. After reports of a threat or an apprehended crank, he would seem to make a point of stopping to mingle with the next large crowd.

And close calls were frequent, long before Dallas. Once, acting on Secret Service information, the Palm Beach police picked up what amounted to a human bomb, a demented New England man with his body belted with dynamite. He had been carefully surveying sites where he might encounter Kennedy in public and blow both himself and the young Chief Executive to bits. In fact, this would-be assassin later told of being within a few feet of

Kennedy in a Palm Beach Catholic church, but decided not to detonate his suicidal bomb because too many other worshipers would have died with Kennedy.

John F. Kennedy actually started the custom of a President plunging into a crowd or "working" an airport fence, but like so many other aspects of the Presidency, it has become obligatory now for each succeeding man. Agents didn't permit people to mob FDR's car, nor was Harry Truman a great mixer in large crowds.

During World War II, of course, security was an unquestioned priority. Hyde Park was turned into an armed camp with search lights, barbed wire, and machine-gun turrets. When FDR went across country, every inch of track was inspected, switches were locked, and up to 150,000 soldiers stood guard on a single trip.

In his time, Dwight D. Eisenhower simply did what the agents told him, and they always told him no when it came to wading into crowds. Certainly he never stopped a motorcade to shake hands in the Kennedy fashion.

President Johnson, however, if anything, topped JFK as an impulsive flesh-presser and, in the Secret Service's eyes, as a chance-taker. And Johnson, more than Kennedy, frequently gave the agents a hard time about their presence in "friendly crowds."

He put down a flat edict against Secret Service men or local police getting between him and the people at airports or rallies. Thus his protectors had to work from behind him or at his side. The principal task of the agents turned out to be keeping temporary fences and barricades from collapsing under the weight of well-wishers.

One agent usually concentrated on warning people just ahead of the President, "Don't squeeze too hard" or "Easy now, take it easy." This did not prevent the President from suffering hand cuts and bruises occasionally when men wearing large rings clamped down on him with that extra power which is supposed to denote special friendship.

Another hazard along the airport fences consisted of the thin sticks on which were stapled the "Welcome L.B.J." signs. The signbearers frequently became excited and dropped their placards just as the President reached them. The edge of a cardboard sign can be as abrasive as a kitchen knife and agents had to grab for these things constantly.

Johnson, however, became quite displeased, sometimes audibly, if an agent came between him and his well-wishers. Because of these strong feelings, agents really didn't do much protecting against their greatest fear, the seeming well-wisher who could step forward and fire a .38 at point blank range. I heard one agent after another bemoan the Johnson restrictions on what they rightly construed as their duty. Under his system, any potential assassin capable of reading the advance schedules published in the newspapers was given a chance at an open attempt, particularly during the campaign swings.

It is a valid question why the Secret Service cannot just veto unsafe Presidential wishes and tell him what to do in cases when it is for his own safety. Theoretically, they can. After the assassination of President McKinley in 1901, agents were assigned to guard Theodore Roosevelt. The Secret Service was charged by law to take whatever means necessary to secure the life and safety of the Chief Executive.

In actuality, however, the Secret Service has no such veto power over the President. He is simply too powerful for individual agents to buck, if his wishes are firm and if the agent values his career and White House assignment.

The Secret Service, then, starts out with the initial handicap of being resented, to a greater or lesser extent, by the First Family it is assigned to protect. Add to this the resentment of people in crowds who are moved aside, local police officials who feel superseded, and many White House visitors and you begin to understand what it's like to be a Secret Service agent.

There are, for instance, over 200,000 business and social visitors to the White House each year, but each, as one would expect, considers his invitation to mean a special sense of importance. Thus, the guest is offended when a stern-looking young man asks, for example, that he please take his hand out of his pocket as the receiving line approaches the President.

"My God, do they think we're criminals?" is not an uncommon response from guests who can rank as high as ambassador. "Don't you want the people to see him?" is the argument of local political officials and "the President surely needs no extra protection on a U.S. Army base" is sometimes the rejoinder of that branch.

And then there are the cases like the men from the Spanish embassy who were suspected of being bombers. An agent accompanying President Roosevelt to an Opening Day baseball game at Washington's old Griffith Stadium once noticed three men directly above the President's box. The three men, obviously foreigners, were peering over the grandstand railing and fidgeting with a small brown box. The agent reached for his shoulder holster and rushed up to the men.

He demanded that they open the box and they did. Inside were six ham on ryes and some deviled eggs. The three men turned out to be attachés at the Spanish embassy and the State Department quickly complained about their rough treatment. A note of apology was dutifully sent, but the incident emphasized that the job of the Secret Service and the White House police is not protocol or politics or anything else except protection.

This fact is usually forgotten—and most of all by Presidents. Secret Service men frequently are used as errand boys. They are asked to carry messages, mind the kids, keep memoranda of appointments and, at times, even fetch groceries or gifts. In the past, I have seen agents pressed into duty as adjuncts of the White House press office; assigned to fetch hats and coats for guests of a President; walk dogs and keep track of gifts received by a President while traveling.

Such tasks are obviously an abuse of a highly-trained security specialist. Over the years, however, Secret Service agents have come to be something akin to political retainers. In fact, a sort of political patronage can be exercised to speed the promotion of a favorite agent. President Johnson's fondness for Rufus Youngblood, the agent who threw himself over LBJ at Dallas, certainly did nothing to hurt Youngblood's career.

Assignments can involve such closeness—for instance, in the case of an agent on the "kiddie detail" guarding First Family children—that an agent becomes associated with a particular President and committed to him personally. An outgoing President often asks to take a particularly friendly agent with him and his family when he leaves the White House.

The problem is that agents start pulling their punches in these situations. They hesitate to get tough in their advice about safety. They willingly carry the groceries instead of pointing out that it isn't their job. And they can even become unable to shift loyalties when Presidents change.

So, for these and other reasons, the Secret Service has traditionally given the President quite a long leash. In days gone by, it seemed harmless enough. Vacationing one summer at Swampscott, Massachusetts, President Calvin Coolidge became so frustrated by the constant presence of agents that one morning, when he thought no one was watching, he burst from his cottage and raced awkwardly through seaside sand toward the nearby village.

Agents in the kitchen were ready to spring into action when they were halted by a wiser and older veteran of the Secret Service.

"Don't catch up with him right away," he advised the younger agents. "Let him think he got away with something."

Franklin Roosevelt had similar instincts. He owned a small Ford phaeton equipped with special controls so his infantile paralysis would not prevent his driving. He took particular delight in trying to race away from his staff and bodyguards at Hyde Park and in Warm Springs, on occasion driving at breakneck speed up lonely, dead-end country roads and sitting in silence until discovered.

After this happened a few times his staff and Secret Service men learned virtually all of the possible secret routes and let him have his fun, within limits. After twenty minutes or so, the Secret Service agents would decide to go get him, and then stumble across his hidden car with loud cries of mock surprise.

There was little need to be strict with the President in these cases. The area was secluded, the danger seemingly slight. Perhaps a case could be constructed for giving a President greater leeway, except that the painful subject of Dallas comes up here.

The Presidential motorcade that day was moving at 11.2 miles an hour. The President wanted it slow. The agents knew from experience he would object if they tried to speed him through the crowded streets. At 30 miles an hour, however, the shot that Lee Harvey Oswald made would have been infinitely more difficult. Politically, it would be a very touchy subject to close, say, the first ten stories of buildings along a parade route. But at heights above this level, the angle is impossible for an accurate shot at a moving target.

Again, politically, it is better to let the local policemen along a motorcade route get a look at the President. After all, they vote, too. But in New York City, the police are trained to watch the crowd, not the motorcade when they are there for the purpose of protection. If they can do it in New York, why not Dallas, Los Angeles, and other big cities?

Some other difficulties of the Secret Service are more standard, but still a hindrance to optimum performance as protectors of the President. Their pay is around that of a middle-level government stenographer. They get no extra clothes allowance for the formal wear they're required to don about once a week or for the suits ruined in crowds or rain or in four-hour laundries around the world.

Their per diem travel allowance will barely get them in the door at some of the hotels they have to stay in to be close to the President. I once knew an agent who was doing so badly on expenses that when the deacon at President Eisenhower's favorite church passed him the collection plate, flashed his badge and said, "Police."

Another internal problem is that organizational pride prevents maximum cooperation with the F.B.I. Much more information could be shared between the two organizations, but like the branches of the armed services, each is somewhat chauvinistic. The Warren Report was convincing on the need for closer cooperation.

I have been listening to the bitches and gripes of Secret Service agents for most of my adult life, but I have never lost my admiration for their dedication and skill. We've shared some terrible moments. A Secret Service agent once came to me months after Dallas and said he still suffered from horrible nightmares in which he would relive the assassination scene. He was losing sleep and weight and, he was afraid, his nerves.

I told him that the same thing had happened to me, and that I had finally gone to a psychiatrist about the problem. The agent just shook his head. That was impossible. A person in his position just couldn't afford to have such treatment on his record. Time gradually solved his problem, but I'll never forget his frustration.

Not all the times were so grim. I remember what served as my initiation into their brotherhood of sorts. It came soon after I started at the White House. I regarded my new job as approaching, if not surpassing, journalistic knighthood, and I guess it must have showed.

Returning from lunch one day, I was stopped at the main gate on Pennsylvania Avenue through which one still reaches the White House offices in the west wing. Tom Qualters, an agent personally assigned to President Roosevelt, was in the booth at the gate and greeted me warmly.

"Would you like a souvenir of your assignment here?" Qualters asked, a picture of friendliness and charm.

Before I could make a proper speech of acceptance, he hauled out a blackjack.

"This is a valuable, historic blackjack," he said. "It was used by a man I sent up to Sing Sing years ago. Here, take it as a souvenir from me."

As I entered the West Wing moments later, the welcome continued—this time from a captain and sergeant of the uniformed White House police. They led me politely and firmly into a small room used by the Secret Service for questioning cranks.

"Tell me, Mr. Smith," the captain said gravely, "are you carrying a weapon of any sort?"

"Why should I carry a weapon?"

"That's what we want to know."

As I was saying indignantly, "Of course, I don't have any

weapon," I felt a chilling, sagging weight in my jacket pocket. I reached for the lethal instrument meekly. "Unless you'd call this a weapon."

The police captain was quite stern and formal.

"I would call it a weapon," he said drily. "My question is— what are you doing with it in the White House?"

"Tommy Qualters gave it to me for a souvenir."

Qualters was quickly summoned and after he arrived and was filled in, he looked at me and stared away unemotionally.

"I never saw this man before and I never saw this blackjack before. Why would I give anybody a blackjack?"

With that he disappeared quickly into the President's suite of offices. I began to perspire profusely as the questioning became more intense. Finally, it seemed ages, the phone rang. The captain listened sourly and then said to the sergeant, "Let him go, Qualters says. But watch him."

There was also the day, also during the FDR years, when the Angel of the Lord came to the White House. He was a tall, lithe man who ran up to the front gate on tiptoe and flapping large and shimmery white wings.

Stopping before the startled policemen, the "angel" proclaimed in Gabrielian tones, "I have a message from the Lord—a message of peace for the President." Besides his wings, he wore ankle-length flowing white robes and carried an ornate scroll.

Letting the angel cool his wings for a minute, the guards called for James Sloan, crank expert of the Secret Service who had been in the business of listening to the impassioned pleas of unexpected White House callers since the days of Teddy Roosevelt.

Sloan, from his experience, could see that the Angel was harmless, so he impressed on the deadly serious herald that the message from the Lord to the President would be accepted, but not by the Chief Executive in person.

Even the most harmless visits, however, are not treated so lightly any more, for it is the undiagnosed psychotic—unknown even to the computers—who poses the greatest threat to a President's life. In 1969, the White House police seized and turned over to the Secret Service 323 "unwelcome visitors," a police term for disoriented persons plus a few drunks and pranksters caught trying to sneak or force their way into the President's presence. They demanded everything from cash to a chance at killing him.

A rather bizarre example occurred one cold day several winters ago. A man arrived at the northwest gate of the White House bundled in a large overcoat and asked to see the President. But the agent on duty spotted a bulge under the man's left armpit.

"You'd better let me have that gun," the agent said and the man calmly handed over a .45 Colt automatic.

"Think you're pretty smart," he said. "Think you've got all my guns." To the agent's surprise he reached inside his coat and brough forth a .38 revolver. But the man continued calmly. "But you still don't have all my guns." The agent gaped as he reached into his hip pockets and brought forth two more.

This man was taken to St. Elizabeth's, the District of Columbia's mental hospital, as was the woman who, on a White House guided tour, lit four separate fires. In fact, there are constant reminders to those who are supposed to protect the President and his family that twisted potential for harm exists in bulk quantities and that First Families act as attractions for it.

An Epilogue:
Presidents and the Press

Merriman Smith had an engaging facility for telling the human side of the presidency through light narrative and amusing anecdotes, but he also had a very serious view of the role of a free press. In fact, in his later years he was deeply worried about what he regarded as encroachments on freedom of the press in Washington and, particularly at the White House.

This epilogue is intended to leave his assessment of this issue—and his philosophy of news-gathering—as the "author's message" of what has been intended as his book.

ABOUT EVERY MONTH or so, President Nixon holds a full dress news conference before microphones, TV cameras and the writing press of Washington. Usually, it is a terribly good show, particularly when seen from inside the East Room of the White House—the majestic old room rimmed with white-hot stage lighting: the long shot-gun microphones pointing among the reporters to pick up questions; banks of cameras mounted on platforms on three sides of the room; the reporters jumping up and down seeking recognition—and then of course the center of attention: the President, himself, in the middle of a small, black-covered platform with only a single microphone stand in front of him. No lectern, no notes, no shuffled sheets of statistics.

The vast television audience is often treated to a virtuoso performance as Mr. Nixon deftly fields twenty-five to thirty questions on a wide range of subjects over about half an hour of prime time. Improved communications and a gradual loosening of the rules of quoting the President have drastically changed the press conference from the days when Herbert Hoover took questions only in writing and in advance.

Yet, over a number of years, the reporting of Presidential activities has expanded and contracted at the same time. It is certainly true that much more is seen and heard of the President, himself, than ever before, but much of this visibility is self-serving and without real news value.

Mr. Roosevelt debated with reporters. He insulted them, lectured them, and made them laugh. He called them liars and used the mighty weight of his high office against the press in pile-driving fashion. Mr. Truman tried to keep everybody happy. His conferences were fast, produced a lot of news and made the reporters wish they had learned shorthand. Truman was the last President to engage in truly head-to-head exchange of not only questions and answers, but also ideas with reporters. News actually originated in his conferences.

Since then, however, the White House presidential press conference has become more and more a one-way street—an avenue by which a chief executive makes careful policy statements and pretty well sticks to them.

Kennedy was a charmer and a talented performer in his TV news conference, but when you analyze what he said, most of it consisted largely of restatement of previously stated positions and policies. He was such a superb performer, though, such a quick wit and so thoroughly comfortable in the theatrical setting of a TV conference, that his meetings with the press vastly added to his national image.

Johnson, once his prepared announcements were out of the

way at the start of the conference, seldom made much startlingly
new news in the question period. For the most part, his answers
amounted to so much salesmanship for various administration
policies and programs. And much the same answers on the same
subjects came through week after week.

On one level coverage was expanding. With Eisenhower came
the quotable transcript and filming of some segments for television. Then Kennedy went the whole route—live TV, a much
bigger auditorium and audience. Each change made for wider
and faster distribution of the President's remarks and thus increased the political value of these gatherings for the President.
But the changes have also caused there to be less interplay between reporter and head of government, and hence less news.

The television format makes follow-up questions nearly impossible. One correspondent asks one question and gets one
answer and then it is the next man's turn. Thus, the President
can answer in general and even ambiguous terms and often escape further questioning on the point he has meant to avoid.
The setting is so formal and the room is so big that exchanges
such as those around FDR's desk would be impossible today.

There is also a school of thought in Washington journalistic
circles that television cuts down on tough, i.e., particularly pen-
etrating, questions. No matter how justified or well-founded, a
question that takes on even the suggestion of an accusatory tone
may sound much more abrasive on television and thus reward the
questioner with bales of scornful letters. So, the theory runs, reporters phrase their inquiries more carefully and more politely
with the thought of millions watching.

(On the other hand, a Columbia University study showed that
press conference questions, which averaged fourteen words in
length during the time of FDR, reached an average length of
over fifty words in President Kennedy's televised conferences.
President Nixon has been getting some questions running up-
wards of a hundred words. Hopefully, the reporters who ask
hundred-word questions do not then sit down and write eighty-
word leads. Without being married to the publisher's daughter.)

Another case which illustrates the simultaneous expansion and contraction of coverage opportunities is the growth of the so-called backgrounder. This term refers to instances in which a top government official discusses sensitive matters with reporters on a more or less confidential basis, but allows them to use what he says provided there is no identifiable attribution. The underlying reason for backgrounders is that the government may want to expand on the bare bones of an official pronouncement without having to make the expansion part of an official record. In the Johnson and Nixon administrations, backgrounders proliferated to an almost daily event.

Background information—if it can be called that—is interesting in that it reflects mood within an administration. But these briefings are most often used as a device to spread patently political propaganda. When a President gives a backgrounder, it can be valuable on occasion for measuring the man's mood against whatever crisis led to the backgrounder. I recall little or no hard news, however, coming from any LBJ Vietnam backgrounder, for example.

The growth of these briefings has also pointed up the fact that with each new President and each new administration, the White House tends to assume unto itself more and more central direction and control of public information originating in the Executive Branch. Jim Hagerty had a very smooth technique of putting out a tremendous volume of material favorable to the administration, giving the impression of great activity even in slack periods.

Bill Moyers took this a step further. He operated on a simple theory—that news from any government department or agency is a matter of legitimate presidential interest. And if it interested President Johnson sufficiently, it should be announced first at the White House. (To paraphrase the immortal bard: good news has a thousand fathers, bad news can stay at Interior.) The Nixon administration finally institutionalized the growing centralization by creating the office of the Director of Communications. Herb Klein now has responsibilities for overseeing public information policies throughout the Executive Branch.

On balance, there has been since the Roosevelt and Truman

administrations, a steadily shrinking opportunity to cover news at the White House, particularly news of policy in the formative stage.

An example of subtle, but important change may be found in the way the White House carefully blacks out public knowledge of many important persons who confer daily with the President. This has been a gradual development. During the Truman administration, most persons, official and otherwise, who conferred with the Chief Executive passed through the west executive lobby leading to the President's office. While these visitors seldom produced big news, they were interviewed by reporters as they left the White House and the public was given a relatively detailed idea of how the President spent his day and the issues under discussion.

When Dwight Eisenhower became President, his chief assistant, Sherman Adams, had an idea. He wanted to move the press out of the White House entirely, across West Executive Avenue to the old Executive Office Building to which they would be confined except on ceremonial occasions. Adams saw no reason why Presidential callers should be identified or questioned by the press unless the White House wanted it. Before the plan could be put into effect, details leaked and the journalistic outcry was such that the Adams muzzle was abandoned before it could be tested.

The late President John Kennedy was more protective of his conferees than either Truman or Eisenhower. The daily visitors passing through the office lobby within sight of reporters became fewer and fewer, although Kennedy, himself, emerged before the country in progressively larger proportions because of his televised news conferences.

Virtually no officials calling on President Johnson were seen or questioned by the press except under very controlled circumstances. The White House in this period often presented officials to discuss administration programs, but much of President Johnson's daily schedule was never announced. Reporters, for example, almost never knew about or had access to the members of the House or Senate or key political figures who saw Johnson daily.

Reporters today have only infrequent opportunities—and most

of these are stage-managed—to interview at the White House those who come to confer with the President on substantive matters. Also, aside from the press office, contacts with presidential advisors must be arranged by appointment.

The move by the Nixon administration of the press from their west wing nest to an area in the basement formerly the White House swimming pool, gave the reporters a roomier locale and freed needed space for additional presidential staff offices. But it also marked the culmination of this trend of isolation.

As a reporter, I regret the trend. News of the presence of White House visitors can provide frequent leads to stories. Informal encounters with advisors and staff during the course of a work day can give a reading of the President's current frame of mind or the existence of policy factions.

News of policy in formation is legitimate. Presidents do not usually like it, of course; they prefer giving the impression of complete unanimity on all policy questions. The press secretary's version often fails to reflect the disagreements and power plays going on behind the scenes. News of this sort has to be pried, cajoled or otherwise extracted from the contestants, and being in an underground sound-proofed, antiseptic location makes it just a little harder.

At this point, two things should be emphasized. First, *legally*, a President is entirely within his rights when he follows a growing pattern of reducing the area of public knowledge of his operations. Reporters and photographers are present at the White House, even under limited conditions, only by sufferance of the President. Any time a chief executive wants to kick out the entire lot and never have any contacts with the world of public information, all he has to do is say so—and he will be within the Constitution. A President is not obliged by law to communicate with the public in any fashion except through messages to Congress.

Second, a President pursues the public information policies that he does out of self-interest. Being human, and being a politician, he will seek the widest possible and most favorable means to accentuate the positive. It follows that he will seek to minimize the means by which reporters can accentuate the actual, if it makes him look bad.

This situation is not necessarily evil. Government information policies are important to a President as they relate to his ability to persuade. Harry Truman once said that successful conduct of the presidency consisted largely of persuading people to do things which they should, but which they did not like doing.

John Kennedy candidly admitted that he used the press conference as a means of putting pressure on the Congress to act on his legislative proposals and he increased the frequency of the conferences when Congress was in session. There is no reason why presidential press relations should not be a legitimate tool of political persuasion.

On the other hand, reporters should remember that the relationship between a President and the press must be, at best, of the batter-pitcher sort.

Gathering news is largely a matter of taking from someone one or more facts which he does not want to give up or have disclosed. The tug-of-war between news source and reporter intensified in proportion to the importance of the news item. I have never seen an administration or a political organization that did not get annoyed when reporters pried out information that they did not want pried out. It is when they get annoyed, though, that the reporter knows he is doing his job.

The real danger is in the other direction. With enough flattery and blandishment, it becomes easy for reporters to start thinking of themselves as participants in the administration—instead of reporting it.

You can make a safe prediction about the start of any new administration. Even as the inauguration band music fades away, certain reporters, columnists and commentators will be told that by sticking with the new President, they will be helping a new and better America. Then will follow those precious little luncheons and dinners at the White House for the new President's wonderful friends in journalism.

But someone will bring thunder into this roseate paradise. A reporter will dig up a story about, say, how a cousin of one of the

President's ranking staff members made a $200,000 profit on lumber for the inauguration stands. Thus the magic circle of those wonderful friends in journalism will shrink by several places at the White House table.

Most reporters are not particularly impressed by first-name relationships with any news source and most resist the temptation to become involved in the success or failure of the administration they are assigned to cover. But this possibility remains a danger and a threat to our professional credibility. People get startled when I vehemently deny being a "friend of the Presidents." They think they are complimenting me, but, as a reporter, they are not.

(I have been criticized for an overly close relationship with some Presidents and even editors have complained sometimes about speeches or television remarks I have made that seemed defensive of one president or another. I have a standard defense. If a critic tells me that long White House tenure is injurious to a reporter's work; that a friendly relationship tends to dampen the reporter's zeal, then I ask him who broke the Walter Jenkins story, who broke the dismissal of Sherman Adams in the face of denunciations and ten days of denials, who broke Truman's dismissal of his Attorney General?)

A short word about another press relations problem: the "credibility gap." It has been with us under different labels for many years. Originally, it must have been called "not telling the truth." In the Eisenhower administration, though, there was something called the "Madison Avenue technique" and, in turn, the Kennedy people were accused of "news management." Lyndon Johnson fell victim to the so-called credibility gap and the tag remains in the Nixon administration.

Let me hazard another fanciful prediction about some future administration. The new president will hold his first press conference, during the course of which he will deny vehemently a story printed that very day, only to discover just after the conference ends that an opposition Senator has just confirmed the entire thing with undeniable detail.

The White House will then insist that the President spoke the truth at the time, but was trapped by unavoidable circumstances.

246

And thus we will witness the birth of a new label—perhaps the Truth Trap. For one thing, it makes a vastly better single column headline than Credibility Gap, or News Management, or the Madison Avenue Technique.

The recurring credibility problems of Presidents can, I think, be traced to one age-old fact. Every president since George Washington has wanted the public to believe his every uttered word— implicitly, completely, and sympathetically. This wish, of course, is based on a rather impossible assumption that any human can be entirely free of exaggeration, error, or the simple peaks and valleys of elation and despondency.

In this situation, a reporter has the same responsibility as a storekeeper. He must stand behind his merchandise. When a president or one of his cabinet officers presents statistics which are inordinately self-serving, then it is the reporter's duty to make this fact clear in his copy. Of such stuff are credibility gaps made.

There is another kind of gap between the press and any administration—a gap between what each judges to be newsworthy.

Any photographer regularly stationed at the White House will tell you that better than half of the pictures they make are little more than political commercials; any reporter will tell you that a great many announcements coming from the government agencies these days should be charged for as paid political advertisements. And most so-called background sessions produce little more than what was printed in last year's edition of the *Encyclopaedia Britannica*—plus a liberal dose of partisan press agentry.

This being the case, perhaps the fourth estate should reexamine its role. The press has the same right to selectivity the government has. Newspapers have no moral or ethical duty to print every word the government puts out and they do not need to print propaganda. This will make some of our friends in public life very angry, but it is time we reach a point in Washington journalism where the writers should be less concerned with the reactions of the people about whom they write.

Presidents should also be less sensitive to every item that is written about them. It is true that a presidential image consists of thousands of little pieces—idiosyncracies of clothing, personal appearance and behavior—which can add up to importance.

Look at the 1948 election. Truman came off as good old, down-to-earth, give-'em-hell Harry. Tom Dewey was the apple-cheeked, mellifluous and dapper man on the wedding cake, never a hair out of place, the perfect grammarian. And against all odds, Truman licked him rather badly.

(It was for image reasons that Pierre Salinger objected to reporters referring to the Kennedy boat *Honey Fitz* as a "yacht." At ninety-two feet, we were reluctant to call it a working-class cabin cruiser.)

But truly, presidents do not have to be so intensely sensitive about virtually every word written about them as some of them are. Lyndon Johnson was a good example. He did not seem to believe entirely the great mandate of 1964 and continued to be super-sensitive about his press.

He went to great effort and expense to assemble a good press staff, then tried in effect to serve as his own press secretary. He resembled FDR somewhat in his unshakable belief that he knew far more than he actually did about the newspaper and broadcasting industries.

I am firmly convinced that his public image would have been more to his own liking if he had delegated more authority in his press relations. At his direction, the flow of routine news from the White House could come in such bursts of volume that little of it got on the air or in print. And this pained him.

All the Presidents I have covered seemed to react with more calmness, deliberation and sure-footedness to genuine crisis than to minor and somewhat personal irritations. Truman, for example, never lost his temper at Stalin as he did when he abused the music critic of the Washington *Post* for having given Margaret's concert voice less than an Academy Award.

I saw Eisenhower much angrier about stories dealing with his catching over the Colorado trout limit than he ever was about his mishandling of the U-2 incident.

Kennedy was bombarded critically for the Bay of Pigs, but he took it with much better grace than stories and pictures of Mrs. Kennedy water skiing.

If a President is upset by what he takes to be distortions of his public image, his first reaction seems to be to blame everybody else before blaming himself. This is a White House syndrome which probably never will change. It is based on a desire to have things both ways—to have on record the events which they choose to publicize and to have complete privacy for those events they do not.

Presidential candidates love to have family scenes shared with the public during a campaign, but are often highly offended when they are successful and find the press wants to come along then, too.

A White House wedding is another example. The Johnsons took the position that Luci's wedding to Pat Nugent was a personal and family affair. They were upset that it became one of the major news stories of the year and as the magic day approached, there inevitably was more and more romantic gush spread upon the public record, some of it having little or no relation to fact.

It could have been a quiet wedding in a small chapel if that is what they really wanted. Quite understandably, however, President Johnson wanted to give his daughter a truly ceremonial send-off. Still, it was the family, not the press, who chose an enormous church and a wedding party about the size of an infantry company.

The Johnsons wanted a colorful, happy and festive affair conducted with dignity and grace, but without the trappings of crowds and sensationalism. Unfortunately, in our society, they could not have it both ways.

Similarly, Mrs. Kennedy had the choice of riding in the hunt or having her privacy (and less of a hunt-cup-set image) and it saddened her to be unable to have both. This, though, is one of the costs of the Presidency.

I foresee no easy solution to the problems I have outlined. (Mine is certainly not a definitive list of all the problems of relations between the press and government. There are many other important issues—for instance, the ongoing controversy over the use of the national security label to protect information which does not fall into that class—which my relatively circumscribed White House assignment does not ordinarily involve.)

Presidents will continue to be increasingly concerned with their images as exposure to the magnifying powers of media inspection grows. They will be increasingly tempted to use television appearances to communicate with the public without the filter of an interpretive and analytical press. I would not even be shocked to find in years hence that the basement space too is needed at the White House or that a future President's doctor feels he really should do some swimming.

If public information policies are loosened from the government side, it will be surprising, but not impossible. This would take an act of statesmanship, and, like all such acts, it would involve short-run political costs. It would be a sacrificial act for a President to provide greater access to the truth about his administration while his political opponents were continuing to follow propagandistic policies.

The more likely, and only partial, solution to the trends of isolating or by-passing the press is for reporters, themselves, to insist on maximum opportunity for coverage of the news and, at the same time, to develop new sources of information for every one that the government attempts to close. If reporters can do this, and if they retain their professional detachment in the face of flattery, their willingness to dig for stories even if it means getting their hands dirty, then the public's right to know has a chance of being fulfilled. Otherwise, it may be in trouble.